The Kennedy Imprisonment

A Meditation on Power

Also by Garry Wills

CHESTERTON

POLITICS AND CATHOLIC FREEDOM

ROMAN CULTURE (EDITOR)

JACK RUBY

SECOND CIVIL WAR

NIXON AGONISTES

BARE RUINED CHOIRS

INVENTING AMERICA

AT BUTTON'S

CONFESSIONS OF A CONSERVATIVE

EXPLAINING AMERICA

The Kennedy Imprisonment

A Meditation on Power

GARRY WILLS

An Atlantic Monthly Press Book

Little, Brown and Company   Boston / Toronto

FIRST EDITION

Portions of this book appeared in *The Atlantic.*

Acknowledgments for material quoted in this book appear on
page 304.

LIBRARY OF CONGRESS CATALOGING IN PUBLICATION DATA

Wills, Garry, 1934–
    The Kennedy imprisonment.

    "An Atlantic Monthly Press book."
    1. Kennedy family.   2. Power (Social sciences)
I. Title.
E843.W54   973.922′092′2   81-18649
ISBN 0-316-94385-1   AACR2

ATLANTIC–LITTLE, BROWN BOOKS
ARE PUBLISHED BY
LITTLE, BROWN AND COMPANY
IN ASSOCIATION WITH
THE ATLANTIC MONTHLY PRESS

MV
Designed by Susan Windheim
*Published simultaneously in Canada
by Little, Brown & Company (Canada) Limited*

PRINTED IN THE UNITED STATES OF AMERICA

To the Other Garry Willses

Garry S. (1884–1956)
Garry L. (1961–)

Contents

There lurks about the fancies of many men and women an imaginary conception of an ideal statesman, resembling the character of which Alcibiades has been the recognized type for centuries. There is a sort of intellectual luxury in the idea which fascinates the human mind. We like to fancy a young man in the first vigour of body and in the first vigour of mind, who is full of bounding enjoyment, who excels all rivals at masculine feasts, who gains the love of women by a magic attraction, but who is also a powerful statesman, who regulates great events, who settles great measures, who guides a great nation. We seem to outstep the moenia mundi, *the recognized limits of human nature, when we conceive a man in the pride of youth to have dominion of the pursuits of age, to rule both the light things of women and the grave things of men. Human imagination so much loves to surpass human power, that we shall never be able to extirpate the conception.*

— WALTER BAGEHOT, of Bolingbroke

The Kennedy Imprisonment

A Meditation on Power

Brothers

Then spake the King: "My house hath been my doom"
— TENNYSON, *The Passing of Arthur*

HAMPTON, NEW HAMPSHIRE, February 22, 1980: This night seems made to vindicate Frank Capra's version of democracy. Hollywood snow falls rhythmically in large wet flakes, late for the ski trade but doubly welcome after delay. The American hockey team has just, unexpectedly, beat the Russians. On the press bus, the Eastern Establishment, in the form of the New York *Times* reporter, is cheering, *"That'll* teach the commie bastards." And, to top it all, an American prince is riding by night to visit the homes of his people; riding on a creaky bus. "Senator Kennedy likes to travel with the press," his aides are explaining, at this very moment, to hostesses along the arranged route. The Secret Service wants to keep Kennedy in its sleek car: every time he gets on the bus, they have to take out reporters' bags, search them for bombs, and seal the doors of the luggage compartment. It's a dangerous thing to be an American prince.

But Edward Kennedy has much to prove, now that there is nothing for him to win. Despite a head cold and his bad back, he remounts this spavined Rosinante and rides it to another doorway. He knows what is ahead — squeezing through small homes packed with people, feigning delight at nibbles on homemade cake, at a ritual slurp of freshly brewed coffee. At one home, after taking something for his dry throat, he assures the housewife: "That's good water."

This is an exercise the Kennedys perfected. Veterans of other campaigns, of other brothers, took it as one of the laws they had written: a Kennedy in the front room of anyone's house means the wife's vote is certain, and the wife will work on the husband. But the woman's vote is a different matter in 1980, and so is the Kennedy technique. Tonight's series of "coffees" is clearly marked on the schedule CLOSED TO THE PRESS. These homes are so jammed that Kennedy will not have room to shrug out of and into his coat — it gets left on the bus. But the pencil press nags at Tom Southwick, the press secretary increasingly insecure (he will soon resign), till he lets us in. The TV crews are just as happy to watch, on their equipment, replays from the Olympic hockey game — which gives Kennedy his opening remark of the evening, repeated from house to house: "I bring you *good* news" (shaking his left hand at "good" as if to get water out of his watch), "the American hockey team beat the Russian team, and *they* were a significant underdog too" (left forefinger points up in a long scooping motion on "they"). It is the epitome of false cheer. Instead of warming the crowd up, he disorients it. What has gone wrong?

These New England houses in a heavily Catholic state should be Kennedy territory. In one of them I study the kitchen calendar, from Our Lady of the Miraculous Medal Parish. Questions are so many "fat balls," served up for Kennedy to knock out of the park — health care, veterans' rights, shipyards. He barely bothers to swing. Phrases out of the past are lifted up, but no longer placed in an architectonic whole, in a Kennedy rhetoric of liberalism overarching local bread-and-butter issues. A woman asks, "What do you think is the future of the UN?" He gives the fending-off answer used to placate right-wing foes of the organization, though she is clearly its friend: the do-gooder agencies *do* do some good — WHO and UNICEF, UNESCO and the FAO. The woman, impatient, asks if the UN can grow toward a world government. "I'm interested in that," Kennedy says, in his uninterested way. But we must also make the world "safe for diversity" (his brother's line from the American University speech, so out of context here as to seem a deliberate caricature). Before leaving the house, I ask the UN questioner if his answers satisfied her. She shrugs: "I guess he can't say more than that in this campaign." By now, she is admitting, Kennedy must bear his liberalism with a shamefaced doggedness, advertising its and his own doom. He actually *ducks* fat balls.

Going from the bright night back into the bus is like entering a rusty muffler. Sniffles blend with cigarette smoke, and with the question endlessly posed here: Why is he, how *can* he be, so bad? He has lost all sense of scale. In little rooms he is too loud, in large halls too mumbly. He seems to be talking to audiences somewhere else — mainly in the past. When a Kennedy cannot do a "coffee" right, things are truly upside down. This very week I saw Howard Baker make hostesses glow in their own homes, complimenting them, giving their coffee cake heartfelt munches. Kennedy cannot even *eat* right — one of the American politician's basic skills.

That is a special problem these days, since everywhere Kennedy goes he is cutting birthday cake. All his years in politics he has reminded people, come February, that he shares a birthday with George Washington. Now, even that reference gets out of hand. Speaking in Newmarket, he shouts: "George Washington was a southern Senator, and *he* was followed in the presidency by a man from Massachusetts." No politician is above making up a little history when it serves, inventing a Senate past for Washington; but Kennedy has done it to equate President Carter with George Washington — not the surest way of diminishing an opponent. Reporters long ago gave up counting Kennedy's malapropisms. Hide and seek is only fun if the quarry will at least pretend to hide. One cannot expose a clumsiness that is proclaimed. "Oliver Wendell Holmes, who was Chief Justice of the United States," Kennedy tells the students at West High School.

So dazed is he and stumbling, now, that some who do not witness the spectacle day by day think the press is picking on him. That was probably true, three months earlier; but since then regard for him has been increasing in the press bus, along with pity. This campaign is out of synch with perception of it — a set of multiple time-lags. When he seemed to be gaining, he was losing; now, in loss, he is subtly growing. At one of the coffees, an angry voice shouts: "Did you anticipate that the press would turn on you as it has?" Kennedy smiles: "We've got a few in the room, so we better look out." The slight laugh makes him provoke a bigger one: "Want me to point 'em *out,* so you can go *get* 'em?" Kennedy, once the darling of the press, is reduced to the ploys of George Wallace, the reporters' bogeyman.

As Kennedy began his campaign in November, flying the huge chartered jet, trailing a presidential entourage, the press resented his arrogance, the assumption that to run was to win, that he would prevail by sheer drift, inheritance, and Carter's default. *Then* his mistakes mattered, his apparent lack of purpose. Then critics were harsh, swift to say this man in the imperial panoply had, intellectually, no clothes on, that "there is no there there." But now a there is beginning to appear, and the press is quick to throw clothes over his nakedness — all too late. The change began a month ago when President Carter beat Kennedy two-to-one in the Iowa caucus votes. Some on Kennedy's own team were counseling withdrawal. They saw the defeats stretch out before him, all through a spring and summer; and so did he. He would, in time, lose twenty-four of the thirty-four primaries, twenty of twenty-five state caucuses. But instead of dropping out, he drew himself together and gave the speech that should have opened the race, the Georgetown speech — wage and price controls, gas rationing, an international commission to study Iran's grievances in the hostage affair; strong stuff, defiant of campaign evasions, an abrupt end to hedging and a declaration of purpose worth all future effort. If he was going down anyway, better to go down for principle, for the embattled liberalism other Senators, running scared, would no longer champion.

Some people thought Kennedy was doing himself, not liberalism, the big favor, drawing it down with him to dignify his fall. Battered as the liberal program might be, it was not so clearly doomed as Kennedy's race. But Kennedy, it turned out, could not be accused of opportunism; which takes, at the least, some clarity of purpose. His mind drifted away again from specifics of his Georgetown speech. Gas rationing disappeared from his rhetoric. The economy was neglected for weeks at a time, though he had declared it the central issue. Scheduling and staff matters were neglected. After his severe effort at focus, Kennedy lapsed back into the daze that numbed others in his campaign. He would rouse himself to eloquence at one stop, and ramble at the next. His attention span seemed to stretch for minutes, not for days (or even hours).

What won grudging respect was his will to go on, the lack of complaint as old allies fell away; the absolute refusal to criticize his critics, to indulge even fleeting bitterness. There was only one thing Kennedy could prove now, that he was not a spoiled kid — the thing on which everything else had depended, back when no one realized that. He campaigned like a dethroned king doing penance. It was painful to watch, even for reporters who had gloated at earlier setbacks.

Ghoulish journalists have for a long time called assignment to Kennedy "the death watch." If there is another Dallas, the networks want to be there. But this is another kind of death watch — not standing by on the chance of assassination, but witnessing the certain dissipation of a vast complex of hopes, the end of the entire Kennedy time in our national life. Rose Kennedy, on the eve of her ninetieth birthday, tells New Hampshire's old folks to vote for her ninth child, and the emotion she calls up is nostalgic regret, not campaign enthusiasm. The emotionally wounded wife and three traumatized children are produced by the candidate like scars, not ornaments. "Come up, Patrick," Kennedy gestures at a morning rally, and the twelve-year-old, so clearly resentful, stands just off the platform edge and refuses. Joan Kennedy, rising to speak, breathless and inducing breathlessness in all who watch, moves as carefully as a wire walker on the first trip over Niagara. Will she fall?

How did it all come apart so fast? Only last summer, Kennedy led Carter two-to-one in the polls. The President was seeking him out for debate, giving up the incumbent's advantage, fearful of the even greater advantage of being a Kennedy. But that, too, had been a lagging perception, one out of synch with events. Edward Kennedy had inherited various simulacra of power, not its reality; he both was and was not "a Kennedy" as his brothers had defined that political entity. And both being and not being like them hurt. His life has become, over the years, a broken chain of tangled memories, full of gaps and overlaps. He lives out of sequence with himself, the youngest child and oldest son alive; the kid brother who must father all his brothers' kids. Nearing fifty, he lives cramped inside the diminutive "Teddy."

At age twenty-nine, Edward Kennedy was Assistant District Attorney for the County of Suffolk, preparing his first Senate race. At the same age, his oldest brother had died in war.

At age forty-three, Edward Kennedy had been a Senator from Massachusetts for thirteen years — the senior Senator for eleven years. He was considered by many (including Jimmy Carter, out of office in Georgia), the strongest contender for the Democratic nomination coming up a year later. At age forty-three his elder brother Robert had been killed while campaigning.

At forty-six, Edward Kennedy ignited the Democratic "mini-convention" in Memphis and seemed to all observers his party's favorite. At the same age, his brother the President was shot in Dallas.

Of his four dead siblings, two died in their twenties, two in their forties. He had become his father's father when he reached the age of thirty: the financier who drove his brothers toward office had a crippling stroke just before Edward won a Senate seat. Later, it was Edward who had to pierce his father's shell of incomprehension with news that the President was dead. It was Edward who buried the father one year after Robert was shot. It was Edward who stood by in smock and face mask to assist at the cesarean birth of Robert's last child after Robert's death, blood from the incision spraying his mask. Day by day, he mixes death and life.

Both press and public were astounded at the way Kennedy bore up under defeat after defeat, Tuesday after Tuesday, in the 1980 campaign. But he has long been initiated into loss. When he was twelve, his brother and his brother-in-law were killed in war. When he was sixteen his sister died in a plane crash. When he was thirty-one, his brother was shot. When he was thirty-two, his aide, and the pilot of a chartered plane, died in the crash that broke Edward Kennedy's back. When he was thirty-six another brother was shot. After that last blow, maudlin in the woozy early hours in Alaska, he kept repeating to reporters, "They're going to shoot my ass off the way they shot Bobby's." He rarely showed fear, however; seemed, indeed, too jaunty to some — with the effort that heaves several lives' weight into the air again. After Robert was killed, he told his aide Dun Gifford: "I can't let go. We have a job to do. If I let go, Ethel will let go, and my mother will let go, and all my sisters."

Because of Kennedy's determination, there is a wounded youthfulness about him that deceives. He will be the kid brother till he dies. Because they died too young, he will be young in a grotesque way when he is old. The proper sequences have been irrevocably mixed. He is allowed neither youth nor age, neither death nor fully living. John, campaigning, had Robert and Edward to work for him. Robert had Edward to advise and be his surrogate. Edward has no one but ghosts at his side, and they count more against than for him, eclipse him with bright images from the past. Where they were praised too fulsomely, he is bound to be judged too harshly. He inherits the illusions of his brothers' followers with the accumulated venoms of their foes; and both tend to disinherit him.

Once brother drew on brother for fresh strength; now brother drains brother, all the dead inhibiting the one that has lived on. Edward has managed to outlast three brothers without ever catching up to one of them. Just as he seems to overtake them, their glory either recedes from him, or fades in the public's eyes. It was pretty evanescent stuff to begin with, the glory; but one can hardly look to him for that perception. To show ingratitude toward the ghosts would just make them harder to shake off. Meanwhile, he inherits all their children, while his own partly slip away from him, victims of his own victimhood, and of his wife's.

There has been too much dying for the Kennedys, which makes the whole nation, not just traveling reporters, mount a kind of death watch over Edward Kennedy. An editor of *Harper's* took offense at the family gift for disaster: "Given the intensity of his family's will to death . . . ," he wrote in 1980. Will to death, indeed. Were Lee Harvey Oswald, and Sirhan Sirhan, Kennedy wish-fulfillments? This almost demented charge shows how deep the Kennedy fascination has entered into the national psyche, and how odd the manifestations of it can become. He only partly died with each brother, and some resent that. What right has he to live?

> *Guthrum the good is fallen,*
> *Are you too good to fall?*

If Kennedys have a will to death, then Edward's life proclaims his lack of willpower. His very courage to go on, his lack of self-pity, are used against him.

James MacGregor Burns called Edward Kennedy "late-born," a description echoed constantly in other people's writings. But, even more important, Kennedy was early stranded, deprived of his own sources of strength and support, forced into the arena by a father and brothers who are not around to help him with the fight. Burton Hersh quotes a friend of the Senator: "When Ted wants to consult with someone he trusts completely he gets in a room alone, and locks the door, and talks to himself." He communes with ghosts. Years ago, one of John Kennedy's mistresses told her son: "The old man would push Joe, Joe would push Jack, Jack would push Bobby, Bobby would push Teddy, and Teddy would fall on his ass." It need not have worked that way, if one or more of the first four men had lived longer. But they did not. Having pushed the younger brother for a while, they could not hold him up or steady him under trial, as each had been steadied, earlier, by the others.

At the end of a campaign day in New Hampshire, I had dinner with reporter Jim Dickenson of the Washington *Star,* and his wife, Molly. How does Kennedy go on, we wondered. Jim said: "If this is the American dream, you can have it. Wealth, looks, family, office, power — he has what his daddy wanted for him, and look where it's got him. Who on earth would want to be Kennedy now?" The center for so long of prying envy, he had become an object of pity for those who watched him up close, what there was to watch. Constantly on display, Kennedy is forever hidden, known only to a few — and those few sometimes wonder if they know him. Does he know himself? Has he a self to know, apart from the vanished older icons of Kennedy self-possession?

We went back to the Wayfarer Inn in Manchester, and met California Governor Jerry Brown wandering with a lone aide down the hall.

"Where you been?" Brown asked me.

"Following Kennedy."

"How's he doing?"

"It seems bleak."

"Yes?" There was no show of glee at this report about a rival candidate. "Well . . . it's hard, I guess, to handle decline." He said it meditatively, knowing his own campaign was gliding down, and knowing that we knew. Jim later remarked, "We just heard Jerry Brown's concession speech."

Molly, a Brown admirer, said, "Yes, but it was more than that. You could tell what was happening to Kennedy affected him." This was more than an unsuccessful campaign. I had thought to pursue the matter with Brown, but just then Theodore White bustled up to lecture Brown on the Roman Empire.

It was more than a campaign ending. Kennedy was being forced, every day, to demonstrate that he was not as good as his brothers. His every effort at recommending himself worked to condemn him. He could not make the counterclaim, that his *brothers* were not as good as his brothers, that Camelot had been a fabric of political unreality. In this campaign, Kennedy was like the last climber in a human chain going up a mountainside, tied to the prowess of the four men above him. But then, in rapid succession, all four men fell, and the very strength that had been drawing him upward now hung a dead weight below him. Each time he stirred to go higher, he just slipped back. The "Kennedy legacy" had become a very literal burden, made his life a constant labor with death.

I

SEX

Sexuality must not be described as a stubborn drive, by nature alien and of necessity disobedient to a power which exhausts itself trying to subdue it and often fails to control it entirely. It appears rather as an especially dense transfer point for relations of power: between men and women, young people and old people, parents and offspring, teachers and students, priests and laity, an administration and a population.

— MICHEL FOUCAULT

1

The Father

Like the other young men of his circle he thought chastity a dangerous state, and he seems early to have taken practical steps to avoid incurring the risks attendant on it.
— DAVID CECIL, *Young Melbourne*

THE TERM "imprisonment" came to mind as I watched Edward Kennedy shake hands with well-wishers at Boston's Pier Four — another stop in his marathon 1980 birthday party. In this ritual of giving himself, every gesture outward was inhibited, visibly checked. He moves, of course, in the stiff constraints of his back brace — at outdoor events, reporters wondered whether it was just the brace or if he wore a bulletproof vest. But there is more to his stiffness with people than medical complaint. That is most obvious when women approach him. With men, he can sometimes do the locker-room punch on the arm, clumsily hug an "old boy." But he subtly tenses when women come near, and puts his hand far out for primmest shaking. He has been burned too often by tabloid pictures of him merely walking near a pretty blonde. A kiss on the cheek may be quite continental, but that is a luxury denied him, now, in public. He lives within an invisible cage of his own forging, sealed in by his own actions outward, by the reputation of his former prowess. The ladies' man can barely shake a lady's hand, so crippled is he by his past.

An air of barely suppressed sexual exuberance was always part of Kennedy campaigns. The day after the Pier Four party, I went with

Steve Neal of the Chicago *Tribune* to look at films of those old campaigns in the Kennedy Library. Even Bobby had been grabbed at by young women as if he were a rock star. The Charles Guggenheim documentary on his life has a touching moment when a girl reaches out to pat his hair, almost reverently, in the turmoil of shouts and handshakes. Of course, the "jumpers" of the 1960 campaign have entered legend. Murray Kempton wrote, of John Kennedy's motorcade:

> John F. Kennedy treated southern Ohio yesterday as Don Giovanni used to treat Seville. His progress, as ever, was an epic in the history of the sexual instinct of the American female. Outside Dayton, a woman of advanced years but intact instinct sat with her dog. Kennedy passed; she waved; he waved back; in that moment of truth she clasped her dog and kissed his wet muzzle. Jack Kennedy is starting to enjoy these moments, and he is starting to enjoy them as a man of taste. He turns back now and goes on waving; the lingering hand gestures and the eye follows; its object is always a quietly pretty girl and the hand says that, if he did not have miles to go and promises to keep, he would like to walk with her where the mad river meets the still water.

For the youngest — in some ways the sexiest — Kennedy to run a sexless campaign in 1980 was a sharp but not a strange reversal. There is a kind of inevitability to it. I have said that Edward forged his own bars around him; but that is only partly true. Family tradition helped put them there. A very important and conscious part of the male Kennedy mystique is a pride in womanizing. Only Robert broke free of this — he had other demons. But, with that exception, what Montaigne wrote of some aristocratic families in his day was literally true of the Kennedys: "We know how some lament being consecreated to celibacy before the age of choice; but I have seen some truly lament their being consecrated to licentiousness before the age of choice. The parent's vice can be the cause. . . ." The Kennedy boys were expected by their father to undertake a competitive discipline of lust; and he let them know that he was still in the competition himself. Here is the testimony of Mary Pitcairn, who dated John Kennedy, but later married Senator Kenneth Keating:

Mr. Kennedy always called up the girls Jack was taking out and asked them to dinner. He came down and took me to the Carleton Hotel — then the fanciest dining room in Washington. He was very charming. He wanted to know his children's friends. He was *very* curious about my personal life. He really wanted to know. He asked a lot of personal questions — *extraordinarily* personal questions. And then — I'll *never* forget this — he told me a lot about Gloria Swanson, how wonderful she was and how he kept in touch with her. When he brought me home, he called her up from my apartment. She was at the Plaza Hotel in New York. He said, "I'm going to call her up and make a date for tomorrow night," or something. Which he did.

Gloria Swanson has described the way Joseph Kennedy flaunted her presence on a ship to Europe, even though Rose Kennedy was traveling with them. According to Mary Pitcairn, he was similarly uninhibited in the home he shared with Rose:

He did something that I heard he did to everyone. After dinner he would take you home and kiss you goodnight as though he were a young so-and-so. One night I was visiting Eunice at the Cape and he came into my bedroom to kiss me goodnight! I was in my nightgown, ready for bed. Eunice was in her bedroom. We had an adjoining bath. The doors were open. He said, "I've come to say goodnight," and kissed me. Really kissed me. It was so silly. I remember thinking, "How embarrassing for Eunice!" . . . I think all this confused Jack. He was a sensitive man and I think it confused him. What kind of object is a woman? To be treated as his father treated them? And his father's behavior that way was blatant. There was always a young, blond beautiful secretary around.

I have been quoting from *The Search for JFK* by Joan and L. Clay Blair, Jr. (1976). The Blairs tried to interview all of John Kennedy's early friends, male and female. The attributes most frequently mentioned in this mass of interviews are John Kennedy's intelligence, his womanizing (often connected with his father's), his bad back and bad stomach, and his habit of expecting others to pay for things because he never carried cash.

The father's "skirt chasing" was notorious. He not only pursued his own sons' "dates," but the dates of those sons' friends. Edward

McLaughlin, John's Navy friend, was engaged to Elizabeth Drake, whom he later married. Mrs. McLaughlin remembers how Kennedy's father took her to dinner:

> He asked me how much I thought Eddie would make when he started working. I said I didn't know but that he hoped to be a lawyer. Mr. Kennedy said he paid his butler more than Ed would ever make. He said I was wasting my time with Ed. I was a nice-looking girl and I could do better than that. I couldn't even eat I was so nervous. And I began to see the handwriting on the wall. I got out of there as fast as I could. I didn't think I'd ever hear from him again, but I did. He called again. And I — foolish me — went again, twice more I think. It was a challenge in a way. I thought I could handle this guy. Nothing was going to happen. But each time he got tougher to fend off. The third time, I really had a rough time getting out of his apartment. I literally ran out. And then I'd see him down at the Cape and he'd be perfectly charming. I've had other girls tell me almost identical stories. He was just that kind of guy.

When the young Charlotte McDonnell went to visit Kathleen Kennedy at her father's Waldorf Towers suite, Kennedy pretended to Will Hays, the movie censor, that she was his "girl in the bedroom":

> I was about sixteen at the time and pretty shook up. I could not imagine *my* father walking in to the room and saying, "Hey, would you believe it? Will Hays thought I had a girl in the bedroom." When you're sixteen years old and you've been born and bred in the convent and you've got a very strict father who never deviated from any line, morally or ethically — it did shake me up. But Kick and Jack didn't seem to care. I think maybe they were so used to it. . . . They just didn't seem to have the same, for lack of a better word, moral values. Although that is not really the proper word. Respect for women.

When the Blairs asked, "Was that also true of Jack?" she answered, "Yes."

Far from covering up his affairs, Joseph Kennedy tried to claim more of them than there were — even when it might hurt his business ventures (shocking Will Hays was not the best way to get motion pictures approved). He obviously thought this was part of his charm; and three of his four boys must have agreed, since they tried to emulate his "conquests."

I have seen it written and heard it said that Joseph — or John or Edward — Kennedy showed an Irish Catholic approach to women, idolizing the wife at home, but recognizing the human frailty caused by original sin, hoping for forgiveness in the confessional. But, as we shall see, the father rarely stressed his own Irish background; and the family line, picked up in a number of the Blairs' interviews, was that the father had an "English" attitude toward women — which meant, they thought, a continental or sophisticated air. Joseph Kennedy was so little Irish that he wanted to ape the English, and his children became intense anglophiles. In calling his attitude "English," they were putting what they considered the best light on it.

Irish Catholics in America have been, if anything, puritanical about sex, and Kennedy wanted people to know he had escaped that particular form of ethnic narrowness; that he was a man of the world, making his own rules, getting what he wanted, ready to indulge without guilt the one sensual pleasure that interested him. His bad stomach forbade drinking, smoking, or fancy foods; he was too restless to enjoy leisure; the arts were nonexistent to him. That left women, where he tried to exhibit a connoisseur's taste and a conquistador's prowess. Here he not only indulged himself; the family indulged him too. The sons seemed to take a borrowed pride in their father's "manliness," and imitated it. Even the daughters put the best face on his philandering. Some of those who told the Blairs that the father's attitude was "English" picked up that designation from Kathleen Kennedy, who became the Marchioness of Hartington. Before her marriage to the Marquis, Kathleen wrote her brother Jack in the Navy: "I can't really understand why I like Englishmen so much, as they treat one in quite an offhand manner and aren't really as nice to their women as Americans, but I suppose it's just that sort of treatment that women really like. That's your technique isn't it?"

Montaigne said that some aristocrats not only claim a license themselves but arrange a similar freedom for their sons: "It is the fashion in our country to put sons in the best homes where, as pages, they may be trained to noble manners. And it is called a discourtesy for anyone to refuse a gentleman his wishes." But if Joseph Kennedy thought sexual freedom an aristocratic trait, he was giving aristocracy a new definition from the jazz age. After his rejection by the brahmins of Boston, he oriented his world around New York and Hollywood, around the sports and journalism and cinema stars of the roaring twenties. A starlet would have disgraced the better Boston families; but Kennedy displayed his actresses as so many decorations, as signs that he was looking to new centers of power and of popular acclaim. The Boston gentry were exclusive. He would be expansive, open and racy. He was steering his family down the course that made them staples of the tabloids. As he told Gloria Swanson: "The Cabots and the Lodges wouldn't be caught dead at the pictures, or let their children go. And that's why their servants know more about what's going on in the world than they do. The working class gets smarter every day, thanks to radio and pictures. It's the snooty Back Bay bankers who are missing the boat."

The father's fascination with starlets, sports heroes, and worldly jounalists was passed on to his sons. Even Robert Kennedy, the most reflective of them, the nonwomanizer, had the family interest in entertainers and athletes — in Rafer Johnson and Andy Williams and Marilyn Monroe. He would ultimately alert his brother against Frank Sinatra's circle — but only after their sister Patricia had married into that circle.

The journalist to whom Joseph Kennedy was closest, over the years, was Arthur Krock of the New York *Times,* a voice of the American journalistic establishment, politically very conservative, but "liberal" in his moral views. The two cemented their joint purposes with a male camaraderie of conquest — exactly the relationship John Kennedy would later have with *Newsweek*'s Ben Bradlee. Krock inadvertently occasioned John Kennedy's first serious trouble over sex. The New York *Times*man tried to find journalistic jobs for his beautiful protégées; Frank Waldrop, editor of the Washington *Times-Herald* in 1941, remembers that when Krock called him and said, "I've got another one for you," Waldrop answered, "What are you, our staff procurer?" The "one" Krock had got was Inga Arvad, a European beauty contest winner who had Nazi connections. Arvad later told her son, "Krock was a skirt-chaser." Women were passed around in the Krock–Kennedy circles; but so was news of them — the FBI soon had tape recordings of Arvad in bed with a naval intelligence officer, John Kennedy. That ended the future President's intelligence days in Washington, and almost ended his military service altogether. Only his father's intervention with James Forrestal, then Undersecretary of the Navy, kept John Kennedy in uniform after this, his first assignment. He later omitted this first tour of duty from his Navy biography.

It seems clear in retrospect that John Kennedy was not jeopardizing his country when he persisted in seeing Inga Arvad (even after his dismissal from intelligence work because of her); but he was certainly jeopardizing his career — which was his father's only concern. Inga Arvad's son remembers: "She thought old Joe was awfully hard — a really mean man. He could be very charming when she and Jack were with him but if she left the room he'd come down on Jack about her and if Jack left the room, he'd try to hop in the sack with her. He did that one weekend at the Cape, she said. She thought it was a totally amoral situation, that there was something incestuous about the whole family."

Krock had earlier helped initiate the Kennedy boys into intrigues, even when the father was giving them a rare warning. Joseph Jr. had struck up a shipboard romance with a movie actress, and was too open about it. His father wanted this son to be President; so he imposed a curfew on Joe, and on John who shared a cabin with him. But once the father had checked the boys in for the night, they escaped out a sealed servant door. In his *Memoirs,* Krock pretends he deduced this from the boys' presence at later carousals; but in the oral history at the Kennedy Library, where he speaks more frankly, he admits he opened the door for them. Despite that cruise's specific injunction, the father radiated a "boys will be boys" ethic around his sons. As Montaigne says, aristocratic pretensions can train one to licentiousness.

Joseph Kennedy's new breed of boys being boys made a questionable aristocracy. Norman Mailer did not quite get the point when he described the situation. In his famous 1960 essay for *Esquire,* "Superman Comes to the Supermarket," Mailer rejoiced that America's "beggars of glamor" were to be given a new kind of political hero-ism: "America's politics would now be also America's favorite movie. . . . America believed in athletes, rum-runners, aviators; even lovers, by the time Valentino died." Now it would believe in Ken-nedys, who — thanks to the father — had a bit of rum-running dash and Valentino glitter to them.

In 1938, Ambassador Kennedy watched the King and Queen of England arrive at Ascot for the Gold Cup races. His wife wrote of that day: "When Joe first saw the royal procession, he commented, 'Well, if that's just not just like Hollywood.' " Kennedy's career in the movies was comparatively short; but it was not a mere incident in his life. He was dazzled by Hollywood, and loved to use its glitter on others. As a movie producer, he had early copies of films to show his family and visitors — something he managed to do long after he had left the business. Even when entertaining the royal couple in London, he showed them early releases of American films. At Hyannis Port there was a movie every night during the summer, which awed the children's visiting friends.

Only John seems to have inherited his father's *consuming* interest in the movies, in the myths and gossip of Hollywood. As President he even called the set where *Advise and Consent* was being filmed, to learn when he could get an early print. He watched films constantly in the White House. And he was as interested in the actors' private lives as in their screen performances. The adoring Kenneth O'Don-nell admits: "His fondness for Frank Sinatra, which perplexed a lot of people, was simply based on the fact that Sinatra told him a lot of inside gossip about celebrities and their romances in Hollywood." Not only was Sinatra the President's private Rona Barrett — he was also one of the President's favorite topics of conversation. Judith Campbell (later Mrs. Exner), who had been recommended to Ken-nedy because "she looks like Elizabeth Taylor" (in 1960, the subject of most movie gossip), says Kennedy's conversations in the White House returned again and again to Frank Sinatra's affairs.

> Oh, but he loved gossip. He adored it. That was something he was always asking me about on the telephone and in person. He would say, "Who's Frank seeing now?" or "I heard Frank is seeing so-and-so and isn't she married?"

He thought Frank's temperament was a riot. He was amused at the havoc Frank could cause and at the way people around him would cower in fear.

Almost immediately Jack started pumping me for gossip, most of it directed at Frank. What was Frank doing? Was it true that he was seeing Janet Leigh? We went through the same routine.

Mrs. Exner does not seem to realize that her own glamour for Kennedy came largely from the fact that she had been Sinatra's mistress.

Every time we talked on the phone, and I am referring to before and after our meeting at the Plaza, he invariably would ask, "Have you seen Frank lately?" I would answer, "No," or "Yes, I saw him on the set," or "He called last night and I wasn't home," or whatever was the circumstance at the moment. Jack would say, "Ohhh, you still want to see Frank?" I would say, "We're just friends, Jack." Then he'd say, "Okay, okay," in almost a little boy's "See if I care" voice. Then the very next day, "See Frank? Where did you go last night? I called and you weren't home."

Kennedy pursued "stars" (Sonja Henie and Gene Tierney) the way his father had. And since his father had taken Gloria Swanson and other mistresses to Hyannis Port, daring any in the family to object, John Kennedy met his women in the White House. The Hyannis Port competition for women, which made that compound partly a fraternity house, was repeated in the executive mansion. Mrs. Exner was a prize up for grabs, not only between brothers but among Kennedy "gofers" as well:

He asked about Frank again, and although I felt that his interest in Frank was genuine, I found it a little annoying that I always seemed to remind him of Frank. Then as we walked into the [White House] dining room, he said, "Have you heard from Teddy?"
That stopped me. "You mean your brother?"
"Yes. Has Teddy called you?"
"Of course not," I said. "You should know that."
"Well, I just wondered."
Jack never forgot what Teddy had tried in Las Vegas. Several times when we were in bed he said, "Boy, if Teddy only knew, he'd

be eating his heart out." I think he got a big kick out of the fact that he had succeeded where Teddy had failed.

When Mrs. Exner ferried Kenneth O'Donnell to the secret apartment kept by Kennedy during the Los Angeles convention, O'Donnell made a grab at her, and was astonished when she resisted. Everyone joined the game, with no preliminary niceties. Part of the father's aggressive charm, passed on to the sons and their imitators, was a merry effrontery, a freshness and candor of rapacity, what Montaigne calls his own "impertinently genital" approach. Burton Hersh has described the family manner, as exemplified by Edward Kennedy: "College girls who went out with him reported back that he made his expectations clear early and with great undisguised feeling, and took it more as a curiosity than an affront if his straightforward-enough offer was not instantly accepted." Even a custodian of the Kennedy legends, James MacGregor Burns, was astounded at the openness of the youngest Kennedy's "series of brief flirtations and longer, more intense involvements," and quotes a friend of his in Congress: "I have told him ten times, 'Ted, you're acting like a fool. Everybody knows you wherever you go. . . . Jack could smuggle girls up the back way of the Carlyle Hotel. But you're not nearly as discreet as you should be.' He looks down with a faint smile and says: 'Yeah, I guess you're right.' But he never listens."

The family game of "chasing" is part of the self that was built up by all three imitators of their magnetic father. Passing women around, and boasting of it, to other men and other women, was a Kennedy achievement:

> As soon as I was introduced to Angie [Dickinson), she let out a shriek: "You're Judy Campbell?" I told her I was and she said, "John has told me so much about you!" All I could say was, "Oh, really?" At first I thought she meant Rosselli [a Giancana associate], but then I realized that she meant John Kennedy. She kept saying, "Oh, I'm so glad to see you. I've heard so much about you."

Kennedy's curiosity and candor about his own and other people's sex lives may indicate why his favorite book was Cecil's *Young Melbourne,* a gossipy and superficial look at "lives of the aristocrats" in Regency England. Betty Spalding was astonished at Kennedy's intrusive questions, as Mary Pitcairn had been by Joseph Kennedy's: "He would say personal things to me. I mean, ask me personal questions about women and marriage — and later he talked to me about his sex life with Jackie."

Ben Bradlee also describes Kennedy's appetite for gossip about the sex life of others: "The four of us got on the subject of a guest at the birthday party last night (who shall here be nameless), who had told Jackie and Tony that he had not slept with his wife for the last sixteen years. This kind of dirt the president of the United States can listen to all day long." It is clear from Bradlee's book what conversation Kennedy enjoyed: "Tonight's last minute miscellany included: Why none of us had women friends with large bosoms." And: "Before we left we reminisced about the night of the West Virginia primary, the dirty movie we had seen, whose plot the president seemed to recall remarkably well, given his preoccupations that night." Kennedy could not even wait for a child to grow up before speculating about its sex life. Complimenting the Bradlees on their infant son, he said: "My God, he's a good looking child. Those eyes. He's going to do a helluva business." That must be what his own father said of the infant Kennedy.

When not gossiping about sex, Kennedy liked to fantasize about it with the help of movies. Even Ben Bradlee was surprised at the President's taste:

> The movie was James Bond, and Kennedy seemed to enjoy the cool and the sex and the brutality.

> The president was determined to see a movie, even though Jackie said the choices were strictly limited. Jackie read off the list of what was available, and the president selected the one we had all unanimously voted against, a brutal sadistic little Western called *Lonely Are the Brave.* Kennedy watched, lying down on a bed placed in the front row, his head propped up on pillows.

Obviously only one vote counted in that room. Those without a taste for low movies must have found the famous Kennedy charm wearing thin come nightfall: "We dined alone with the president last night. Jackie did not appear. We saw a dreadful movie about some Englishmen in a German prison camp."

Joseph Kennedy, a man of strong will and low tastes, passed on both traits to his son. He aspired upward to the White House and downward to tabloid heaven. John Kennedy reached both places; and though the tabloids cruelly exploited his widow in later years, the son had been groomed for the one place just as surely as he was for the other. It is difficult to become an American prince.

2

The President

He had been at Eton and Oxford, but he had not learnt, what is
often learned there, a decorum in profligacy.
— WALTER BAGEHOT, of Bolingbroke

IN 1960, as a graduate student in New Haven, I was discussing
Mailer's *Esquire* article with another graduate student, a woman.
What, I asked her, would happen if Kennedy's womanizing became
even better known? (The reputation was already there, winked at
several times by Mailer in his piece.) "That will help him," she replied. Why? "It will show he knows how to get what he wants."
The liberal world was so bored with avuncular "Ike" that it welcomed a President who had the nerve to wear a rake's rather dingy
halo. It is easy to forget that the Sinatra "rat pack" was considered a
liberal phenomenon in the late fifties. After all, it admitted one black
performer to its carousings.

The graduate student in New Haven, afire for liberal causes, was
also excited by John Kennedy's sexual image, which was not "irrelevant" for her — as it later became for those trying to hide Kennedy's
affairs. It was, precisely, a basis of *political* appeal. Power was one,
over women or over Khrushchev. As Kathleen had written to her
brother in the South Pacific, "It's just that sort of treatment that
women really like." Women could trust a man who "treats 'em
rough" to be tough in other contexts too.

I thought of that graduate student when I went to work for a
magazine where a female writer was described to me as "a Kennedy-

style celebrity-fucker." She too admired New Frontiersmen for their macho. But by the time Sammy Davis, Jr. was embracing Nixon and Frank Sinatra was subsidizing Agnew, that woman had become a feminist — and a critic of Edward Kennedy. Mailer was right to see things poised for a massive swing of mood in 1960; but he could not see how wide the mood would ultimately veer from his own (and the Kennedy) view of male heroism. The sexual revolution launched with a glorification of aggression would lead, finally, to profound criticism of it.

But all that was far ahead when John Kennedy became the first movie-star President. It is hard to remember that the "sexual revolutionaries" of the 1950s — male *and* female — had been brought up on the cult of Hemingway, of dominating men, hunters, bull-fighters, risk-takers. This was the Hemingway called on in the first sentence of Kennedy's *Profiles in Courage*. Mailer voiced the creed of that time during and after the 1960 campaign:

> The film studios threw up their searchlights as the frontier was fi-
> nally sealed, and the romantic possibilities of the old conquest of
> land turned into a vertical myth, trapped within the skull, of a new
> kind of heroic life, each choosing his own archetype of a neo-renais-
> sance man, be it Barrymore, Cagney, Flynn, Bogart, Brando or Sin-
> atra, but it was almost as if there were no peace unless one could
> fight well, kill well (if always with honor), love well and love
> many, be cool, be daring, be dashing, be wild, be wily, be resource-
> ful, be a brave gun.

Naturally, there was no occasion to talk of female heroism. Woman's role was to be one of the "many" getting "well loved." They were to revolve (replaceably) about the hero, like the freshets of nubile bodies circling Sean Connery in James Bond movies, the favorite entertainment of Mailer's "Superman" in the White House.

It may seem pointless to notice that John Kennedy had extra-marital affairs. Politicians are not famous for fidelity. The male politician's ego reaches out to manipulate others, to dominate; and with women that domination often takes a crude sexual form. Lyndon Johnson, for instance, tried to put his brand on everyone around him, and was colorfully direct about the nature of the branding iron used on women. But John Kennedy's womanizing was different in both scale and intensity. It led him to take political and personal risks, from the time of Inga Arvad to that of Sam Giancana's lover, Judith Campbell; risks even his father and brothers thought foolhardy. It would in time enmesh most of his entourage in a complex set of lies and cover-ups. And it seems never to have abated. Few politicians — much less Presidents — would candidly inform a Prime Minister of England that they get headaches if they go for long without a woman.

When Kennedy said that to Harold Macmillan, he was assuming his sister Kathleen's view of the *English* attitude toward sex — an attitude celebrated in Kennedy's favorite book, Cecil's life of Melbourne: " 'I was afraid I was going to have the gout the other day,' writes Lord Carlisle to a friend. 'I believe I live too chaste: it is not a common fault with me.' It was not a common fault with any of them. In fact, an unmarried man was thought unpleasantly queer if he did not keep under his protection some sprightly full-bosomed Kitty Clive or Mrs. Bellamy, whose embraces he repaid with a house in Montpelier Square, a box at the opera and a smart cabriolet in which to drive her down to Brighthelmstone for a week's amorous relaxation."

The sheer pace of Kennedy's sex life, its serial and simultaneous variety, awed his friends and competitors. Rip Horton, a Choate friend who was with the teenage John Kennedy at his sexual initiation in a bordello, remembers what Congressman Kennedy's bachelor pad was like in the fifties:

> I went to his house in Georgetown for dinner. A lovely looking blonde from West Palm Beach joined us to go to a movie. After the movie we went back to the house, and I remember Jack saying something like, "Well, I want to shake this one. She has ideas." Shortly thereafter, another girl walked in. Ted Reardon was there, so he went home and I went to bed figuring this was the girl for the night. The next morning, a completely different girl came wandering down for breakfast. They were a dime a dozen.

They were, in fact, so interchangeable he had trouble keeping them straight, according to Charlotte McDonnell: "I got a letter from Jack from the South Pacific. When I opened it up, I saw it wasn't meant for me. He had written two letters and got the envelopes mixed up. The salutation was 'Dearest ———.' She must have been some starlet." Anthony Gallucio, a friend of Joseph Jr., who worked in John Kennedy's campaign, told the Blairs:

> The male side of the family were all like that. They came by it naturally — from the father, who chased anything in skirts. Girls would come around and Jack would get all excited. He was like a kid. He really liked girls. But it was just physical and social activity for him. He'd just keep moving. Italians get emotionally involved. But Kennedy never got emotionally involved. He'd sleep with a girl, and then he'd have Billy [Sutton] take her to the airport the next day.

Senator George Smathers of Florida, known as a ladies' man himself, was Kennedy's closest social friend on the Hill during their early Washington days. He says: "Jack liked girls. He liked girls very much. He came by it naturally. His daddy liked girls. He was a chaser."

But according to the English tennis star Katherine Stammers, who dated Kennedy just after the war, Kennedy did not so much "like" girls as use them, at a fast turnover rate: "He really didn't give a damn. He liked to have them around and he liked to enjoy himself, but he was quite unreliable. He did as he pleased. I think he was probably spoiled by women. I think he could snap his fingers and they'd come running."

We have seen that his father tried to discourage a woman from marrying one of John Kennedy's friends. The Blairs found that the son, too, tried to discourage others from getting married. And the wives of those already married resented his attempt to keep their husbands still "on the chase." The wife of a Navy friend, James Reed, complained:

> Jack would frequently ask Jim to parties — but not me! It was a male prowling thing and Jack couldn't understand why Jim couldn't leave me behind and prowl with him. Maybe this is acceptable in the "upper class" [her husband, too, called Kennedy's attitude an aristocratic "English attitude"]. I think Jack felt this was being manly. But, it seemed to me, he had a contempt for women, possibly because of his father's attitude toward women.

Friend after friend traces the speed of female turnover to a total lack of emotional involvement. Leonard Nikoloric, another Navy pal, said: "Girls were almost an obsession with him. We liked them too, but we didn't make a career of it the way he did." The journalist John White, who dated Kathleen Kennedy, told Herbert Parmet: "He was completely driven to dominate them. Once he got them, he lost interest and moved on to the next." It is the classic Don Juan attitude: by putting them on the list, you cross them out of existence. Conquest erases the conquered. In Montaigne's words: "As soon as we can make them ours, we are no longer theirs." The cancellation could take place so fast that a woman might well wonder if she was still *there*. Judith Campbell contrasts the active lovemaking of Frank Sinatra with Kennedy's supine passivity:

> I understood about the position he had to assume in lovemaking when his back was troubling him, but slowly he began excluding all other positions, until finally our lovemaking was reduced to this one position. It is impossible for me to pinpoint when I first realized it, because it was such a gradual process, but slowly I began to feel that he expected me to come into bed and just perform. There would be a moment of stillness when I came into bed and it was almost like he expected me to roll over and put my arms around him and make love to him. . . . I was there to service him.

Inga Arvad's son heard the same complaint from her: "If he wanted to make love, you'd make love — now. They'd have fifteen minutes to get to a party and she'd say she didn't want to. He'd look at his watch and say we've got ten minutes, let's go. There was a certain amount of insensitiveness, an awful lot of self-centeredness." He had this terrible itch that needed constant scratching, and the attention was on the itch, not on the replaceable scratchers. As Lord Rochester wrote of a profligate duchess:

> *She'll still drudge on in tasteless vice*
> *As if she sinn'd for exercise.*

The crowded, compulsive schedule of Kennedy's sex life went beyond that of most politicians, beyond even that of his father or brothers, though it was grounded in the father's code. Charles Spalding, one of Kennedy's closest friends, said:

> He was always interested in seeing whether he had it or didn't have it. Can I do it or can't I do it? To me, that always accounted for a lot of the numbers, if you will. And the other thing I think is having a very, very strong father. All kids, I suppose, want to be better than their fathers. That's part of the game. Mr. Kennedy was a very strong and also a very worldly fellow.

Besides the competition with other males, and especially his father, there was a testing of himself, his potency. Did he "have it" for girl after girl? Could he maintain the numbers? To understand this discipline of lust, it is useful to turn again to Montaigne, that shrewd observer of sexual behavior, who says the ill or aging sometimes must rely on the tickle of lust to reanimate them. This was especially true of the chronically ailing Kennedy, who had the physical assertiveness of the partly crippled.

It is becoming more obvious as time passes, and the sequestration of medical records is pierced, that Robert Kennedy was not exaggerating when he said his brother passed half his days on earth in terrible pain. He was sickly from birth, with allergies, an unstable back, and other unspecified illnesses that shuttled him in and out of hospitals all through his youth, and that were followed by the carefully hidden Addison's disease of his later years. With a truly staggering willpower Kennedy refused to acquiesce in his own debilities; not only rose again and again after collapsing, but took on further challenges. He seems to have needed danger and risk and adventure, physical or moral, to keep an edge on his life. If he took to his bed, it would not be to die. He courted danger — driving fast (he turned a car over on himself and Torbert Macdonald in Europe, and crashed into a dock with his PT boat in the Pacific). He went out for sports that were clearly beyond his physical capacity — spurred on, as always, by his father, who wrote him at Harvard: "Good luck to you on the swimming and as to football, remember to be as good as the spirit is." He volunteered for PT boat service, though a boat that size, repeatedly slamming the water, would rattle his back viciously. He had a cult of courage that helps explain his interest in football players, war heroes, and astronauts.

Some thought Kennedy could not have approved James Roosevelt's slurs, in the 1960 campaign, at Hubert Humphrey's "draft dodging"; but Kennedy advised journalists to look up his opponents' war records. Referring to Nelson Rockefeller's diplomatic service in Latin America during World War II, he asked *Newsweek*'s Ben Bradlee, "Where was old Nels when you and I were dodging bullets in the Solomon Islands?" Kenneth O'Donnell says that President Kennedy stopped mocking Douglas MacArthur after reading his World War I citation for bravery on the battlefield. Military service and manhood went together in his mind, and he was quick to accuse an opponent of shirking. During his youngest brother's Senate race against Eddie McCormack, he asked Bradlee, "When are you going to send one of your ace reporters to look into Eddie's record?" Bradlee asked what that meant, and Kennedy said McCormack had resigned from the Navy, the day he graduated from Annapolis, on flimsy medical excuses. "Dave Powers had all the information and he'll give it to you."

I think it is only fair to assume that Kennedy's constant self-testing, the lashing of his body back to a sense of its powers, contributed to his continual, almost heroic sexual performance — a way of cackling at the gods of bodily debility who plagued him, "I'm not dead yet." This performance would be especially important in the macho world he admired, the Hemingway–Mailer–Sinatra world, because he was denied two items in its trinity of manliness, broads and booze and brawls. Among his many ailments, Kennedy had inherited his father's weak stomach, which precluded drinking — which, de facto, eliminates most occasions for brawling.

Kennedy senior, who had or thought he had ulcers most of his life, drank no alcohol and ate bland food. His way of taking a young girl out to lunch was to show up in her hotel room, invite himself in, and send two eggs down to be soft-boiled not more than three minutes — according to Charlotte McDonnell he carried the fresh eggs in his pockets, and wrote his instructions on their shells. His second son, too, did not drink or eat rich foods. The Blairs quote many people wondering at his huge appetite for ice cream, though he disconcerted hostesses by picking without interest at the meals they served him. Abstention from drinking is very noticeable when you spend long hours in nightclubs, as John and his father did — in fact, it takes an almost inexplicable taste for such places to stay in them while not drinking. During long nights in the Solomon Islands, where there was little to do but drink, Kennedy gave away his liquor coupons. But even a teetotaler can keep his macho credentials in order if he doubles the order on broads to compensate for non-performance at the booze.

Kennedy's ailments no doubt gave him license with some women, beginning with those of his family. Even the puritanical Eunice, aware of the courage of his daily life, remained as loyal to the President as did the puritanical Robert. They realized how many pleasures were denied him. Cripples are often very strong in that part of them that is not directly incapacitated. Those closest to Kennedy understood his need to demonstrate virility to himself and others.

But, if anything, this understanding at the personal level raises in more pointed fashion the political implications of large-scale satyriasis. Risk-taking may be the right therapy for an individual; but the commander of a PT squadron should know ahead of time if one of his officers administers self-therapy by crashing expensive boats into valuable docks.

In the same way, a woman a day might help keep the doctor away; but an omnivorous approach to women can compromise the presidential policy as well as reputation. Kennedy had more reason than most people to know this — he was certain, from an early age, that the FBI had at least one set of tapes taken while he made love to a woman suspected of espionage. His father had told him to fear J. Edgar Hoover's use of such tapes. And his grandfather Fitzgerald had been driven from a political campaign by threats to reveal his relationship with a "Toodles" Ryan. Yet, incredibly, John Kennedy continued to make compromising assignations in the White House itself. When he inherited Judith Campbell from Frank Sinatra, he was making love to another woman who might be under investigation — and, as it turned out, was. Overlapping her affair with the candidate, and then with the President, she was intimate with Sam Giancana, who was (a) more or less permanently under investigation for suspected criminal activities, and (b) being approached by the CIA to help assassinate Castro. On several grounds the President's love life was bound to end up in another FBI folder.

Why would a man take such risks? The answer seems obvious: *be-*

cause they were risks. (Montaigne: "Both the act and depictions of it should have a whiff of the criminal about them.") According to Campbell, he tried to arrange even more compromising meetings than their White House trysts, including a threesome arrangement in a hotel room. Like his father inviting Gloria Swanson to travel openly with him on the steamer to France, Kennedy asked Campbell to fly on Air Force One. As she comments on this incident: "I think he just loved intrigue." Setting up risky meetings could take more of his energy than did completion of the tryst. As John Buchan's hero, Richard Hannay, says in *The Thirty-nine Steps,* "It was risks after all that he was chiefly greedy about."

The love of risk, the taste for compromising intrigues and hair-breadth escapes, may lead to an "interesting" life; but it can lead, as well, to international trouble if indulged in the White House. Kennedy admired risk-takers, not only on the football field or the field of battle, but in everyday life. People around him were constantly challenged to display their macho. Those who advised against the Bay of Pigs invasion, Harris Wofford has revealed, were mocked by the President for "grabbing their nuts" in fear. On the other hand, told that his appointment of Robert Kennedy as Attorney General would cause a storm of protest, he turned to his brother and said, "Let's grab our balls and go." Ballsiness was a category as important to him as to Hemingway or Mailer, and he must have been delighted when Joseph Alsop began referring to him at Washington dinner parties as "a Stevenson with balls." The adventurous services appealed to Kennedy, while President as well as in his Navy years — the PT raiders, the Green Berets (whose romantic symbol he invented), the CIA's "special action" teams, the counterinsurgents who promised to perform for him like real-life James Bonds (and who did some of their jungle exercises to an admiring audience at Hyannis Port). Kennedy was intrigued by the U-2 pilot Gary Francis Powers, considering him weird but brave. Later, he admired the legendary counterinsurgent Edward Lansdale.

Admiration for the courage that takes risks can have odd policy consequences, as we shall see. But this very love of dash and freedom had conspicuous exceptions on the "new frontier." The Kennedy administration, brashly taking on bureaucrats, was timorous if not obsequious with the oldest bureaucrat in town, J. Edgar Hoover.

When Robert Kennedy needed information on the layout of the University of Alabama, during the integration struggle there, he did not ask the FBI field office to check facts, but caused a terrible flap by asking the Pentagon to make air photos of the campus. While Justice Department marshals risked their lives at black demonstrations in the South, FBI agents stood on the sidelines taking notes. The series of unworthy southern choices for the federal bench was caused, in part, by superficial FBI reports on the candidates.

These derelictions continued, as Victor Navasky notes in his book on the Kennedy Justice Department; yet J. Edgar Hoover was mysteriously immune to the Kennedy feistiness. Not only did Robert allow Hoover's noncooperation; the Attorney General himself cooperated with requests from Hoover — like that for a phone tap on Martin Luther King. Granted, Hoover was a sacred cow; but the Kennedys showed a passivity toward him out of keeping with their activism in other areas, an activism that positively courted risk. Arthur Schlesinger remembers the priorities of postelection euphoria:

> On Wednesday night after the election he relaxed at dinner with several friends. The group fell into an animated discussion of what the President-elect should do first. One guest suggested that he fire J. Edgar Hoover of the Federal Bureau of Investigation, another that he fire Allen W. Dulles of the Central Intelligence Agency. Kennedy, listening with apparent interest, egged his friends on. When they opened their papers the next morning, they were therefore a little irritated to read a Kennedy announcement that Hoover and Dulles were staying in their jobs.

No explanation was given. Dulles would have to go after the Bay of Pigs. But Hoover kept doing outrageous things, and remained. The President would take on U.S. Steel and Nikita Khrushchev, but not Mr. Hoover. The Attorney General would cut corners to "get Hoffa," but he breathed no wish to get, or even check, his own subordinate at the Justice Department. To guarantee protection for civil rights demonstrators, he formed new kinds of legal posses, but he let FBI agents stand on the sidelines useless and unrebuked. As Navasky wrote: "It was ironic that the FBI — the only intelligence agency directly under the Attorney General's jurisdiction — was the only agency which he did not feel free to bully, pressure, harass, and pull rank on." There was no "ballsiness" in either Kennedy's attitude toward Hoover.

The strange passivity of Robert, this most energetic man, is noticeable in one other area, the investigation of his brother's death. He not only showed a lack of curiosity about the killer (or killers); he took steps to quash rumors of conspiracy — gave exclusive post-assassination interview rights to William Manchester, who opposed any conspiracy talk; sequestered the autopsy report; supported the Warren Commission without even reading its report. Harris Wofford argues persuasively that Robert feared the uncovering of CIA plots to kill Castro, since these involved Sam Giancana, who involved Judith Campbell, who would involve the dead President. As Navasky says: "Any list of RFK priorities would have to begin with his brother's reputation." If that is the case, then the Kennedy servility toward Hoover is explained. From the time of Inga Arvad, Hoover had knowledge that could have ruined the Kennedy reputation and career. Hoover was willing to use that kind of information on targets like Dr. King and Philip Berrigan; but the information was more potent *unused* where men in power were concerned. The mere threat of its use kept such men "in line."

In fact, one of John Kennedy's motives in appointing Robert to the Justice Department was no doubt to have his most trusted agent "handle" Hoover. That appointment was risky at the public level; Kennedy courted charges of nepotism, and Robert was young for the job. But it was a *caution* taken at the private level — no other man was Kennedy's intimate as Robert was, privy to the family secrets, certain to do anything to keep them secret, speaking for the family in sessions with Hoover. Another person, given the choice of ruining Dr. King's reputation or John Kennedy's, might hesitate. But not John Kennedy's brother.

To many people's surprise, Robert Kennedy earned a reputation as his brother's "best appointment." His record at Justice was mixed, as Navasky has argued, but it included many achievements. There may, indeed, have been a compensatory ardor in Kennedy's work for civil rights. He had to assemble his own team and use his own devices, since he had denied himself any opposition to Hoover's wiretapping, to his obstruction in the integration cases, to his slipshod screening of federal judges. There is an air, in the later Robert Kennedy, of doing penance — not, I think, for his own earlier "ruthlessness," as it is fashionable to say; but for his own later sense of helplessness against a man who brazenly frustrated the government's support of civil rights. Robert had been appointed by his brother to contain the threat of Hoover — which made him acquiesce in Hoover's campaign to destroy King. That was a terrible burden to sustain; and it makes a mockery of any talk that John Kennedy's sexual affairs were irrelevant to his politics. His brother's earlier freedoms put Robert Kennedy in a moral prison.

3

Sisters and Wives

And the old man — having his mistresses there at the house for lunch and supper. I couldn't understand it! It was unheard of!

— BETTY SPALDING, visitor at Hyannis Port

IN 1970, my wife and I were at Eunice and Sargent Shriver's house in Rockville, Maryland, for a dinner welcoming Patricia Lawford back from Europe. It was the first time we had seen Joan Kennedy, who was a natural beauty with little makeup on, still looking much younger than her years. Edward Kennedy came late from the Senate floor; we were already seated. But from the moment he arrived there was a hum of invisible wires strung across the room, from Kennedy to Kennedy, alive with continual semiprivate communication. Eunice, no matter what the conversation in her vicinity, heard and laughed at each of Edward's jokes at another table, and vice versa.

When their nurse took the Kennedy children swimming at Taggert's Pier, back in the thirties, they all wore the same color bathing hats, so they could be distinguished from the other children — you knew at once if it was a *Kennedy* in trouble, or if one had not been rounded up for the trip home. Ever since they have been wearing invisible caps that signal to each other on a radio frequency no one else can use.

Driving home, I asked my wife if she had noticed this phenomenon, and its corollary — she had. The corollary was that Joan Kennedy barely said a word at table, or was addressed, after her husband arrived. She wears no invisible cap; she sends no signals. There are honorary Kennedys and real Kennedys, as Sargent Shriver has had occasion to learn. But Joan Bennett Kennedy suffered a double disadvantage at the family table — she is not only not a Kennedy, but not a man. My wife and I were not surprised, a few years later, when reports of Joan Kennedy's drinking became public.

One has to be tough to marry into so close a family, to fight for attention, for one's own space to turn around in. Inga Arvad's son claimed there was something almost incestuous in the closeness of Kennedys to Kennedys; and, in her innocent way, Rose Kennedy bears out that insight: "Joe thought the children would never be married because they all enjoyed going out together so much. They were stimulated by each other's interests and plans, problems and ambitions." Ethel Skakel could become a Super-Kennedy, taking all their competitive games (even the breeding one) to new extremes. Jacqueline Bouvier could make her bargain, mark off her space, and let the family flow, a little bit awed, around her quiet pose. But Joan Bennett was shoved, half a century after the mold had been broken, into Rose Kennedy's role; and not even Rose's own daughters can live that way anymore.

Gloria Swanson, having agreed to Rose's humiliation on a steamer trip to Europe, ingenuously wonders how the wife could put up with such boorishness:

Virginia [Swanson's friend] grasped the curious situation in which she was taking part the first day on the ship, but whether Mrs. Kennedy did or not I couldn't tell. Only a few years older than me, Rose Kennedy was sweet and motherly in every respect. Most of the time she and her female relative treated Virginia and me like a pair of debutantes it was their bounden duty to chaperon. . . . If she suspected me of having relations not quite proper with her husband, or resented me for it, she never once gave any indication of it. In fact, at those times during the voyage when Joe Kennedy behaved in an alarmingly possessive or oversolicitous fashion toward me, Rose joined right in and supported him. In the salon after dinner one evening, he openly and without apology talked and joked confidentially with me and left the other three women to converse among themselves; but when a man at the next table turned his chair around to look at me, Joe became white as chalk, leaped to his feet and loudly ordered the other man to mind his own business and stop staring at me. Before I could think of how to conceal my mortification, I heard Rose emphatically agreeing with Joe's action, saying she didn't understand how I stood being on constant public display, unable to travel two steps without my husband or somebody else to protect me. She thought it was shocking. Was she a fool, I asked myself as I listened with disbelief, or a saint? Or just a better actress than I was?

Of course Rose knew. And of course she had to pretend she did not. That kind of acting came naturally to women of her generation and faith and social position. The men in the family, and even her daughters, were not embarrassed by the mother's plight, but proud of her submissiveness to it. If courage is ballsiness, that is by definition not a quality for women. Their nobility is in patience, in long-suffering, in just those things that would disgrace a man. This attitude is displayed by Tito Gobbi, the great baritone, in his 1979 autobiography. Boasting of his mother's uncomplaining virtue, he wrote:

> My good-looking father had been playing the Don Giovanni and my grandfather — who had a patriarchal tendency to summon the family together when advice or reproof was called for — did so then. I think he principally wished to assure my mother of his support, but before he could say anything *she* addressed *him*, together with the rest of the assembled family. "Thank you very much for your concern for me," she said, "and I hope what I am going to say will not lessen your affection for me. But one thing I must ask you to understand. I am proud of my husband and will not have anything said against him." In point of fact I suppose it might be said that my wise mama was the winner in the end. For the last twenty years of her life my father never left her side and he adored her to the end.

The woman should wait for her wandering husband to come home, and then take care of him in his old age. Meanwhile, she must never complain, never let on that she knows what everyone around her knows. Not only will Joseph Kennedy take Gloria Swanson into his home, Rose Kennedy will talk of that in her own book as an honor done to their abode:

Gloria Swanson was our house guest for a couple of days in Bronxville and brought along her small daughter, who was about the age of our Pat, who was about ten. They got along well together, and Pat took her down to show her the Bronxville public school and meet her classmates and perhaps show off a little, as she did by introducing her as "Gloria Swanson's daughter." Nobody believed her. They all just grinned, thinking it was a joke. After all, Gloria Swanson was, to them, practically a supernatural being, so she wouldn't be in Bronxville.

But Rose knew why she was in Bronxville. As she knew why she was on the boat to France.

When Joseph Kennedy was in Hollywood, during his many long absences, Rose took it as her duty not to disturb his work:

> It may seem unusual, but I did not think it was vital for my husband to be on hand for the birth of the babies . . . I knew he worked hard for us. . . . In the same spirit and for the same reason, as the years went on and our children grew and went through the inevitable period of childhood accidents and diseases (though the latter were more frightening then than now), I saw no point in mentioning these to Joe if he was away and telephoned me for the family news. There was little or nothing he could do to help the situation at a distance, so why worry him? How could he do his own work well if his thoughts were preoccupied with concern for a beloved child? I remember once, for instance, when he was in California and telephoned me within a matter of minutes after I arrived home from a car accident that had put a good-sized gash in my forehead. I was feeling shaky. In fact, when the call came I was lying on my bed pulling myself together and drinking coffee. But I spoke naturally, gave him news of the children and told him what a fine day it was: a perfect day for golf. Then I drove to the hospital where the doctor took five stitches in my forehead.

When Rose was at the Court of St. James's, Eunice heard of her mother's appendectomy from the newspapers — she had not wanted to worry the children. When Rose saw her son John at Mass on the morning of his inauguration, she avoided him — she did not want to embarrass the President-Elect with her makeshift snow garb. A woman's virtue is not to embarrass the men of the family, obstruct their careers, dim their accomplishments. In fact, she must not only excuse her husband's lack of attention to her, but make her forgiveness so manifest that no one else will have trouble forgiving him. Arthur Krock told the Blairs that Rose's attitude made it unnecessary for any outsider to feel sorry about Joseph Kennedy's wanderings: "It was the way of the world as far as I knew it and the way of *his* world. I was not concerned about what happened to him in that respect. It never bothered me at all because Rose acted as if they didn't exist, and that was her business, not mine."

There can, as singer Gobbi says, be a noble pride in such refusal to complain. Once, when Rose almost broke into tears after the death of her second son, she pulled herself together again and told her companion, "No one will ever feel sorry for me." But that was something beyond her control. Others did feel sorry. Mary Pitcairn Keating, who visited Hyannis Port while dating John Kennedy, says:

> Of course, she never saw things or acknowledged things she didn't want to, which was great. I had the feeling that the children just totally ignored her. Daddy was it. I mean, I was the one who went out and picked her up when she was coming down to Washington for dinner. When the children went to Europe, Mr. Kennedy would come down to the boat with a couple of his Catholic legmen, but Mrs. Kennedy never did. At the Cape, Mrs. Kennedy was always by herself. You know that little house she had by the beach? She'd take her robe and her book down there. When she went to play golf, she'd go by herself. She did everything by herself. I never saw her walking with one of the children on the beach. . . . She was sort of a non-person.

Rose said she put up her separate little cottage at Hyannis Port to get away from the noise of a large family. It became a cell, not of loneliness but of study and prayer. Rose Kennedy belonged to the last generation of Catholic women who could combine, in some measure, the two vocations held up to them by the nuns — marriage and the convent. Rose traveled, prayed, and read much of her life in a chosen solitude. My own Irish grandmother, who was also called Rose and raised a large family, came to live with my parents after her husband died; and she turned her room, complete with prie-dieu and statues, into a chapel for her spiritual reading and rosaries. This double life was easier for Rose Kennedy, since she had nursemaids to bring up the children till they were old enough for boarding school. As she herself writes, "I did little diaper changing." Her file card, to keep track of the children's health records, became famous when she went to England. But that was surely a minimal labor for one with nine children to keep track of. There is no questioning her deep affection for her children, her duties gladly performed. But she was soon shut out of the active philandering life of her sons; and though she traveled some with Eunice, even the girls preferred the company of their father and the games of their brothers.

"Joe and I had agreed that the responsibility for education of the boys was primarily his, and that of the girls, primarily mine." Which meant that the boys went to secular schools, which would promote their careers in the world, while the girls were sent to convent schools. There was a division of labor. Boys play, girls pray. But the Kennedy girls wanted to play, too — and did it as strenuously as the boys. Women visitors at Hyannis Port found themselves forced into games where the Kennedy boys and Kennedy girls were equally ferocious. Kate Thom, wife of a Navy friend of John's, told the Blairs:

> I remember Eunice was in a sailing race and didn't have a crew. I'd never been in a boat in my life and I was made her crew. They were in everything to win, not just to participate. I remember how cruel I thought she was because she kept barking orders at me and if I did something wrong she'd scream. But she knew what she was doing and what she had to to win. And we won the race. . . . And I was pregnant at the time.

There is a famous story of Joseph Jr. throwing Edward out of his boat, during a race, for clumsy handling of a jib. Mrs. Thom may not know how close she came to going overboard herself. Mary Pitcairn Keating says, in the Blairs' interviews: "I was a bridesmaid in Eunice's wedding. She was highly nervous, highly geared, and worshipped Jack. I always thought she should have been a boy."

Another woman who visited the Kennedy home with Mrs. Thom remembers: "We were organized from the moment we arrived. The Kennedys organized everybody. I hated playing tennis, so Eunice invited me to play golf. The next day we played touch football, which was hideous. But we *had* to play and it was relentless." Later, Jac-

queline Kennedy's independence was marked by her successful refusal to play "dumb football." But in her engagement days, as one
can see from photographs in the Kennedy Library, even she was
dragged into the family softball game.

What rebellion the girls expressed was not in defense of their
mother, but in efforts to join their father's world, the world of male
play and politics. They were expected to work only in wartime; they
could not run for office themselves. Their task was to marry and raise
children. But the oldest marriageable sister did not take up the pious
role of Rose — she would marry a non-Catholic, an anti-Irish
Englishman, part of that world Joseph Kennedy aspired to. It was
Kathleen, who thought of womanizing as an English trait, who
married the Marquis of Hartington.

The next sister, Patricia, joined her father's world in a different
way, marrying not only an Englishman but a movie star who ran
with Sinatra's crowd. Eunice, the strongest of the sisters, helped her
brothers campaign but married a man who was given part control of
the family business; Jean did the same. These sons-in-law did work
the father thought of as below his own boys, but still above the girls.
The in-laws would help service the careers of Kennedy after Kennedy. They had married all of them. Torbert Macdonald, John's
friend from Harvard football days, fell in love with Kathleen; but he
realized he was too independent to become what he called "a corporate son-in-law," and broke off the attachment.

The exceptional Kennedy in-laws married the brothers who were
murdered. Ethel Skakel had several advantages in her own right. She
came from a large and competitive Catholic family, and she was the
strong one, the Eunice, of her sisters. But, more important, she married the brother who was not a "chaser," the one male in whom the
mother's piety took root. If the rule of the father was that boys play
while girls pray, pious Robert was to that extent womanish. He did
not challenge his father's rakish habits; but neither did he try to
emulate them. He was left out of his brother's carousings, and felt
excluded from the friendships John formed at Choate and in the
Navy. John often called his brother a puritan. A visitor to Hyannis
Port during the war told the Blairs: "Bobby came home from Harvard. He was a scrawny little guy in a white sailor suit. He was very
upset that we were sneaking booze in the kitchen. He was afraid his

father might catch us and he knew his father's wrath. But Kathleen handled him. She told him to get lost." On another occasion he came in while John was entertaining friends, and was ignored; going up the stairs he asked plaintively, "Aren't you glad to see me?" He was left out of the fraternity house side of Hyannis Port. Herbert Parmet claims that "Not until after Jack's death did Bobby Kennedy shed his jealousy over his brother's closeness to Torby [Torbert Macdonald]."

Unlike his brothers — Joseph Jr. was unmarried when he died at twenty-nine, and John did not marry until he was thirty-six — Robert settled down early. He was married by the age of twenty-five, and started raising his large family, to which he was devoted. Around children, Robert was almost maternal — not the strict disciplinarian his father had been, the man whose wrath he feared when grown-up children "sneaked" Scotch to Navy friends. The "boiler room girls," who became famous after Chappaquiddick, said he indulged his children when they came into his Senate office, sat on the laps of secretaries and pretended to type. Esther Newberg recalled, in her oral history for the Kennedy Library:

> Christopher said to Matthew, when he was sitting on my lap eating a mouthful of crackers and the Senator was in his doorway, "Show the lady how you learned to whistle." And he turned around all over a brand new suit and he showed me how he learned to whistle. Crackers everywhere! It was just a mess! The Senator thought it was amusing. I wanted to slap the kid in the face, but it really was kind of cute.

But if Robert was "feminine" in his piety and maternal instinct toward those he loved, he was the fiercest Kennedy competitor, the one who played touch football with a grim determination worthy of war, all bony elbows and fierce beaked face. The first time he met James Hoffa, Robert said he thought him "not so tough" — and challenged him to a push-up contest. Robert's ruthlessness became a family joke — and, like most such jokes, would have lacked point if it lacked a basis in fact. When Robert visited Edward after the plane crash that almost killed the youngest brother, the patient opened his eyes and smiled groggily, "Is it true you're ruthless?"

Robert's piety just made his fighting spirit more awesome — he

not only wanted to win but to destroy evil, whether that was embodied in the Communists he helped Joseph McCarthy hunt for a
while or in Hoffa's corrupt teamsters. John did not ask Robert to or-
ganize his campaigns out of mere family loyalty. He knew that Robert would be demanding on subordinates, up to and past the point
of abrasiveness. Friends of Robert regretted, when he ran for office
himself, that he had no "Bobby" of his own to "kick ass" in the
lower echelons of aides. It was this harsh and ruthless side of Robert
that gave poignancy to his later concern for the poor, and made his
brother take seriously his plea for restraint in the Cuban missile
crisis.

Joseph Kennedy might not have recognized himself in the puritan
Robert but for the latter's almost kamikaze physical daring and cult
of athletic prowess. He would prove he was a true Kennedy down to
his final days — climbing mountains, shooting rapids. If he was a
more cautious skier and driver than his brothers, it was because he
calculated risks with a more economical insistence on what is needed
to *win*. In remorseless determination to reach his goal, the puritan
resembled his predator father more than did any other son (or
daughter). And he married a scrapper of his own sort. Ben Bradlee
wonders at Ethel's will to win:

> Another time Kennedy and I were playing at Hyannis Port with
> Ethel and she was about seven months pregnant. I had not played
> golf for a couple of years, as I remember, and I had never played
> that course. The stakes were again ten cents a hole. Once I asked
> Ethel what club she thought I should use, because I was unfamiliar
> with the course and unsure of my own judgment. She suggested a
> five iron, and I clocked it pretty good, only to see it go sailing way
> over the green. I turned around to the sound of gales of laughter
> from Ethel and the president. She wanted to win so badly she had
> purposely suggested too much club.

Jacqueline Bouvier was tough in a different way. John Kennedy
did not marry her until the bachelor state began to pose a threat to
his career. Even as late as 1980, Governor Brown of California found
that an unmarried presidential candidate is suspected either of homosexuality or of promiscuity — he was damned if he traveled with
Linda Ronstadt, and damned if he didn't. It seems unlikely that

John Kennedy would have been accused of homosexuality. But his large and growing number of heterosexual affairs might prove damaging to any effort at the White House. It was during the 1952 race for the Senate that speculation about Kennedy's marrying came to a head. The *Saturday Evening Post* ran an article calling him "just about the most eligible bachelor in the United States, and the least justifiable one." Kennedy obviously took those last five words in several senses; after delaying the announcement long enough to let the article have its impact, he told the world he was marrying Jacqueline Bouvier, twelve years his junior, an ideal political choice. She was a Catholic by upbringing, but with a worldly background as well. She had not gone to convent schools, but to Vassar. Her father, whom she deeply admired, was a famous rake, "Black Jack" Bouvier. Like Kathleen Kennedy, she married a man who resembled her father in his attitude toward women. When Senator Jack met Black Jack, she recalled: "They were very much alike. We three had dinner before we were engaged, and they talked about politics and sports and girls — what all red-blooded men like to talk about." Like Rose Kennedy, but for very different reasons, she would not criticize her husband's affairs with other women. It was part of the world she knew, where fame and money and glamour cost something.

The political calculus of John's wedding was so obvious that even Professor Burns, in his early biography, wrote: "At least one good friend doubts that Kennedy would be married today if he had lost his Senate battle." And Burton Hersh calls that remark "as sybilline and penetrating as any ever made concerning the oncoming President." But if he had struck a good bargain with his marriage, so had she. Her later arrangement with Onassis showed what was transferable from the Kennedy contract — power, money, fame. No other coin was current in both realms. She too, even the ethereal Jacqueline, was more than half in love with Hollywood. And if Onassis was a womanizer, one might expect better taste in one who chased Maria Callas than in Judith Campbell's lover — though one hesitates at the report of whale-testicle coverings for the bar stools on Onassis's yacht. Jacqueline Kennedy did not enter tabloid heaven when it came time to marry Onassis — that had been done earlier; she merely achieved its empyrean.

Joan Bennett Kennedy was not in the league of these tough

ladies. Like Ethel, she was a Manhattanville student, with the Madames of the Sacred Heart, when she met a law student named Kennedy. But her Kennedy was not the monogamous Robert. It was Edward, the nicest of the Kennedy playboys, but playboy still, at least for some crucial years of their marriage. She tried to play touch football like Ethel. As if to prove her worth, the new Kennedy bride told journalists: "Ted taught me to play tennis and golf, to waterski and be a much better skier than I was."

But, try as she would, she was on the outmost rim of the concentered Kennedy family. The nucleus was the father. Around him circled the sons, near to the point of disappearing, at times, into this center of family gravity. Outside that tight ring came the women Kennedys, wife and daughers. Outside that, the male in-laws, Sargent Shriver running the Merchandise Mart, Stephen Smith financing campaigns out of the patriarchal stock. Outside that ring, the female in-laws — but even here Joan was not an equal to the other two; she came in a distant third, farthest from the family's animating center — till she spun out, alone, into darkness.

The caution with which she bore her barely mended pride, during the 1980 campaign, impressed many viewers. But it was miraculous that any mending had occurred. She had been, over the years, systematically broken down and almost discarded in a world of men who shy superstitiously from losers and of women who go with their men no matter what. Myra McPherson, in her book on political wives, interviewed a frequent visitor to Hyannis Port, who told her: "They all really got on Joan, to the point where I felt sorry for her. I remember one day we were all going sailing, and everyone had on old blue jeans and Joan came down in a leopard skin bathing suit. Ethel said, 'Really, Joan, did you expect the photographer?' Everyone snickered. Joan was helpless, unable to quip back with some smart crack. That's what you had to do."

The results of this long attritive living with the Kennedys came to frighten Edward Kennedy at last. And no wonder. Burton Hersh's book contains this searing passage: "A longstanding journalistic friend of the Kennedy family remembers stopping at Kennedy's house in Hyannis Port a couple of summers ago to talk and have a drink. As he was leaving, Kennedy suggested that the visitor hadn't had a chance yet to say hello to Joan, and led him around to the back of the house; Joan lay crumpled up, passed out in the back seat of one of the Kennedy cars. 'She was a rag mop,' the friend observes. 'I've seen drunks often enough, but what I was looking at there was the result of a two- or three-day bender. I think Kennedy just wanted me to see what he was up against. If something got printed, he was prepared for that." In a man's world of winners one must be tough enough to go on, even when the losers can't.

4

The Prisoner of Sex

By a kind of compensation the source of his power was the cause also of his downfall.

— WALTER BAGEHOT, of Bolingbroke

THE NIGHT AFTER that Pier Four rally where I first noticed how checked are all Edward Kennedy's public gestures out toward women, there was a little "birthday party" for staff and press in the motel we stayed at. Joan Kennedy was just ahead of me in the buffet line, and I tried to kid her gently about adding a year to her husband's age in a speech earlier that day. She knitted her brow in an effort to understand, but said nothing. Her husband saw her talking to me and hastened over. "Come join us, Joansy." She was swept to a small protective table with familiar aides around her.

Kennedy's task during the campaign was to produce Joan and protect her at the same time, and these were antithetical aims. Her absence would be an indictment of him as a family man. Yet her presence was an absence even more startling — she was so clearly disoriented by the glare; misread her short, carefully prepared speeches; wore an orange mask of makeup which cracked, on occasion, and let the tears seep through.

Kennedy's "Joan problem" was not simply that he had to protect her while producing her, hide and expose simultaneously. The real problem was that he *could* not protect her. Often as he thanked her, guided her, deferred to her, he touched her as cautiously as he did the women who gushed up to him for handshakes. There was a troubled space between them; each reached across it only rarely, tentatively. During the St. Patrick's Day parade in Chicago, when security problems were anticipated, she skittered at noises and clutched for him, but he was marching defiantly forward and did not notice. The few times they tried to kiss in public were tense moments for them both. It is hard to put together sundered intimacies with half a nation watching.

So the imprisonment was complete. Not only could he not reach out in public, even innocently, to women supporters. He could not reach out to his own wife with any confidence of finding her. Once he may have neglected her. Now, try though he would, he could barely locate her.

The philanderer's compiling of lists means crossing women off, erasing them. The philanderer's punishment is the inability to call back the one woman he may want once she has been erased. The very word "conquests," used of seduction, poses the problem in a military metaphor. It is one thing to conquer a people, quite another to rule it, to win it over. The power to conquer is often a delusion, even at the national level; and almost always at the personal level. Power to destroy hurts the destroyer if there is not a concomitant power to restore. The child, angry at not getting the station he wants on a radio, has the power to smash it; but this is not useful power, the power to make it speak again. It is easy to smash the intricate circuitry of a marriage; but what if one should want to make the other partner speak again some day? Edward Kennedy was trying, all thumbs, to put back the most costly and complicated inner workings of a delicate speaking apparatus, a marriage, in front of the voters of New Hampshire. And he was failing.

The failure was not his alone. The entire Kennedy family was too much for Joan (or for most people) to cope with. Nor was Edward the worst husband she might have found in that family. It puzzled me all through the 1980 campaign to hear people say they would vote again for one of the older brothers, but not for Edward; he lacked character. His character flaws, such as an outsider can judge, seemed to me neither as deep nor as crippling as those displayed by other Kennedys, beginning with the father. Then why was the judgment on Edward's shortcomings so harsh?

One reason may be that he seems to have got caught more than a reasonably prudent man should. If the others symbolically "got away with murder," getting away with it took managerial discipline that might be relevant to presidential performance. William Buckley even wrote that what disqualified Edward Kennedy, in the light of Chappaquiddick, was his poor head for cover-ups. It was not important that he was, in Buckley's words, "drunk and horny" that night (questionable assertions), but that he could not tidy up the mess more deftly.

The friend of Richard Nixon and Spiro Agnew may place cover-up skills higher on the list of presidential qualities than others would, but this youngest son *does* seem to have been caught a good deal — repeatedly caught speeding, caught cheating in college, caught doing God-knows-what at Chappaquiddick. Some amateur psychiatrists put this down to a death wish in the last brother left alive, claim that he may subconsciously desire the comparative immunity that has come to his brothers after death. That kind of speculation is amusing to the speculator but of little use to anyone else. The trouble with it is that Kennedy started getting caught — at Harvard, at the University of Virginia — long before there was any "legacy of death" for the Kennedys.

One reason for this brother's public indiscretions may simply be the fact that he is the first Kennedy male in three generations to break the family taboo on drinking. His grandfather kept a tavern, but did not touch his own wares. His father did not drink himself, and strictly rationed the family's predinner drink to one, even for visitors. Joseph Jr., John, and Robert drank rarely, and very little on the rare occasions. By all accounts, none was seen drunk, in private or in public; which means that when they took risks, they were calculated risks, not the improvisations of befuddlement. Some of Edward's getting caught may be the result of lowered defenses. When he sped away from police in Charlottesville, then hid in the back seat after parking his car, he may have been avoiding the suspicion of driving while intoxicated. He was hiding the evidence — himself. The late-night session at which a whole group schemed up a solution to Kennedy's Spanish problem sounds well lubricated. If Kennedy had determined in any cold-headed way to cheat, he would hardly have invited in so many witnesses to the decision. And at Chappaquiddick there was just enough drinking to make the impulse to hide that fact affect the complex of decisions and, mainly, nondecisions that undid Kennedy.

It may seem no defense to say a man gets himself into trouble by appearing intoxicated in public. But there is a sense in which this gives Joan somewhat less to complain of than Jacqueline had. For Edward, handsome and besieged by beautiful admirers, to slip on occasion out of weakness should be more acceptable to a wife than the calculated regimen of John Kennedy, the daily dose of sex taken, as it were, for muscle tone. One can say, by the standards of cover-up artistry, that John Kennedy showed political skill in marrying a woman who would not object to this regimen (not terminally, at least); but there is a coldbloodedness to this that seems less admirable in a person, no matter how useful it may be to a leader.

As for other charges against Edward's character, I cannot (since I am a teacher) condone cheating on exams. But I do not regard that act as dishonorable as lying about one's authorship of a book in order to keep the Pulitzer Prize. And if we are to measure public virtue by public service, as the founders of this nation did, Edward Kennedy has served his constituency and the nation in the Senate long after it became clear that such service involved risking his life. He has bent the Kennedy ego to cooperative work among his peers. He has shown legislative concern for refugees, the aged, the ill, by doing the drudgery of his Senate homework. He does not try to take the glamour and leave hard work to others. He labors at being a good Senator — the only Kennedy who has ever done that. This Kennedy has not misused the power of his office as Robert did, wiretapping Martin Luther King. He has not risked the national dignity as John did, taking a "gangster's moll" into White House bedrooms.

Ah, but this Kennedy was involved in a woman's death on Chappaquiddick Island. Much as there is to criticize in Kennedy's behavior that night — and the thing most to the criticized is that we still know so little of that behavior — the narrowly sexual charges leveled at Kennedy seem, in this case, a bum rap. It is the irony of Don Juan's life to get caught on a night when he is not prowling for women. There were many knowing winks about the idea of six married men getting six single "girls" together in an isolated spot — as if Edward Kennedy needed this elaborate arrangement to find female companionship. The irony is completed when we learn that, though Kennedy has a hard time showing respect for women, he *did* respect the six assembled at Chappaquiddick. For that we have the best pre-Chappaquiddick evidence, that of the women themselves.

One of the most touching transcripts in the Kennedy Library's oral history project comes from Esther Newberg and Rosemary Keough, and was made on May 22, 1969, a year after Robert Kennedy's murder, not long before their own attendance at the Chappaquiddick party. They were asked to speak about Robert Kennedy's last campaign, for which they ran the nerve center of information called "the boiler room." They admit they had trouble impressing old political types with the importance of clearing all information through them; but they said that one exception to this was the candidate's younger brother, who *did* look to them for information, on a professional basis. Esther Newberg said: "He really knew that even if we didn't have it written down in books, we had it in our heads. He didn't look down on us, as you might expect, as a group of pool secretaries for instance. I think he respected what some of us knew."

Much that has been written about Chappaquiddick either asserts or implies that the party was based on a *lack* of respect, was an "office party" in the stereotypical sense. Yet Kennedy's respect was shown not only during the campaign, but afterward, well before Chappaquiddick. In the summer of 1968, after the murder of Robert Kennedy, Joseph Gargan arranged the *first* party for the boiler room girls at Cape Cod. This was to thank them for their work in Robert's ill-fated campaign. Edward and Joan Kennedy threw a cocktail party for them. The women were put up at various Kennedy homes — Mary Jo Kopechne stayed with the Shrivers. The Chappaquiddick party was to be a repetition of that innocent first gathering. Since it was to be held at the Edgartown races, there were no Kennedy homes to put them in — the women stayed at a motel. The Hyannis Port compound could not be used to entertain them, so Gargan rented a cottage. Kennedy's attitude toward this party, as to the first one, was dutiful; he was discharging a debt for his brother, not arranging an orgy. I delay discussion of his later conduct for a later page, since my topic here is sex. Chappaquiddick is discussed in a haze of innuendo, typified by a 1980 bumper sticker in New Hampshire: "Ted Kennedy drives women to the drink." Yet sex was the least important aspect of the Chappaquiddick tragedy.

It may seem Kennedy has such a genius for getting caught that he is caught even when there is nothing to catch him out in. Well, not quite. But he does receive a kind and intensity of criticism he has not earned all by himself. His father and brother were more single-minded philanderers than he, but their activity was kept away from the mass of the electorate. Now that their record is better known, Edward alone survives to take the brunt of moral dismay these revelations caused in naive admirers. A nun who taught my daughter in parochial school kept a picture of President Kennedy in her classroom and spoke of him as a saint. It is fairly certain she will not look at Edward Kennedy through the same haze of hagiography. Even those who claim that their opinion of the dead President has not been altered are ready to look with sharper eyes of suspicion on his brother — and would have done so at the President if they had known then what they do now.

But a deeper cultural reason for Edward Kennedy's difficulties comes from the vitality of modern feminism. John Kennedy was the beneficiary of a first sexual revolution, the one proclaimed in Norman Mailer's gushy welcome to Superman at the Supermarket. But Mailer and Hugh Hefner — and Edward Kennedy — are the victims of a counterrevolution, one that says woman's highest destiny is *not* to become another notch on some hero's gun. Joan Kennedy, a victim in so many ways, is the beneficiary of this counterrevolution; she says the liberation movement helped get her out on her own, continue her education and her music, without looking to her husband's family for applause that never came. And if she is to be the beneficiary, her husband must be the victim. The graduate student of my era, who rejoiced in John Kennedy's sexual reputation, has been replaced by "sisters" on campus, twenty years later, who think of such "chauvinism" as a political issue, just as the earlier liberal had — but one, now, that works against the Kennedys, not for them.

This criticism of Kennedy macho was first mounted in a massive and rather clumsy way by Nancy Gager Clinch, in her book *The Kennedy Neurosis* (1973), which had all the faults of "psychobiography" at its worst. But by the time Edward actually ran for President, the criticism had become more refined. Suzannah Lessard's article "Kennedy's Woman Problem, Women's Kennedy Problem" was rejected by *The New Republic,* which had commissioned it; but the piece ran (to an audience made more attentive by the rejection), in *The Washington Monthly,* and some at *The New Republic* felt embarrassed by the rejection. Lessard admitted: "In the Bible Belt, it would take courage to say that philandering is of no importance. But in New York the danger lies in saying that it matters." Yet she found Kennedy's pattern of "semi-covert, just barely personal and ultimately discardable encounters" degrading to women and revelatory of the Kennedy attitude toward power.

Kennedy's voting record on "women's issues" like the Equal Rights Amendment and abortion has been praised by the National Organization for Women. But people notice that he has few women in high positions on his staff, and those few are not among the most intimate or powerful. Here his imprisonment takes on its exquisite, its cruel thoroughness. Just when it is important for him to show a greater trust in and reliance on women, his reputation makes him hold them off in public. He cannot win. Some ask him to take women into his political apparatus; but a suspicious public whispers about any women who get near him. He suffered for trying to honor Robert's boiler room workers. Even innocent meetings have been given tabloid treatment. Burnt so often, how can he work intimately with a woman, keep her late at the office, thank her fondly for good work done?

The moralizers at the end of *Don Giovanni* lay it on rather thick for most of us; but it is true, in quite specific ways, that licentiousness throws chains around itself. Earlier Kennedys were more subtly bound — the father's mistreatment of his wife was more obvious than the callousness he formed around himself. But Edward inherits the handiwork of his elders as well as the links he has added on his own, and by now he is so heavily chained he can hardly move naturally in the presence of women.

It may seem unfair for the inheritor of all that libidinous imperialism to live in the postcolonial era of sexual reations. The power over women that was promised him, almost as his birthright, has turned on him, has tripped him up. Power has a way of doing that.

II

FAMILY

You will hear everlastingly, in all discussions about newspapers, companies, aristocracies, or party politics, this argument that the rich man cannot be bribed. The fact is, of course, that the rich man is bribed; he has been bribed already. That is why he is a rich man.

— GILBERT CHESTERTON

5

Semi-Irish

We have again been cheated of the prospect of a Catholic President.

— MURRAY KEMPTON, 1961

IT IS THE OLD STORY: for "one of your own" to get elected, he must go out of his way to prove he is not *just* one of your own. The first Catholic President had to be secular to the point (as we used to say in Catholic schools) of supererogation. And John Kennedy had the right credentials. Theodore Sorensen vouched for the fact that "he cared not a whit for theology." Jacqueline Kennedy told Arthur Krock: "I think it is unfair for Jack to be opposed because he is a Catholic. After all, he's such a poor Catholic. Now if it were Bobby: he never misses mass and prays all the time." Herbert Parmet quotes a close friend's judgment that Kennedy had "no sense of piety as an internal characteristic." As Charles Kinsella puts it in Edwin O'Connor's novel: "I got the Catholic vote because everybody knows I am one. I got the non-Catholic vote because the others don't think I'm a very good one. Or, as they'd put it, I'm not 'typical.' "

But one must quote O'Connor with care. The Kennedy legend makes much of the Boston Irish background on both sides of John Kennedy's family. It sees him growing up in a world of bowler-hatted Boston pols with outlandish nicknames like Knocko and Onions, where Honey Fitz is always singing "Sweet Adeline." But Murray Kempton saw through it all during the 1960 campaign:

"There is a myth that Boston is his home. It is only the place where he went to college. He is a Cambridge man and he looks at Boston as Harvard looks at Boston, in some middle distance between amusement and disgust." Kennedy's parents moved from Brookline to New York in 1926, when he was nine years old, and he grew up there, went to school there, before going to prep school in Connecticut. True, he spent summer vacations at Hyannis Port, just as he spent winter vacations in Palm Springs — but that did not make him a resident of Massachusetts or of Florida. When he decided to run for Congress in 1946, he had not lived in Boston for twenty years; he had to take out rooms at the Bellevue Hotel to be his official residence.

Later, people would remember the cry of "carpetbagger" raised against Robert Kennedy when he ran for the Senate in New York. But the charge had first been leveled at John Kennedy, and with better reason. Robert had been only one year old when his family moved to New York. That state was his home for all his young life. And, just to make the border-crossing story more complex, Edward was actually born in New York, though he would follow John's example — and claim his old residential apartment — in running for the Senate from Massachusetts.

The loyal Kenneth O'Donnell admits that "Jack Kennedy himself was a stranger in Boston, having lived as a youth in New York and at Hyannis Port on Cape Cod." But he suppresses the accusation that hurt most: Kennedy was called the Miami candidate, a Floridian like his father. In 1946, Kennedy senior had to hire local politicians to instruct his son in the state's ways. David Powers remembered with wonder that "It took Jack three months before he found out that Mather Galvin wasn't a woman" but a pol known for bounty in dispensing favors. So much for the Edwin O'Connor view of Kennedy as a kind of Ivy Shamrock sprung from Honey Fitz, the Purple Shamrock himself.

Though Joseph Kennedy was the first in the family to get out of Boston, his father had taken care to make that departure possible. The state legislator's son was educated at Boston Latin School and Harvard, where he could learn to talk like the brahmins. During the war John Kennedy got mad at a Navy friend's surprise over his father's diction — he did not have the "lower class" Boston accent.

The son was angry that anyone would *expect* his father to "talk mick."

The grandfather of the future President, Patrick Joseph Kennedy, had a cerain contempt for the Irish weaknesses he ministered to as a bartender. He did not drink himself — asked to celebrate some occasion with a toast, he would fill a shot glass with beer. He was a man anxious to forget his own origins. Elected to the state legislature, he could put "liquor dealer" as his occupation — he did not tend bar anymore. Later, with sensitivities further honed, he would identify himself only as "trader." His son, in turn, got out of the liquor business just before John Kennedy's campaign for the House of Representatives.

Though Joseph Kennedy would later be embarrassed by his florid father-in-law, John (Honey Fitz) Fitzgerald, it should be remembered that Fitzgerald too went to Boston Latin and was enrolled at the Harvard Medical School when his father died and he had to go to work. As soon as he rose in the world, John Fitzgerald affected brahmin ways, playing polo, hobnobbing with Sir Thomas Lipton, fox hunting. Later, when Edward Kennedy thought of riding with a polo team, his father told him Kennedys were not polo society. He was referring to John Fitzgerald's unsuccessful attempts to become assimilated on horseback.

But if John Fitzgerald was only semidetached from his own father's "shanty" background, he sprang his daughter almost entirely free. She was schooled not only at Manhattanville, the "best" school for Catholic ladies, but abroad with German aristocrats. She was a catch for the young bank president, who first suffered the condescension of Honey Fitz, and then spent years repaying it a thousand-fold.

With this beautiful wife at his side, Joseph Kennedy did everything he could to be accepted by the "real" Boston. Not content to vacation with the wealthy Irish at Nantasket, he went to the WASP playground at Cohasset — where the country club blackballed him. Years later he recalled every such rebuff; and, according to Ben Bradlee, so did his son. Even the tranquil and pious Rose Kennedy once asked a Harvard student from one of the brahmin families, "When are the nice people of Boston going to accept us?" As late as 1957, the New York *Times* could quote her husband's protest at being called an Irishman: "I was born in America. My children were born here. What the hell do I have to do to be called an American?" After his graduation from Harvard, where he was not accepted into the best clubs, Joseph Kennedy kept trying to ingratiate himself at class reunions, furnishing the beer and entertainment; but when he was booed at the twenty-fifth one, he attended no others. Richard Whalen wrote: "In years to come, for a number of reasons he found sufficient, Kennedy adopted an attitude toward Harvard that friends and classmates sadly described as hatred." The family sensitivity was passed down. To paraphrase Jacqueline Kennedy, it was unfair for the Kennedys to be treated as Irish, they were such poor Irishmen; they tried so hard to be anything but.

Convinced at last that he would always be just another Irishman in Boston, Kennedy decided in 1926 to "purge his trousers cuff of the Boston Irish" (in Kempton's words) by moving to fashionable New York addresses: Riverdale, Westchester, Bronxville. When he did not get the cabinet position he aspired to under Roosevelt (Secretary of the Treasury), the only honorific that appealed to him was Ambassador to the Court of St. James's, the diplomatic post even brahmins look up to. There was no Irish hatred of the English among Kennedys. Just the opposite. Most of the heroes (and some of the in-laws) of the Kennedys were English.

Though he realized that his son would have to learn the Irish wards in Boston, he carefully put him in hands other than Honey Fitz's, and he approved when his chosen mentor blew up at the ex-Mayor for entering the campaign headquarters. Joe Kane shouted, "Get that son of a bitch out of here," and John Kennedy did not defend his grandfather. He was learning, like his father, to use the Irish connection only when necessary.

If anything, John Kennedy went further than his father in dissociating himself from Irish ways. His famous reluctance to wear hats was put down to vanity — he must not have thought they became him. But doing interviews for their book, the Blairs soon learned that an Irish politician's hat was his trademark in Boston — just as Al Smith's had been in New York: "Talk of hats — style, size, and so on — cropped up all through our political interviews." Edward Gallagher, one of those deputed by John's father to instruct him in Boston politicking, bought the candidate a hat and tried to make him wear it. John refused. He had not come to join the Irish pols, and certainly not to look like them. He just wanted their votes.

Six of Joseph Kennedy's children married — not one to an Irish spouse. They had not been brought up to respect their own. In fact, only four of the six married fellow Catholics. Nor were "vocations" ever a serious prospect for any Kennedy in this large family. The mother's was not the strongest voice in domestic matters. The parish priest was no figure of importance. There was no hint of jansenist views on sex. In all these ways, the Catholic families of Edwin O'Connor's stories — or Elizabeth Cullinan's — have little to do with the secular and rootless environment of the Kennedy family. Joseph Kennedy took his family with him to various parts of America and the world, trying to win acceptance on his own terms in several societies — New York, Florida, Hollywood, London — where he could "make a splash" without fully belonging. Phil Kinsella, speaking for the family O'Connor partly modeled on the Kennedys, could say of the novel's fictionalized Boston, "This has always been our base." Joseph Kennedy's children could not say that. They had a floating base. Their base was the father.

Joseph Kennedy's loyal inner circle of business subordinates was all Irish; but they were flunkies. They did the work for which Kennedy felt his sons would be too good — only sons-in-law were expected to perform the chores of his lifelong henchmen, the personal attendants Gloria Swanson called his "Four Horsemen." In the words of Richard Whalen: "Throughout his career, it was Kennedy's standard operating procedure to move from job to job behind a protective cordon of cronies." Dragonflying from this venture to that, he needed a mobile team of men he could trust entirely, who had no other interest than his own shifting concerns, whose base was his person as fully as the children's base was paternal.

The father's rootlessness is reflected in his business attitude. When President Roosevelt put him in charge of the Securities and Exchange Commission, he was called a traitor to the business community he came from. But he was never part of any "community." He operated in a series of raids — saw opportunity, struck fast, and moved on. Banking, movies, liquor, land — he was in and out of these ventures, cutting his losses, always moving. He did not stay long enough to get entangled in the stable concerns of business, certainly not in any business responsibility to the circumambient community. He was a predator on other businessmen, not their partner. He looked down on them, just as he did on the Boston Irish. If he was forced to be one of them, he would make sure that his sons were not. He must earn enough from other capitalists to keep his family clean of any further contact. When President Kennedy, in the midst of the steel dispute, said his father "always told me that businessmen are sons-of-bitches," he was not joking; it was the literal truth. Even for associates of higher standing than businessmen, there was little real respect. Through the years Kennedy cultivated and, when necessary, flattered Arthur Krock. But Krock told the Blairs, "I've often reflected since those days that he probably never liked me at all, but found me useful and thought he might be able to make use of me." All others were to be used; but not the family. That was what the others were being used *for*.

Joseph Kennedy scrambled up with a desperate ambition. His constant emphasis on self-improvement was the other side, the escape side, of his self-contempt. If he was not always rising, he would be just a Boston Irishman, just another businessman — a crass mick. As he told Arthur Krock, "For the Kennedys it is the shit house or the castle — nothing in between." The castle was what he hoped to arrive at; the shit house was where he had been. He had no credentials but his latest achievement — no community to lean back on, no base but the one he forged for himself every day, the clearing he made for his family in a hostile environment. The endless catechizing of his children on the need to win, the competitive edge he sharpened in each of them, reflected his own inner urgencies. If he did not keep winning, there was nothing to support him. The dragonfly, with nothing to light on, would just fall straight down forever.

Gloria Swanson gives a convincing picture of the threat failure presented to Kennedy. The film Kennedy had tailored for her, *Queen Kelly*, was unshowable; he stood to lose over a million dollars and — worse — to appear ludicrous, to hear the boos that drove him from the Harvard class reunion echoing all around the nation.

An hour later he charged into the living room of the bungalow, alone, cursing Von Stroheim and Le Baron and Glazer. Stopping abruptly, he slumped into a deep chair. He turned away from me, struggling to control himself. He held his head in his hands, and little, high-pitched sounds escaped from his rigid body, like those of a wounded animal whimpering in a trap. He finally found his voice. It was quiet, controlled. "I've never had a failure in my life," were his first words. Then he rose, ashen, and went into another searing rage at the people who had let this happen. . . . Bravo, I wanted to say. If you're forty years old and you've never had a failure, you've been deprived. Failure is a part of life, too.

But failure could not be part of Kennedy's life. One failure was enough to send him all the way back to the shit house, to prove he was nothing but a shanty mick. Kennedys don't lose. If they do, they are not Kennedys, as Joseph defined them, with their own code and their own excellence, hovering without props in the air by sheer energy of levitating ambition. If (God forbid) they should fail, they would simply be Honey Fitz's in-laws.

When Joseph Kennedy's own ambitions for the presidency were frustrated, he turned to his surrogates, his sons. They would become a tiny and enclosed aristocracy of talent, with a material base entirely provided by him. They need not scramble, or be predators. They would live on the heights to which he lifted them. It was an astonishing act of will, to create a kind of space platform out of his own career, one from which the children could fly out to their own achievements and come back for refueling. As this one or that one took on a new challenge, the children were informed by the custodian of their patrimony that "You have just made a political donation" to the new flight.

The wonder is not simply that the whole thing could be held together by the fierce drive of one man's will, but that, under the blowtorch of that willpower, none of the children rebelled. Of course, the sons would edge away from some of the old man's prejudices, his anti-Semitism, his attitude toward blacks. But it is nonsense to say they differed from him deeply in politics. He had no ideology but achievement, and that became theirs. I spoke earlier of the way Kennedys have of talking mainly with other Kennedys, of forming a circle that others are only partly let into. That is the circuit forged by the old man's desires, the communications system of the little society made to hover in air by his sheer energy. That circuitry animates them all, and to drop out of it would be death for them.

The semi-Irishness of the Kennedys can be gauged by a comparison that was often raised *because* the Kennedys were Irish. Another large Irish family, cosmopolitan, talented, tight-knit, has been likened to them over the years — sometimes in mirror-image formulae, such as: the Kennedys are the Buckleys of the Left, or the Buckleys are the Kennedys of the Right. Granted, neither side of this comparison seems to have relished the conjunction. When Robert Kennedy refused to go on William Buckley's TV show *Firing Line* and a reporter asked why, Buckley ferociously answered: "Why does the meat shun the grinder?"

Both sides rightly sense the comparison is ill-grounded just because it relies on the Irish Catholic connection. But there are real similarities, precisely in terms of this rejection. They resemble each other negatively, by their strenuous push *off from* the stereotypes people keep trying to use in order to link them. The suggested first comparison not only misses the point, but reverses it: the two families are similar only to the extent that they have ceased, deliberately, to be Irish in the accepted sense.

William Frank Buckley (1881–1958) deserves his own Richard Whalen — who would, no doubt, get as little cooperation from the Buckleys as the Kennedys gave to Whalen. The son of a Texas sheriff, young Will Buckley was a frontier scrambler who anticipated some of Lyndon Johnson's experiences. Born on the Brazos River, he grew up in San Antonio, where an educated Basque priest made him yearn for a more cultured world. He taught school to Mexican Americans, and worked his way through the University of Texas, where he became a campus leader, editor of the school paper. After finishing law school, he became an oil speculator — as natural an entry into the financial world, for a Texan, as was Joseph Kennedy's apprenticeship to banking in Boston.

Like the Kennedy patriarch, Buckley was a loner, launching individual raids on targets of opportunity, defying the big oil companies. Kennedy, however, diversified, jumped from one successful enterprise to others of entirely different sorts. Buckley, after hitting oil in Mexico, kept free-lancing on the same lines all his life. Thus the

Buckleys ended up land rich and oil poor, with too many options on sites with too little oil. The father's "big killings" came at longer and longer intervals and almost ceased with his retirement. When James Buckley was dragged, kicking and screaming, to the revelation of his income during the 1980 Senate race in Connecticut, people were surprised at how little it was. But Buckleys had never reached the financial stratosphere Joseph Kennedy moved in.

For one thing, the Buckley father seemed less driven. Given financial competence, he broadened his interests. He admired good prose, and exacted it from his children with the sort of dedication that made Joseph Kennedy try to plaster a Harvard football letter on each of his sons' chests. Here, at least, Buckley was more successful. Only one Kennedy son — Robert, the least likely — won his H. Every Buckley child, so far as I know, writes well — though no Kennedy, without a ghost, found it easy to commit English prose. The elder Buckley, who once taught Spanish, kept Spanish servants and insisted that his children speak both that language and French. He had them all tutored in music. (Joseph Kennedy liked to play classical records as background to conversations, which made Arthur Schlesinger claim that he had a taste for the stuff — it seems to others to belie that fact. Kennedy did not want to go to concerts, just to have classical muzak to soothe him — and, on one recorded occasion, to irritate others.)

The Kennedys liked to work and play as a team — on boats, footballing over the lawn (more ardent than deft), or in politics. The Buckleys are individualists in practice as well as theory. They take their sports and politics in comparative isolation from each other — John Buckley hunting, Priscilla golfing, James bird-watching, William skiing.

While less single-mindedly attached to each other, the Buckleys are also less thoroughly detached from their origins — some have even married Irish spouses. Religion gets more than lip service from most Buckley children. Their father not only stuck to one line of business, but was ideologically single-tracked as well. Both patriarchs were America-Firsters who opposed entry into World War II, though their sons were quick to enlist in that struggle. Both were anti-Communists in the Cold War period — indeed, both were friends of Joseph McCarthy. But Joseph Kennedy was flexible in his politics in order to be undeviating in support of his sons' political ambitions. John Kennedy told Dorothy Schiff, "My father would be for me if I were running as head of the Communist Party." No Buckley son felt he could make that boast.

Despite these and other differences, there are remarkable similarities between the two clans — some, of course, just accidental. There is no deep significance to the fact that James Buckley succeeded in time to the Senate seat Robert Kennedy had held, or that both ran as "carpetbaggers." The size of the families is not a matter for surprise, given the religious upbringing of both mothers. Rose Kennedy began her family of nine children before Aloise Buckley (a New Orleans belle) began hers of ten — the oldest Kennedy son was born in 1915, the oldest Buckley in 1920. During the twenties, the two women were more or less continuously pregnant (William Jr. was born in 1925, the same year as Robert Kennedy). The last Kennedy child (Edward) was born in 1936, the last Buckley (Carol) in 1940.

More profound similarities lie in the relation of the children to their parents. The mother was, in both cases, pretty, cultured, and retiring; clearly not the major force in the family. Kenneth O'Donnell, stressing the importance of the women's vote in Boston, said: "In an Irish home, the mother's word is law." If that is the case, then neither the Buckley nor the Kennedy home was Irish. One daughter of Aloise Buckley told me that her first memories of her mother's room — where she retired as Rose Kennedy did to her "hut" on the beach — were of holy water and perfume.

In both families the father was dominant, though he traveled much away from home. Both men combined the discipline of an executive driving his underlings with a paternal affection that showed best in memos. Each man was rootless, restless, going where the action took him, living in a variety of homes simultaneously — south in winter, north in summer, Europe often. The children were tutored and sent to secular schools that would advance their careers — eventually Yale became for the Buckleys what Harvard was for Kennedys. To some degree the Buckleys freed their daughters from convent backgrounds — while Kennedy girls were at Manhattanville, the Buckleys were at Smith. But neither father liked to see his daughters aim at anything but homemaking.

Though Buckley's cultural aspirations were deeper than Kennedy's, they were no less anglophile, in defiance of Irish memories. John Kennedy grew up admiring Lords Tweedsmuir and Cecil, at an age when William Buckley's hero was Albert Jay Nock, who modeled his *Freeman* on the English *Spectator,* the better to mock American vulgarity. As Joseph Kennedy exchanged his "low Boston" accent for brahmin, the Buckleys acquired a "mid-Atlantic" mode of speech partly modeled, in William Jr.'s case, on the Oxford diction of Willmore Kendall. It is no wonder this same Buckley told an interviewer: "I simply wasn't aware that we were somewhere along the line taxonomized as Irish Catholics until somebody told me, and that was fifteen years after I graduated from college." That was not a thing his own family would have impressed on him.

Buckleys, no more than Kennedys, rebelled against their strong father. The children gradually rid themselves of their parents' anti-Semitism and prejudice against blacks, but this was seen as a forgivable generation lag in the admired rulers of the clans. There were no open breaks. Buckley, having less financial power, had to welcome his sons into the family business — something unthinkable for Kennedy. But even Buckley seems to have been happier at the thought that some of his boys would become writers or scholars than that they would keep poking at the largely dry holes he left them. Buckleys, though less fused in a single system than the Kennedys, do have special antennae for each other, making it hard sometimes for in-laws fully to belong.

The main difference between the families is that the Kennedy father pushed farther out, aspired higher, and fueled more ambitious flights than did the Buckley father. This means the Buckleys are only semi-semi-Irish, when compared with the Kennedys' full semi-Irishness (the condition of John's rise to the presidency). But if that differentiates them, the thing that makes them similar is the fact that each man *did* push off from his point of origin, to create a private world for his children, a rootless aristocracy of merit. Though no one is entirely free of ancestral influence, these men's families do not exemplify their ethnic heritage so much as the American *escape* from origins toward opportunity.

6

Semi-English

Irish-Americans, particularly those who live in the Boston area, are almost to a man staunchly anti-British.

— DAVID NUNNERLY, *President Kennedy and Britain*

WHEN JOHN KENNEDY WENT to Washington for his work in naval intelligence (and his trysts with Inga Arvad), he met John White, a journalist who was dating his sister Kathleen. White, who thought Kennedy a shallow playboy, was surprised by one sign of depth: "He said his favorite book was *Seven Pillars of Wisdom* by T. E. Lawrence. That was extraordinary taste. Genuine taste."

Perhaps. In 1941 Kennedy was enthusiastic about John Buchan's memoir, *Pilgrim's Way,* in which Buchan praised his friend "Lawrence of Arabia" and said, "I could have followed Lawrence over the edge of the world." Lawrence lived the kind of adventure story Buchan wrote — he served, in fact, as model for "Sandy" in *Greenmantle.* Lawrence could write, in *Seven Pillars:* "Blood was always on our hands; we were licensed to it." James Bond's agent number, remember, is his license to kill. Lawrence presented his qualifications as a translator of Homer this way: "I have hunted wild boars and watched wild lions, sailed the Aegean (and sailed ships), bent bows, lived with pastoral peoples, woven textiles, built boats and killed many men." It is the code of Norman Mailer's neo-Renaissance man: "kill well (if always with honor), love well and love many, be cool, be daring, be dashing, be wild, be wily, be resourceful, be a brave gun."

It did not hurt that Buchan was made Lord Tweedsmuir for his services to the British government. Kathleen Kennedy married an English lord, which was not possible for John Kennedy; but the two books he always referred to as his favorites were by British lords — *Pilgrim's Way* by Tweedsmuir, and *The Young Melbourne* by Lord David Cecil. Both books came out within a year of his own *Why England Slept,* at a time when Kennedy was a defender of England's imperialist politicians. Both books gave him a wildly romantic view of aristocrats. From Cecil's *Melbourne* he seems to have derived his impression that English aristocrats have naked women emerge from silver dishes at their banquets (the moral *Time* magazine drew from the book). The Melbourne described by Cecil, a doting descendant, was all the things Kennedy wanted to be — secular, combining the bookish and the active life, supported by a family that defied outsiders. The Arthur Schlesinger line on Kennedys as "slow maturers" was laid down by Cecil: "He was the sort of character that, in any circumstances, does not come of age till middle life. His nature was composed of such diverse elements that it took a long time to fuse them into a stable whole."

The family loyalty of the Kennedys is presented by Cecil as a Melbourne trait. Melbourne House must have seemed to Kennedy a remarkable anticipation of Hyannis Port:

Children brought up in gay and patrician surroundings seldom react against them with the violence common in more circumscribed lives. If their tastes differ from those of the people round them, they have the leisure and money to follow them up in some degree; and anyway, their ordinary mode of living is too agreeable for them to conceive any strong aversion to it. Further, the Milbanke half of William's nature was perfectly suited by his home. He loved the parties and the sport and the gossip; he felt at home in the great world. Nor was his other side starved at Melbourne House. He had all the books he liked, he could listen enthralled to the clever men cleverly disputing, while his native tenderness bloomed in the steady sunshine of the family affection. His brothers and sisters were as fond of him as of one another. And, in the half-laughing, unsentimental way approved by Lamb standards, they showed their feelings. He returned them. His brothers were always his closest men friends, his favourite boon companions. What could be better fun than acting with George, arguing with Frederick, racing with Peniston? He was equally attached to his sisters, especially "that little devil, Emily."

The Melbourne set described in such a dreamy glow is the fulfillment of Joseph Kennedy's dream for his own children, aristocratically free of the need to climb, to do business, to court others: "Born in the centre of its most entertaining circle, he found himself, without any effort on his part, elected to its best clubs, invited to its most brilliant parties. And he had the talents to make the most of his advantages." Some resemblances were almost eerie — Melbourne, for instance, had a retarded son he cared for with great affection. Other resemblances John Kennedy could arrange — both Melbourne's wife and one of his lovers were named Caroline.

Cecil was sentimental in describing Melbourne as an eighteenth-century man whose circle and class kept wit alive into Queen Victoria's time. But John Kennedy must have felt that Cecil was a contemporary reporter on the English ruling class when he took six months off from Harvard studies to be a "courier" for his father in London. David Nunnerly, in *President Kennedy and Britain* (1972), describes the undergraduate's initiation into English country life:

> Englishmen of his own generation, like David Ormsby-Gore and "Billy" Hartington, he found altogether more sophisticated and confident than his American contemporaries. They were hardly the angry young men of the 1930s: in fact politics was for them rather light-hearted, certainly no obsession, though this very idea of politics invigorating rather than dominating society much appealed to Kennedy. But the other aspects of the British way of life equally appealed to him. He immensely enjoyed his leisured week-ends in the country homes of the great aristocratic families. At first through his father's position, he found himself regularly invited for week-ends at the Chatsworths and Lismores, respectively the English and Irish ancestral homes of the Devonshires, with whom he later strengthened his ties through his sister Kathleen's marriage to the Marquis of Hartington. The presence of other house guests, many of whom were public figures, like the Edens and the Randolph Churchills, was in a sense history come alive for him. It had, as Arthur Schlesinger put it, "a careless elegance he had not previously encountered." The new perspective on life to which he was exposed

was of special importance since it was acquired in his formative and impressionable years, during which period he might otherwise have been content to have remained a shy and somewhat introverted personality. Instead, and as one of his intimate friends later recalled, somewhat to his own surprise, "He found his British friends very agreeable and he got on very well with them; and gradually what I would call the anti-British elements he grew out of and by the end you couldn't have found a more British person."

Nunnerly properly stresses the confidence of the class Kennedy was meeting. The Harvard undergraduate naively extended that trait to every single Englishman in his first published book, *Why England Slept:* "No discussion of Britain's psychology would be complete unless some mention were made of the natural feeling of confidence, even of superiority, that every Englishman feels." It was a heady vision to take back with him into classrooms where even Boston brahmins looked provincial now.

John Buchan, in *Pilgrim's Way,* takes a view of English aristocrats at least as rosy as Lord Cecil's. Here, for instance, is his Lord Asquith: "The Prime Minister, Mr. Asquith, had in his character every traditional virtue — dignity, honour, courage, and a fine selflessness." If Lytton Strachey was less dazzled by Asquith, his view would not alter Kennedy's admiration for these aristocrats:

> Who would guess from this book [of Asquith's] which has just come out (*Occasional Addresses*) with its high-minded orotundities and cultivated respectabilities, that the writer of it would take a lady's hand, as she sat behind him on the sofa, and make her feel his erected instrument under his trousers? (this I had very directly from Brett, to whose sister it happened at Garsington, and who told me as much of it as her maiden modesty allowed — egged on by Ottoline — and all of it to Carrington).

But Buchan, an imperialist admirer of Cecil Rhodes who served as a colonial official in several countries, had more to tell Kennedy about aristocratic *politics.* He presents himself as a defender of democracy "properly understood," but says this must not amount to a denigration of the "great men" England needs to survive. He thought the people of England had gone soft, and hoped his adventure tales would brace them for new risks. His ideal was T. E. Lawrence, worshipped as a superman on the James Bond scale:

> Physically he looked slight, but, as boxers say, he stripped well, and he was as strong as many people twice his size, while he had a bodily toughness and endurance far beyond anything I have ever met. In 1920 his whole being was in grave disequilibrium. You cannot in any case be nine times wounded, four times in an air crash, have many bouts of fever and dysentery, and finally at the age of twentynine take Damascus at the head of an Arab army, without living pretty near the edge of your strength.

For Kennedy, who lived at the edge of his slight strength — defying illness, risking dangerous sports, driving recklessly — Buchan's "crush" on his hero proved contagious, as we learn from John White. Kennedy's statistics-laden senior paper, published as *Why England Slept,* should be read in conjunction with Buchan's memoir. The latter supplies the romantic ideology partly covered over by the scholastic pose of the former. Both books appeared in the same year (1940), and their attitudes came from the same class, one that Ambassador Kennedy was cultivating as he supplied his son with evaluations of the British leaders, journals, and problems.

Since Joseph Kennedy opposed America's entry into England's war, and was harshly criticized by the British after Roosevelt recalled him, there has been a tendency to treat him as just another "isolationist" like Senator Borah or Colonel McCormick. But Kennedy considered Borah a pacificist, and his son's book castigates him for trying to disarm America. No Kennedy shared McCormick's anglophobia. In fact, Joseph Kennedy dearly loved a lord, and did not throw his strong will — the only one that mattered — against his daughter's decision to marry one. Rose Kennedy remembers how her husband glowed with pride in their suite at Windsor Castle: "Well, Rose, this is a helluva long way from East Boston, isn't it?" Arrived in England, Kennedy quickly joined the fashionable Cliveden Set, and imbibed its antiwar position. Franklin Roosevelt was soon wondering to Henry Morgenthau: "Who would have thought that the English could take into camp a red-headed Irishman?" To James Farley he said: "Joe has been taken in by the British government people and the royal family." The wonder of it, according to Heywood Broun, was that this American cultivating lords and ladies came from an Irish background "where the kids are taught to twist the lion's tail even before they learn to roll their hoops."

The distinctive mark of Joseph Kennedy's "isolationism" was its paradoxical nourishment from *foreign* sources. This circumstance set Kennedy at some distance from other Americans who opposed the war. Since British "appeasers" claimed their policy was meant to buy time for rearming, Kennedy was not opposed to war preparation as such, like Borah. Nor was he optimistic about America's avoiding "entanglement." He wanted the country armed to the teeth, for any emergency. It was England's failure to do this that trapped her in a position where rapid mobilization could only be accomplished by adopting totalitarian disciplines herself. This was the background of Kennedy's disastrous later press conference in Boston — the one that ended all his presidential hopes when he said that "democracy is finished in England."

Because Kennedy's views fit imperfectly with those of other American isolationists, his son's book *Why England Slept* — which reflects those views — has regularly been misread. It is customary for authors to tell us the book departed from the elder Kennedy's position. Arthur Schlesinger makes an even stranger claim: *"Why England Slept* was a singularly dispassionate statement to be flung into America's most passionate foreign policy debate of the century — so dispassionate, indeed, that it was impossible to conclude from the text whether the author was an interventionist or isolationist."

No one who reads the book's original foreword can think it rose above foreign policy debates. Henry Luce cut all but a few paragraphs of that foreword in the book's 1961 reprint, the version familiar to most readers now. But in 1940, a campaign year, *Why England Slept* was recommended between its own covers as an attack on Roosevelt for not alerting the public to impending war dangers. Luce, of course, was backing Wendell Willkie's candidacy in 1940, as was Arthur Krock, who gave the book what little style it possesses. In arranging for these two sponsors, Joseph Kennedy was easing away from what he thought would be the disaster of Roosevelt's policies — he hoped to inherit the Democratic party for himself if Roosevelt fell. He was playing for big stakes at this period, but without Roosevelt's cold nerve. Having set up a confrontation with his leader, Kennedy shied off at the last minute. By that time, his son's book was out.

In the 1940 foreword, Luce argued that Roosevelt was unrealistic in his dismissal of the war threat. He denied that this was just a campaign ploy: "Surely Mr. Roosevelt couldn't just be playing politics if he really thought we might be in for a war." Luce had to admit that Willkie, too, had presented himself to the Republicans as a peace candidate. But this was understandable in the first stage of an outsider's campaign. "Since his opponents (in both parties) have had eight years to play politics, Mr. Willkie may reasonably be given eight days." But this newcomer was not frozen in the antiwar stance Luce attributed to Roosevelt: "Very soon Mr. Willkie must meet the psychological test which Mr. Kennedy has so ably staged. Perhaps he will have met it magnificently before this book is off the press."

The "test" proposed by the book was this: How can a modern democracy be brought to arm itself in peacetime sufficiently to deter war, or to win it, without having to adopt totalitarian ways? England failed that test, according to Kennedy, for two reasons, one structural, one specific to the thirties. The structural problem arises from the very nature of democracy, which caters to people's present wants instead of addressing future threats. The more transitory problem was England's pacifism of the thirties, fed on unrealistic hopes raised by the League of Nations. America, necessarily, suffers from the first problem; but it might still bring itself to arm, because it had not been fatally infected with the League's pacifism.

Throughout his book, Kennedy accepts and repeats Stanley Baldwin's assertion that "a democracy is always two years behind the dictator." Absolute rulers can plan ahead, free of the necessity of coaxing votes from the populace: "A democracy will merely try to counter-balance the menaces that are actually staring it in the face." Thus the effort to rearm England had to be abandoned in the crucial year, 1935, because of the General Election: "For election year is the time when the public rules — it is then that the politicians acknowledge its superiority. Then, as at no other time, do they try to strike on the policy most acceptable to the mass of voters." Dictators manage the news to alarm their subjects into activity, while a free press lulls the citizenry: "A democracy's free press gives the speeches of the totalitarian leaders, who state their case in such a 'reasonable' manner that it is hard always to see them as a menace." Even Hitler had a plausible case to make in such a press: "As Hitler pointed out with some truth, in his cleverly worded letter to Daladier in August, 1939, shortly before the outbreak of the war, much of what he had done in Europe rectified wrongs that had been done at Versailles, and which should have been righted long before."

Beyond this continuing problem of a democracy, England of the 1930s had gone soft under the preaching of idealists (the John Buchan view). "Numerous political federations and councils throughout the country opposed it [rearmament] also. Groups, like the League of Nations, protested that it was a desertion of collective security; and others, like the National Peace Council, the National League of Young Liberals, the National Council of Evangelical Free Churches, were equally outspoken in their opposition. In any discussion of groups opposed to rearmament, no list would be complete without including the completely pacifist wing of the Labour Party led by men like George Lansbury and Dick Shepherd. Though the number of people who supported their advocacy of complete and final abolition of all weapons of warfare was limited, yet their indirect influence was considerable."

England, in short, had an enemy within, for which young Kennedy was supplying a kind of Attorney General's List. The country's spirit had been sapped by dangerous books: "The whole spirit of the country was pacifistic — probably more strongly than it had ever been. Numerous books against war like *Cry Havoc!* by Beverly Nichols were widely circulated and avidly read. In an article on *Illusions of Pacifists,* the writer began, 'Disarmament and peace are among the most discussed topics of the day.' " Kennedy repeatedly denounces "the strength of the pacifist movement and the general feeling against disarmament," "the strongly peaceful attitude of the people."

The structural and the incidental problems, combined, posed the dilemma for British statesmen (who were wise enough to see the danger): how to flatter the people's pacific instincts enough to get elected, yet defy them enough to rearm? The resolution of this problem depended on buying time. Since that was the goal, it became for Kennedy the justification of the appeasers:

> In his [1936] acceptance address, Chamberlain announced the policy that was to become known as "appeasement." Appeasement to us now has a bad sound — it connotes Munich and backing down. In a vague way we blame it for much of Europe's present trouble, but there was more to it than that when Chamberlain announced it back in 1937. It was a double-barreled policy; he would "continue our program of the re-establishment of our defence forces, combined with a substantial effort to remove the causes which are delaying the return of confidence in Europe." That Chamberlain's policy was not merely an unsuccessful effort "to remove the causes delaying the return of confidence" is not popularly realized. It is the other part of his program, "continuing our program of the re-establishment of our defence forces," with which we are chiefly concerned.

> The policy of appeasement, while it was partly based on a sincere belief that a permanent basis could be built for peace, was also formulated on the realization that Britain's defence program, due to its tardiness in getting started, would not come to harvest until 1939.

> Taking all these factors into consideration, the Munich Pact appears in a different light from that of a doddering old man being completely "taken in." It shows that appeasement did have some realism; it was the inevitable result of conditions that permitted no other decision.

But time ran out on the men trying to overcome the mass's dangerous reluctance to face danger, and Baldwin became a scapegoat while Chamberlain became a figure of sad comedy.

The Cliveden Set had taught Joseph Kennedy that the British public was at fault for the country's weakness — especially the labor unions:

> The question has come up again and again, as the great increase in production has been made by the recent great sacrifices of labor in England — why wasn't this done more than a year ago? Why didn't the Chamberlain Government organize labor in this way? Why

weren't strikes outlawed months before, as was done on June 6? Why wasn't labor conscripted and the country organzied at the end of 1938 and through 1939? This has all been done by Mr. Bevin, the new Minister for Labor under the Churchill Government. But Mr. Bevin was the great leader of the Trade Unions in England before the war. What was his and Mr. Greenwood's attitude at that time about this problem?

So strong was John Kennedy's defense of the ruling class in his earlier draft that even his father told him to tone it down. The book should not look like a whitewash. So there is a perfunctory "blame all around" conclusion, which — like the book's rambling struc- ture — encourages people to call it evenhanded where it is just con- fused. The only real criticism of the rulers in the body of the book is directed at Baldwin's "great mistake" in telling the truth about the 1935 election — admitting that he played down the need to rearm during the election period, to gain time for developing his plans:

> The speech Baldwin delivered was one of the gravest political "boners" that any politician ever made. His "appalling frankness" has resulted in his being blamed for the entire condition of Britain's armaments. Although a master politician, he made the most ele- mentary mistakes in phrasing, and from this time on he became the political scapegoat for Britain's failure to rearm. Much of what Baldwin said was true, but the manner in which he worded the truth made it appear that he had put his party's interest above the national interest, and that was fatal.

It is hard to see, in retrospect, how reviewers took seriously a book that presented Baldwin's speech as the appeasers' one great mistake. The whole book is a hodgepodge of disconnected and ill-grounded assertions: "There is no lobby for armaments as there is for relief or for agriculture." The basic argument was hard to follow, since the volume was first planned as a chronological treatment of military production, year by year. For this Ambassador Kennedy supplied masses of ill-related statistics and charts, shoved into the different time slots. The argument was made, as it were, in the interstices of this less ambitious account — and it derives less from a reasoned chain of thought than from the father's odd blend of prejudices, fears, and ambitions. The book, like the Ambassador, is anglophile-isolationist and warhawk-appeasing. Even in its amended version it struck Luce as too charitable to the appeasers: "On the very difficult subject of Munich, I agree with Mr. Kennedy to the extent that he rebuts the cheap-and-easy vilification of Mr. Chamberlain by many American writers. I do so even though, on balance, I cast my own jury-vote against Mr. Chamberlain."

Why England Slept was a passable undergraduate paper that never quite became a book. The disparate things stuffed into it have obscured its principal argument; its only unity comes from a cluster of attitudes John Kennedy had drawn from his reading, his experience of England, and his dependence on his father for information and point of view. That is why the book should be read in relation to his contemporary enthusiasms for Lords Cecil and Tweedsmuir. The "English attitude" toward politics was, for young Kennedy, the English attitude toward sex. He admired adventurer-aristocrats, who could save the people by guiding them, sometimes without their knowledge. The book's only importance is its way of striking these notes. They would sound for a long time in Kennedy's political career.

It is said that Kennedy's early friendship for Joseph McCarthy derived simply from his father's ties to the man, or from the Irish Catholic constituency of Massachusetts. But the heated attack on pacifist books, authors, and organizations in *Why England Slept* shows that Kennedy thought subversive ideas could undermine people's will to resist. It might be necessary, in such circumstances, to limit civil rights — the right to strike, the "misleading" tendency of a free press. A country exposed to peril by an enemy within may have to submit to a period of voluntary totalitarianism:

> The nation had failed to realize that if it hoped to compete successfully with a dictatorship on an equal plane, it would have to renounce temporarily its democratic privileges. All of its energies would have to be molded in one direction, just as all the energies of Germany had been molded since 1933. It meant voluntary totalitarianism because, after all, the essence of a totalitarian state is that the national purpose will not permit group interest to interfere with its fulfillment.

This is the earliest formulation of "Ask not what your country can do for you, but what you can do for your country."

Sometimes enlightened leaders must hide from their subjects the reasons for their acts (avoiding Baldwin's mistaken candor with the electorate), or even the acts themselves. The world of aristocratic rakes like Melbourne has an underside, the dark area where T. E. Lawrence moves, and Richard Hannay, and James Bond, all the Green Berets and gentlemen spies of the CIA. Presiding over this potentially dangerous world is the honor of the aristocrats, their code of national service. When it came time for Kennedy to praise his forebears in the United States Senate, he sought men with Melbourne's sense of personal honor, which precludes a servile deference to constituents. All eight of his heroes are praised for defying the electorate, sometimes quixotically:

> It may take courage to battle one's President, one's party or the overwhelming sentiment of one's nation; but these do not compare, it seems to me, to the courage required of the Senator defying the angry power of the very constituents who control his future. It is for this reason that I have not included in this work the stories of this nation's most famous "insurgents" — John Randolph, Thaddeus Stevens, Robert LaFollette, and all the rest — men of courage and integrity, but men whose battles were fought with the knowledge that they enjoyed the support of the voters back home.

Kennedy's father tried to instill in each of his children a sense of their own worth. It was a miniature aristocracy he created, hovering above the Irish-American scene. Those clustered on that space platform did not so much have roots as sources — and the principal source was an imagined English aristocracy of public service.

7

Honorary Kennedys

I would have the courtier devote all his thought and strength of
spirit to loving and almost adoring the prince he serves above all
else, devoting his every desire and habit and manner to pleasing
him.

— CASTIGLIONE

VICTOR NAVASKY ATTRIBUTES much of Robert Kennedy's success
in the Justice Department to the talented circle of men he calls
"honorary Kennedys." Though Kennedys are attuned mainly to
Kennedys, their superheated mutual admiration sets up a magnetic
field energizing others in their vicinity. Without being fully admitted to the family (even by marriage), friends and allies rotate loyally
and lend their skills. Navasky studied the resources this system made
available to Attorney General Kennedy. Not only could he recruit
from his own cluster of friends and past associates, but from those of
his father and brothers. People who would not have served at second
or third level posts, just for a minor title, were happy to serve a
Kennedy. And their performance was spirited, not only from a sense
of obligation or office, but from reinforcing motives of pride and
ambition — to make a *Kennedy* recognize their ability.

The use of honorary Kennedys was not restricted to formal ap-
pointments at the Justice Department. When the Attorney General
took it as a family obligation to free those captured at the Bay of
Pigs invasion, powerful friends organized a private ransom fund.
Cardinal Cushing, for instance, pledged the first million dollars. In
Navasky's words: "He called upon a Kennedy potpourri, a public-

private mix of family, friends, ad hoc committees, free-lance lawyers, sympathizers, bankers and power brokers within, without and throughout the government, the network, the charismatic authority structure, the honorary Kennedys."

When, as Senator from New York, Kennedy decided to do something about slum conditions in Bedford-Stuyvesant, he set up the same kind of task force. McGeorge Bundy was now at the Ford Foundation, Burke Marshall at IBM, Douglas Dillon back at his firm — the voices of wealth and influence. Civil rights workers from Robert's Justice Department — including the admired John Doar — dropped other work and took up Robert's project. Money and talent were instantly available for the Senator's personal poverty program.

When, sudden and late, Kennedy decided to run for President in 1968, he could compensate for prior delay by turning to this instantly mobilizable network. Jack Newfield describes his first move: "So the phone calls began to go out, and dozens of men agreed to abandon their families, and their jobs with law firms, newspapers, and universities, and go to Indiana, or Oregon, or California, to work for the Restoration."

Joseph Kennedy had organized the first generation of honorary Kennedys, which included Arthur Krock, William Douglas, and James Landis. The fast-moving businessman knew how to use the talents of such adjuncts, but he had neither the leisure nor the reputation to acquire them on the scale that his sons later did. To have courtiers, you must maintain a court — something he made possible for his family rather than himself. For every Krock he collected, his sons would have dozens of bright journalists in tow. At different times, the honorary Kennedys included Philip Graham, Ben Bradlee, Joseph Alsop, Bill Lawrence, Roland Evans, Sander Vanocur, Hugh Sidey, Hayes Gorey, Henry Brandon, Theodore White, Charles Bartlett, Anthony Lewis, Art Buchwald, Pete Hamill, Jack Newfield, Jeff Greenfield, John Bartlow Martin, and — ironically — Roger Mudd. For every Dean Landis of Harvard Law, the sons would have courtier-professors bowing in with book after book. Arthur Schlesinger abandoned his major work on the New Deal to write — endlessly — for and about the Kennedys. He and James MacGregor Burns alternate volumes on the Kennedys, creating one-man libraries.

Service for one brother became a claim on the next, building up ring on ring of variously influential allies. Loyalty was expected of them, understandably. If the real Kennedys set family above all else, those who share in the Kennedy magic without owning it by birth should, clearly, take up their share of service to the clan. Navasky describes the reaction when Nicholas Katzenbach, Robert's friend and successor as Attorney General, "disloyally" refused to issue a statement exonerating Kennedy from all complicity in FBI buggings.

> Katzenbach rationalized his resolution of the conflict between loyalty to law and loyalty to friend by arguing — to himself and to RFK — that there was no conflict, that by leaving out the requested language he was acting in Robert Kennedy's best interest as well as the Justice Department's. Nevertheless, he had violated one of the unspoken tenets of the Kennedy code — that when there is a disagreement between a hard-core Kennedy and an honorary Kennedy such as Katzenbach, the former prevails, even when a non-Kennedy like Johnson happens to be President — and the relationship was never quite the same thereafter. The story is important less for what it shows about Katzenbach's decision than for what it suggests about Kennedy's assumption in dealing with other members of the extended Kennedy family: that where the formal requirements of the legal system and the informal requirements of politics or personal obligation conflict, the code of the Kennedys should prevail, or at least be given great weight.

In the 1968 campaign, Robert told Jack Newfield how McNamara had observed the Kennedy-first rule: "Bob McNamara twice turned down the Vice Presidency just because he felt I should get it." The standards varied as one went up or down the social scale of Kennedy attendants. A *gran rifiuto* was expected of Robert McNamara. For Paul ("Red") Fay, an aborted checkers game would show proper respect for John Kennedy's supremacy: "I was winning the first game when I noticed a warning look in his eyes. He coughed suddenly, sending the checkers onto the floor or helter-skelter across the checkerboard. 'One of those unfortunate incidents of life, Redhead,' he said with a touch of a smile. 'We'll never really know if the

Under Secretary was going to strategically outmaneuver the Commander-in-Chief.' "

The natural order of things was several times enforced on Sargent Shriver, as Harris Wofford describes in his book *Of Kennedys and Kings*. Shriver's interest in running for governor of Illinois had to be sacrificed in 1960 to the presidential race of John Kennedy — lest he distract people with another Catholic who was part of the senior Kennedy's business world. When Lyndon Johnson thought of offering the vice-presidency to Shriver, and Bill Moyers said that Robert would not object, Kenneth O'Donnell blurted, "The hell he wouldn't." Then, when Humphrey considered Shriver for the same post, Edward Kennedy vetoed the idea. When Shriver did accept appointments from President Johnson — to the poverty program, and as Ambassador to France — this caused hard feelings in the family, reaching their climax in the 1968 race. Wofford writes: "It was the first time when family loyalty broke down, to the disservice of both Shriver and Kennedy — and Johnson — each of whose effectiveness would have been greater if they could all have worked together."

But Shriver remained an in-law, so no final break occurred. With those less bound to the family, retaliation for disloyalty could be savage. Arthur Krock, who had spent decades serving the career of Joseph Kennedy, was bitterly opposed to the civil rights movement of the sixties. He refused to endorse John Kennedy because of the 1960 platform statement on civil rights. Kennedy, once in office, arranged for attacks on Krock to run in *Newsweek,* and was disappointed that they were so mild. "Tuck it to Krock," he told Ben Bradlee. "Bust it off in old Arthur. He can't take it, and when you go after him he folds."

Bradlee, meanwhile, was serving Krock's old functions, clearing things he wrote about Kennedy with Kennedy himself, informing the President when *Newsweek* planned to publish anything critical of the administration. But Fletcher Knebel quoted in print a Bradlee remark about Kennedy's sensitivity to criticism, and the punishment that followed confirmed the accusation: for three months Bradlee was banned from Kennedy festivities, and from other social gatherings where the President's influence extended. In front of Bradlee himself, Kennedy told the British Ambassador not to invite *News-*

week's man to an embassy party. Only after he had been fully chastened was he readmitted to court — never to make the same mistake of risking candor while Kennedy lived.

Loyalty, which won honorary Kennedys their reflected glory, also exacted a price. Kennedy's bright staff at Justice worked hard, cut corners, got things done. But the cost was a certain suspension of judgment before Kennedy priorities. Family pride was forfeit to the task of "getting Hoffa," and the loyalists supported this effort, even when it meant prosecuting on a dubious charge, with no issue at stake, by a major commitment of resources to the hunt. Navasky says of Hoffa's Nashville indictment, "Never in history had the government devoted so much money, manpower and top level brainpower to a misdemeanor case." The charge, which would have brought a maximum penalty of one year, was conflict of interest in a truck-leasing firm Hoffa openly set up. This was not a crime that cried to heaven; it was just an opportunity to get Hoffa, and the honorary Kennedys — with one honorable exception — dutifully went along (though they would not, in fact, win a conviction):

> Within the Department, Byron White, Nicholas Katzenbach, Burke Marshall (who flew down in the middle of the trial with Howard Willens, First Assistant in the Criminal Division), former labor law professor Archibald Cox and Ramsey Clark were among those consulted on the case, and with the exception of Clark — whose experience as a private attorney with the trucking industry convinced him that the evidence was insufficient to show a significant departure from the practices of the trucking industry — they all felt a legitimate case might be made.

Honorary membership in the family could entail dangers. And why not? Being a real Kennedy is even more dangerous. Dean James Landis, loyal to the Kennedys for many years, was one of those people who suffer a mental block in dealing with the IRS. For some years, he had deposited his income tax payments in a special account rather than with the government. When this came to light, he paid taxes, interest, and penalty; there was no evidence of attempt to defraud; with anyone else, the case would have been dropped. But that might open the Kennedys to a charge of favoritism, so the Justice

Department was compensatorily rigorous. Navasky concludes his analysis of the case:

> The code of the Kennedys was profoundly entangled with James Landis's fate. His tax delinquency was discovered because he was on the Kennedy White House staff. It was brought to old Joe's attention because the district Director of the IRS shared the nation's image of the clannish, behind-the-scenes way the Kennedys do business. The case proceeded through channels partly because the Kennedys had officially disqualified themselves, partly because it was *not* part of the Kennedy way of doing business for Robert to tell his old University of Virginia tax professor, Mortimer Caplin, to get him off the hook at the expense of the integrity of the tax code, partly because Kennedy loyalists didn't want the Kennedy Administration vulnerable to charges of fix. Landis pleaded guilty so as not to embarrass the Kennedys, despite evidence that a not-guilty plea might have been sustained. He was sentenced to confinement, seldom the case in failure-to-file convictions, undoubtedly in part as a tribute to his importance as a member of the Kennedy family.

To circle in tight family orbits, ringed about with powerful satellites, is to create a field of influence very gratifying — until the satellites, reversing nature, begin to tug at the center of their own system, pulling it in contrary directions. This happened to Robert when the number of real Kennedys diminished, and the honorary family members were all concentered on him. Other galaxies collapsed inward, around his, after his father's stroke, his brother's death. Edward, the youngest Kennedy, was more Robert's satellite, at this stage, than a center in his own right. The subordinates, neatly sorted out before, now collided; clogged the air around Robert, inhibiting his motions with their friendly crowding; deafened him with advice.

This problem became acute when Robert Kennedy tried to free himself of the Vietnam war his brother helped initiate. Robert had named three of his children after powerful men in his brother's administration — Averell Harriman, Douglas Dillon, and Maxwell Taylor. It was a way of binding the system together; the honorary Kennedys around the older brother were honored in their turn by the younger brother. But in the period leading up to the 1968 campaign, these three "wise men" were supporting the war they helped President Kennedy launch. The natural order of things is for honorary Kennedys to move toward the oldest living heir; but one test of President Kennedy's growing influence had been his ability to attract ever more powerful men toward him, men who — even while serving Kennedy — had positions and reputations of their own at stake. Besides, the Kennedy heir had himself supported the Johnson escalations when they first occurred — along with stellar members of the Kennedy team like Robert McNamara, the Bundy brothers, the Rostow brothers. These people all felt they were being true to a Kennedy legacy. *Robert* had departed from the course his brother set.

Even some of those closest to Robert — including his younger brother — joined those who had been close to John Kennedy (e.g., Schlesinger, Sorensen, Salinger) in urging Robert not to run against Lyndon Johnson in 1968. Other members of the Kennedy team were dropping out of the Johnson White House — but, like McNamara, they went quietly, not risking outright confrontation with an incumbent Democratic President. And when Robert Kennedy began to critize the war, his comments were cautious, muted, contrite ("there is blame enough for everyone"), and invariably joined with some expression of good will toward President Johnson. This meant that the "old guard" was still welcome at Robert's home, Hickory Hill, where their voices were raised in the rivalry of friendly advisers, all with claims on Robert through his brother or his father. They were part of the dead man's legacy, the Kennedy promise. Many resented Kennedy's apparent willingness to squander the family's future hopes in a quixotic race against Johnson. They thought of *him* as disloyal to his name.

In this period, Robert showed signs of wanting to break out of his own protective cordon of family powers. He sought new and younger advisers — creating, inevitably, more honorary Kennedys who would clash with the older ones. Generations of such family retainers now clamored for his ear. The "first generation" were veterans of the Adlai Stevenson campaigns who had switched to Kennedy. They claimed to uphold the authentic liberal tradition — Arthur Schlesinger, for instance, and Kenneth Galbraith. Schlesinger began with doubts that Robert should take on Johnson, then shifted as the candidate's own desires became clearer. Galbraith thought he should run from the start; and, when he didn't, joined Eugene McCarthy's campaign. This member of the old guard outran Robert's own hot-headed young staffers.

The second generation was made up of those who had run his brother's campaigns. They, too, were divided — Kenneth O'Donnell, for instance, wanted to take on Johnson. But the weightiest members of that team thought this would be foolish — and theirs were the arguments Robert himself had used when advising his brother. Don't make gestures; go in to win; forget liberal sentiment; count the votes. The vote counters could not come up with the right numbers, so they told him not to run.

Another generation was made up of those recruited into President Kennedy's cabinet and staff. The "big guns" here were all supporters of Johnson and the war. They spoke, for the public, as Kennedy men. They made the war Kennedy's war — how dare Robert attack it?

The fourth generation of honorary Kennedys came from Robert's associates in the Justice Department — men like Burke Marshall, John Seigenthaler, Edwin Guthman. They, too, initially opposed a 1968 campaign.

Last came Kennedy's Senate staffers, the press secretary Frank Mankiewicz and the two "kids" who served as administrative assistants, speechwriter Adam Walinsky and legislation-drafter Peter Edelman. These people were free of echoes and memories from President Kennedy's time, and vividly alert to the distress of college students over the war. Often Robert's heart slipped off from his head's calculations to share the sentiments of these "kids." And, while the older Kennedy guard of journalists upheld the Vietnam war — Joseph Alsop outstanding in this group — Kennedy cultivated a new circle of adversary journalists: Jack Newfield, Jeff Greenfield, Pete Hamill, Jimmy Breslin, David Halberstam. When Robert died, these writers would be his elegists — as Theodore White and Hugh Sidey had been for his assassinated brother.

Naturally, the young staffers and newsmen were resented by older servants of family glory — not simply because they were Johnnys-come-lately, but because they were reckless with the family's future hopes. They seemed to think in terms of a demonstration rather than a restoration. Guardians of the legacy were rightly upset when the young firebrands dragged Robert Kennedy off to consult with Tom Hayden, or with street gang leaders. If Kennedy was willing to take communion with Cesar Chavez today, to recommend sending blood to the Viet Cong, what might he do tomorrow? Take communion with a pacifist like Dorothy Day? Become Eldridge Cleaver's friend? Go — as his Justice Department colleague, Ramsey Clark, finally did — to Hanoi? Or, like Clark, defend the Berrigan brothers? Where would it all end?

At least part of Robert Kennedy — and that the oldest part, the successful campaign manager — shared these reservations about his new cohorts. Kennedys do not run campaigns as a form of moral gesture. They run to win; and know what that takes; and do what is necessary. The young guard around Kennedy had an open contempt for "old politicians" like Mayor Daley. But longstanding associates of the Kennedys knew what Daley had done for them in the past and could do in the future — and Robert knew that best of all. Shortly before his death, he told Jimmy Breslin, "Daley is the ball game." But if that was so, what was he doing in a different ball park entirely, palling around with Cesar Chavez?

The truth is that Robert Kennedy agreed to run, not out of total agreement with his "kids," but in the belief that he could beat Eugene McCarthy first and then win back the old machine types he would need. That is why Robert ran a "law and order" campaign, and refused to debate McCarthy in Indiana and Oregon, though all his younger aides felt he was honor-bound to do so. The strains of the coalition Kennedy was trying to put together showed over and over in Oregon. And then, when he agreed to debate in California, Robert was willing to win in his old ruthless way — he played on white fears of blacks moving into lily-white Orange County, a ploy even Schlesinger called "demagogic."

In Oregon the honorary Kennedys were fighting for custody of "their" man. Those who felt he had to debate McCarthy went to his suite hoping to make him reverse his decision. Kennedy, standing there in his shorts, blew up. Jules Witcover describes the scene:

Kennedy ordered the room cleared except for a few of the old professionals. He called one of them into the bedroom. "They're pressing in on me," Kennedy told him. And then, looking at the old pro, he added: "Don't tell me you're buying these guys." It was a political crunch, and time for political decision making. "I don't know what they're doing here," Kennedy said of his young speechwriters. "I didn't even want them out here." Outside in the corridor, Walinsky, Greenfield and others were milling around, talking loudly. Kennedy, still dressed only in his shorts, went to the door, opened it and stalked out. "I thought we decided that," he told them angrily. "Why are you standing around here making noise? If you want to do something, go out and ring doorbells." And then, turning to Adam [Walinsky] and Jeff [Greenfield] he barked: "Besides, I don't see why my speechwriters aren't writing speeches instead of playing the guitar all the time." And he stormed back inside. This last was a slow burn erupting. Sometimes during the campaign, Walinsky and Greenfield would get aboard the campaign plane and start playing and singing folk songs while others, including the candidate, tried to work. Now the group in the corridor broke up, and Kennedy dressed for the rally. Adam and Jeff came to [Fred] Dutton's room later, properly chastised, announcing they were returning to Washington to write their speeches. Dutton laughed it off, and told them to do the same. That was the end of it — but there was no debate in Oregon.

Kennedy's young followers were acutely embarrassed by the way their candidate deferred to McCarthy when he could not avoid him. The man who made such a cult of courage, the man who had challenged Jimmy Hoffa to do push-ups, actually turned and ran when his path crossed McCarthy's in Oregon. The two men, without knowing it, were touring the same park outside Portland. Jeremy Larner, on McCarthy's staff, saw the rival press bus and sent three of his aides to block Kennedy's car while Larner brought McCarthy to it. Larner's candidate would only saunter toward the car, so Larner ran ahead to hold it:

My charge carried me right up to Kennedy, who was sitting on top of the back seat with his brown and white spaniel next to him, just like in the photographs. Kennedy shrank a little, as if I were going to grab him. He was smaller than I thought, and his eyes were a brilliant blue. Every second I could hold him talking would bring McCarthy that much closer into camera range.

"Senator McCarthy is coming," I grinned. "Why don't you stick around and talk with him?" I was standing over him and he was looking at me with a look of exquisite hurt. Did we think he was running from fear?

"Isn't that too bad!" he said. He turned to his driver and the driver floored it, the kids jumped for their lives. So Kennedy rolled down the hill without looking back, and I stood with the *Life* photographer shouting "Coward! Chicken!" — for truly he was running away. It turned out that we had held him just long enough for the TV crews to get McCarthy coming and Kennedy speeding off. That night all Oregon saw our backs, and heard the shouts of Coward. Followed by McCarthy capturing the Kennedy press bus and shaking hands with Kennedy's abandoned press.

After Kennedy's death, Larner felt contrite about taunting him; but even Kennedy's people were a bit sickened at the thought that their man was following the old politics — not risking his greater name in debate — even at the cost of running out on the young. There was no way to please all the honorary Kennedys; and their division had left the aggressive Robert Kennedy inwardly divided and uncharacteristically wavering.

Those closest to him at that point sensed that his resort to old political ways violated something that had come to birth in Kennedy out of his brother's death. Now he talked wistfully of leaving politics, of becoming a social worker. His feats of brave mountain-climbing and rapids-shooting were nonpolitical ways of recapturing the headlong spirit with which he once campaigned. He ruefully admired the young McCarthyites with nothing to lose, working for their cause with never a compromise. That was how he had fought when he knew no cause higher than his brother's election. But he could not fight for himself that way. When friends regretted that "Bobby" did not have his own Bobby to do his dirty work for him, they were confessing, indirectly, that "Bobby" no longer existed. It was a deeply changed man who was running for office now. Depth had come to him, and with it indecision — the very thing he despised in Adlai Stevenson while working on his 1956 campaign staff.

No one can tell how the 1968 election might have gone if Kennedy had lived. But David Halberstam rightly observes: "Because he had come in late, McCarthy had picked up Kennedy's natural base and as a result Kennedy was forced to appeal to blue-collar people, which contradicted his appeal to blacks and liberals." And Lawrence O'Brien, who had seen more of all the candidates' camps than any other man that year, was overheard on Robert's funeral train: "Couldn't they see? Couldn't they see? He didn't have a chance." Kennedy had given himself an assignment he probably could not live up to — itself a sign of his change from the win-at-all-costs days. He intended to woo Johnson democrats, and Humphrey, through Richard Daley, after polishing off the McCarthy threat. But that would give him hostages in too many camps. The South, with enmities toward him nurtured from civil rights days, thought him a traitor for advocating that blood be sent to the Viet Cong. His "kids" would deny him that superpatriot bloc so necessary to a Democratic candidate. And would his kids themselves stay with him when he went, hat in hand, back to Johnson, to the man they greeted with the shout, "Hey, hey, LBJ, How many kids did you kill today?" Would Johnson receive him? Would Daley?

Robert's hopes from Daley can be gauged by the way he went through a farce of reconciliation for Daley's sake, just at the time when he was deciding to run against Johnson. When Daley made the suggestion, Kennedy had to go along. He had a lingering respect for the man, who had some of his father's gifts and abrasive strength. In fact, the young Robert Kennedy once seemed destined to become a kind of Richard Daley, a tough political manager. Certainly, when he looked back at his earlier career, Kennedy did not find there a Tom Hayden or Jimmy Breslin. Breslin and Hayden and Hamill, like Michael Harrington, were Catholics who broke away from the Daleys and Cushings and Spellmans — from the people young Bobby had revered.

Mayor Daley went to Mass every morning; he never missed his Easter duty — and never forgot an enemy. Kennedy had been that kind of pious gut-fighter. Like Daley, he was not personally corrupt; but he could deal with corruption to achieve some "greater good." The memory of that fact no doubt galled Robert Kennedy in 1968 — the memory of campaign tricks in West Virginia, the nastier memories of plots against Castro. He had shed much of that older self — but he had to confront it again if he meant to deal with Richard Daley.

Daley's intrusion could not have come at a worse time. McCarthy, while losing the popular vote in New Hampshire, had won twenty of its twenty-four delegates. Kennedy had decided to run, and knew he would be called a spoiler after McCarthy had risked the first challenge to the President. Kennedy informed Mayor Daley of his decision — and Daley asked him, first, to explore the idea of an outside commission to review Vietnam policy. It was a project doomed from the outset — President Johnson was not going to let Robert Kennedy set up a panel to criticize him; and Kennedy did not want to work for such a commission while his chance to campaign slipped by. Yet Daley's influence was so great in the party that all sides had to go through the motions of desiring a review panel just because "Hizzoner" did. Johnson asked Sorensen for a list of names, to be delivered to McNamara's replacement at the Department of Defense, Clark Clifford. Robert Kennedy went to the meeting with Clifford. Unwilling to serve on the review board, he had to *say* he would consent, if asked. That gave Johnson his chance to say Robert wanted to use the panel against him. The episode exacerbated conflict with the President, whose response in turn fueled anger in Kennedy's supporters. The honorary Kennedy from days past, Richard Daley, was tripping up new arrivals at that status.

Accounts differ on the timing of Kennedy's decision to run — before New Hampshire, or after; *well* before New Hampshire, or *just* before. Kennedy was sending different signals to different parts of his own support system; agreeing now with one group, now with another; seeing too many sides of the matter to set a simple course. He caused conflicting impressions in others because he was in conflict with himself. That was clear down to the eve of his announcement, when the kick-off speech had been composed and the team of consultants had gone off to whatever empty beds they could find about his house. Even at this point, Robert had dispatched his brother to see Eugene McCarthy, campaigning in Wisconsin, with a proposal out of character for Kennedys in general and for Robert in particular: the two men would be friendly rivals, raising the war issue but not confronting each other in the same primaries. In short, "Let's fight, but not really." Kennedy wanted to take the war issue away from McCarthy without upsetting McCarthy's troops too much — a proposal fully as unworkable as Daley's, and one McCarthy rightly dismissed. Robert was entering the campaign and not entering it at the same time — which accurately reflected his mood on the sleepless night before he announced.

Arthur Schlesinger, having gone to bed at one-thirty, was awakened by a whisper, "Ted! Ted!" It was Edward Kennedy trying to find Sorensen with the unsurprising news that McCarthy had said no. He did not want to wake his brother, who must be fresh for the morning press conference; but Robert was already awake, and he soon wandered into Schlesinger's room, looking morose: "Well, I have to say something in three hours." Schlesinger, who wanted no bitter or final division between Kennedy and McCarthy's followers, said, "Why not come out for McCarthy? Every McCarthy delegate will be a potential Kennedy delegate. He can't possibly win, so you will be certain inheritor of his support." Kennedy gave him a stony stare and said, "Kennedys don't act that way." Kennedys *didn't* act that way. But they didn't back halfway into fights, either. When Schlesinger went down to breakfast and asked Sorensen where the candidate was, he said, "He is upstairs looking for someone else to wake up in the hope of finding someone who agrees with him." Schlesinger continues:

> Ted Kennedy raised his arms in the air: "I just can't believe it. It is too incredible. I just can't believe that we are sitting around the table discussing anything as incredible as this." Vanden Heuvel and I proposed that, as an interim measure, he come out for McCarthy. My impression was that both Teds thought this might be preferable to his declaring for himself. Then Robert entered the room, still in his pajamas. He had heard the last part of our talk. He said, "Look, fellows, I can't do that. I can't come out for McCarthy. Let's not talk about that any more. I'm going ahead, and there is no point in talking about anything else." With that he left. I proposed taking one more look at the situation. There must be some other course besides endorsing McCarthy or running himself. Teddy said, "No. He's made up his mind. If we discuss it any longer, it will shake his confidence and put him on the defensive. He has to be at his best at this damned press conference. So we can't talk about it any more."

The real and honorary Kennedys, who basked in the light of power and moved so confidently, were broken and divided among themselves, serving a divided man, finally abandoning advice in favor of therapy. The Kennedy pride was engaged, but had to be forsworn — Robert would have to fight Johnson while deferring to him. The family glamour had been eclipsed by McCarthy, who claimed the young constituency Robert thought belonged to his brother by right. The support Robert had *assumed,* McCarthy had gone out and *earned;* and now McCarthy could neither be wooed nor fought outright.

Every move Robert made was opposed by one cluster of Kennedy friends. He had to get away from them; yet he could not. He wandered the house asking, listening, for what no one could say. He talked with everyone, with too many, because he could not talk it through by himself. Yet that was the one thing necessary. It was like being back in his father's house, going with questions at night where certain answers would be given — all the sprawl of family and friends united by the fierce will that made everything cohere on the inside, defiant of anything outside. Robert was struggling to lift up the whole complex of Kennedy loyalties and personal ties, make it hover above difficulty, bright as his father had made it shine for a while. But the sheer accumulation weighed him down. He was a captive of his own courtiers, of those who were urging him on and those who were dragging him back, of the different worlds littered about him, of the dead man's teams and the dead man's shadow, of a legacy divided beyond reassembling.

8

Ghosts

It's narrowed down to Bobby and me. So far he's run with the
ghost of his brother. Now we're going to make him run against it.
It's purely Greek: he either has to kill him or be killed by him.
We'll make him run against Jack. . . . And I'm Jack.

— EUGENE MCCARTHY, 1968

IF ROBERT KENNEDY COULD SEE an older self in Mayor Daley, he
faced in Eugene McCarthy a kind of antiself. For years McCarthy had
been considered the "other Catholic" Senator of presidential stature;
and when McCarthy looked at John Kennedy he clearly thought
there was only one *real* Catholic in the running. During the 1960
convention McCarthy tugged at liberal heartstrings with his tribute
to Adlai Stevenson. But the Kennedys knew he was talking with
Lyndon Johnson about a spot on the Texan's ticket if Kennedy
could be stopped. They took all the praise of Stevenson as an attack
on John Kennedy, on the fake liberal. McCarthy was a natural for a
Johnson ticket, just as Johnson was for Kennedy's — to balance a
northern Catholic with a Southerner.

Unlike John Kennedy, McCarthy took his religion seriously; had
even spent time in a Benedictine monastery. But in other ways Robert could see much of his brother's appeal in this lazy Senator who
moved easily with intellectuals. McCarthy's poems had not won a
Pulitzer Prize; but at least he had written them himself. He had a
buttoned and unrumpled self-possession, a wit that could flick out
and wound, a handsome poise, an equilibrium maintained by mockery. If anything, he made more of personal style than the Kennedys

could — unlike them, he was not afraid to show his contempt for political hacks.

McCarthy is an interesting study in the pride of people trained to embrace humility. He had given up most of the means of satisfying his ambition without giving up the ambition itself. By 1968 he had arrived at a desire for power whose purity was guaranteed by his unwillingness to take any practical steps toward power. He *should* be President because he would not *try* very hard to be. The American people were being tested. If he was not elected, they had failed, not he. All through the 1968 campaign he sought to legitimate a principled indifference as the true prophetic stance. "Don't get excited," he kept telling his enthusiastic young followers. Excitement is undignified. It musses one's hair.

While his young recruits worked day and night for him, he quietly disdained their zealotry. I watched him, that summer, come out of a meeting of Michigan delegates in East Lansing to answer waiting newsmen's questions. "Do you think you won any votes in there?" Well, McCarthy said, these meetings with delegates are mainly a waste of time — a comment that became a self-fulfilling prophecy when the delegates read it the next day in their newspapers.

McCarthy had been stung once by his own ambition, when Lyndon Johnson renewed in 1964 the talk, from 1960, about becoming his Vice-President. Merely continuing that negotiation meant that McCarthy had to undercut his own senior colleague from Minnesota, Hubert Humphrey. But McCarthy crawled partway toward Johnson before being rejected. The humiliation mattered less than his own guilt at yielding to the base scramble for advancement. He would not yield again. So far from bowing to the voters in 1968, he barely bothered, on many occasions, to notice them. He closeted himself with Robert Lowell and made fun of the demeaning aspects of running for office. Refusing to stoop for the crown, he showed his contempt for all those who did — and principally for Robert Kennedy. If the world would not give him the presidency, over the clowns who were running for it, then the world owed him something just for his refusal to join the clowns.

He is still trying to collect what the world owes him — as my wife and I found out later, after a National Book Award presentation: he and a young woman he was escorting saw us sitting with some friends at a restaurant, sat down uninvited, ate an expensive meal, and, after the brandy, left us with the check. It did not come as a surprise, in 1976, when he repeated the campaign act he had disdained in 1968 (when he had a chance) — all, a friend of his assured me, to keep his lecture fees high enough to support him.

As a liberal "Commonweal Catholic" of the forties and fifties, Eugene McCarthy did not share some Irish Catholics' fondness for the other Senator McCarthy. And he still felt, in 1968, that Robert Kennedy was just Joe McCarthy's ex-goon — a cut above Roy Cohn perhaps, but not even up to his older brother's pretensions. Even after Robert was murdered, McCarthy would not utter the minimum words of praise that would unite the two peace campaigns. Robert's team, rebuffed, went to the convention with a new leader, George McGovern, dividing the dissenters' energies. Then, to top it all, McCarthy seemed intent on repairing his treachery to Humphrey in 1964 by refusing to attack the Vice-President for the President's Indochina war.

Yet, despite all his personal flaws and the pettiness of his attitude toward Kennedys, McCarthy was immune to attack from Robert Kennedy. He had done what Robert wished, too late, he had undertaken. He had challenged his party's incumbent, even before Tet; and many thought he deserved the fruits of that challenge. When McCarthy first announced, Robert knew his own young staffers felt disappointed in their boss and envied their rival. Some wore McCarthy buttons on the inside of their lapels. Old Kennedy hands, leaderless after their appeals to Robert, joined McCarthy's effort — Kenneth Galbraith would stay on even after Robert joined the race, after Richard Goodwin went back to his first loyalty. Robert spent the last months of his life lamenting that McCarthy had the "A kids," the ones who went first with the courageous man, the kind who had looked up to his brother. Kennedy Robert had to run with the "B kids."

Having disappointed his followers by inaction, Robert infuriated many when he did act, coming in as a "spoiler" after McCarthy's New Hampshire upset. Murray Kempton, who had learned to respect Kennedy's concern for the poor, manifested after he won his Senate seat, reacted bitterly to the late entry into competition with

McCarthy. In a telegram to Edward Kennedy, turning down an invitation to his book party, he said: "Sorry I can't join you. Your brother's announcement makes it clear that St. Patrick did not drive all the snakes from Ireland." Kennedy could not feed this resentment by overt attacks on McCarthy. He had to defer to him, praise him, hope for his followers somewhere down the road. That was the odd story of 1968 for this old gut-fighter — he could not attack Daley, nor McCarthy, nor Johnson himself. He had to run against men while bowing to them constantly and asking their pardon. One side of the Kennedy legacy now belonged to the hawks around Johnson, who invoked the late President's pledge to fight all over the globe. It was hard enough for Kennedy to see Johnson usurping his brother's tough rhetoric with the help of President Kennedy's most warlike cabinet members. But when Robert turned to the other side of his brother's legacy — the side that inspired youth — he found an even more dangerous, because more charming, usurper in place, mocking him with a smile and saying, "I'm Jack."

John Kennedy, without any trace of radicalism himself, ignited the hopes of young people in the early sixties. The authorized aspect of this was the Peace Corps. An unplanned — and undesired — result of it led to sit-ins and the march on Washington, the Free Speech movement, the Port Huron Statement. John Kennedy would never, like Robert, consort with Tom Hayden; but he helped, like an inadvertent Dr. Frankenstein, bring Hayden into being. Now Eugene McCarthy had captivated and partially tamed the Kennedy monster, made the shaggier types cut their hair and go "clean for Gene," brought civility back to the protest movement. He had not only inherited the Kennedy youth following, but seemed to have elevated it. Thus, when Robert Kennedy appeared late on the scene, McCarthy could say to his speechwriter Jeremy Larner, "We'll make him run against Jack." Arthur Schlesinger finds this statement meaningless, mere verbal posturing. But the meaning is not hard to find. McCarthy, the man who should (in his own eyes) have been the first Catholic President, now stood where the next Kennedy should have, blocking the mere physical heir with a higher spiritual claim. "So far he's run with the ghost of his brother. Now we're going to make him run against it." Lyndon Johnson feared Kennedy because he was the heir; McCarthy felt that Robert was no heir at all, and had no claim. For Robert Kennedy to attack McCarthy would be to attack the A kids who belonged by right to John Kennedy. It would be attacking his brother.

Kennedy shunned debate with McCarthy in Indiana and Oregon, not simply from the "old politics" rule that the better known does not share platforms with the lesser known. He feared confrontation because, on too many points, he had no good case to make against McCarthy — none that could not have been made against his brother. "He either has to kill him or be killed by him."

McCarthy seemed to have a malignant gift for doing what would diminish Kennedy. He moved ostentatiously free of the constraints that were hobbling his rival. Kennedy attacked the war; but McCarthy pointed out that his opponent would not criticize those who had escalated the war — McNamara and other Kennedy appointees. John Kennedy's first official appointment had reconfirmed J. Edgar Hoover in office; so McCarthy campaigned in 1968 on a pledge to fire Hoover — something Robert Kennedy could not promise. Most important of all, McCarthy attacked President Johnson — the way he spoke of "my" helicopters and "my" fighting men and "my" war. McCarthy indeed had reason to resent the man who had humiliated him in 1964; but his attacks were mild next to those of his followers who asked Johnson, chanting, for his daily "kill count" of Americans. McCarthy only looked daring next to Kennedy, who was strangely tongue-tied about the President.

This restraint puzzled Kennedy's followers. The explanation given was that Kennedy should not trigger Johnson's paranoia. As he told Jack Newfield: "I don't want to drive Johnson into doing something really crazy. I don't want to hurt the doves in the Senate who are up for re-election." Now we know that, with Johnson as with Hoover, Kennedy's hands were tied. He feared what Johnson might release about his brother, going all the way back to the Inga Arvad tapes. In 1967 Johnson started dropping hints to the press that he knew about the Kennedy plots against Castro. He even told Leo Janos of *Time* that the Kennedys "had been operating a damned Murder Incorporated in the Caribbean." Robert could not be certain how much else Johnson had learned from Hoover or the CIA. He had to assume Judith Campbell's simultaneous affair with John Kennedy and Sam Giancana was known to the President from files in either agency.

His own service as Attorney General had not endeared him to Hoover. He did not want to provoke either man into campaign leaks or revelations.

Robert's Johnson problem had been both typified and exacerbated by the Manchester affair in 1966. After the President's assassination, Robert and Jacqueline Kennedy had many reasons for controlling the family image. They wanted a dignified treatment of the national tragedy. They did not want to be pestered by a thousand writers seeking interviews. The high-handedness of some Kennedy aides in dealing with Dallas authorities would need soft-pedaling. The autopsy follow-up could be embarrassing on the matter of Addison's disease. And the search for other assassins could lead in the direction of Cuba, of CIA attempts to use the Mafia against Castro.

To all these motives must be added the problem of future relations with President Johnson. In the aftermath of the assassination, Kennedy friends and aides expressed a hatred of Texas and Texans that focused, understandably if unfairly, on Lyndon Johnson. And, as usual, the resentment of the honorary Kennedys outran that of the real ones. The emotion at the center of things was exaggerated by outsiders, who compensated for their distance from the original fire. On the flight back from Dallas, there were ugly little outbursts, anguished rude comments — some of which Johnson had heard about, some he had not. It was important to control the reporting of these events — and, if possible, to delay any reporting of them. The Kennedy team had to work with Johnson, for a while at least — to appear patriotic (and to be patriotic), to avoid charges of pettiness and desertion when the nation was in crisis. Besides, Robert Kennedy felt Johnson was an aberration, an intruder, whose harmful effect could be controlled if he were forced to accept Robert as his running mate in 1964. As long as that option remained, he told his people to express their loyalty to the new President. Frank reporting of those people's real feelings had to be prevented.

The best way to delay and mute reports on the mood in and after Dallas was to find a sufficiently pliant writer, to exact submissiveness to censorship from him, and to prevent him from publishing for almost five years (till after the 1968 election). The Kennedys were especially worried by the prospect that Jim Bishop would do one of his "day" books — *The Day the President Was Shot*. Bishop liked drama and conflict; and the "us against them" mood of the Kennedy aides would lend itself well to his skills. He must be prevented from interviewing the more outspoken members of the Kennedy entourage.

A cooperative author was ready to hand, respectable enough, but with a record of accommodation to the Kennedys. In 1961, William Manchester sent Pierre Salinger a request for interviews with the President, to be turned into articles and then a book: "I should be eager to have you review the facts in the completed articles." When Manchester finished typing his *Portrait of a President,* the publisher sent proofs to Salinger for review — but not a word had to be changed in a White House very touchy about its image.

To Manchester's credit, it must be said that his adoration was sincere. He had been smitten by the glamour of the Kennedys, and his 1961 book records this case of puppy love:

> Dwight Eisenhower, the painter, declared that he wasn't too certain what was art, but he knew what he liked, and Harry Truman, the pianist, said of something he didn't like that if it was art, he was a Hottentot. Jacqueline Kennedy, the connoisseur, makes both look like Hottentots, if not outright clods. She has a rare visual eye. . . . Cultivated families admire elegance, and John Kennedy sets great store by good form. His circle doesn't include men who wear clocks on their socks, or call Shakespeare the Bard, or say budgetwise.

Manchester was thoroughly dazzled after interviewing the President: "It is an encyclopedic performance, and any writer who has condescended to climbers on the political ladder (while he himself has remained in journalism, which is more of a trampoline) is likely to feel a bit contrite." The President is "frank as St. Augustine," a writer with imperfect spelling "like Fitzgerald," who has "more than ideas in common with" William James, and shared traits with "Caesar and Napoleon" — "and, for that matter, with Tacitus." Jacqueline Kennedy's poetry appears in fragments "like Emily Dickinson's."

Both the President and his wife liked this performance — a proof that they would accept incense from the tinniest thurible. Caroline Kennedy was praised for showing her "membership in the Quality," and Jacqueline because "she has moved from the trivial to the aesthetic, and is, in her *comme il faut* way, just as U as her husband."

Finally, "her fastidiousness has been endorsed by Russell Lynes" — a man, it must be presumed, without clocks on his socks.

There could be no problem in manipulating such a man. Indeed, when Salinger mentioned the assassination book early in 1964, Manchester anticipated demands on him by a preemptive surrender. He wrote to Robert Kennedy: "I agree that it is important that Mrs. Kennedy and you should review the manuscript. If you had not suggested this, I would have. I also agree that no film should ever be made from the book. That would be unthinkable." To manage all aspects of the book's production, Robert demanded that Manchester be released from an option clause with his own publisher and issue the book from Harper & Row, where Evan Thomas would be its editor. Thomas had worked with John Seigenthaler on Robert's *The Enemy Within.* Harper & Row, whose president, Cass Canfield, was related to Jacqueline Kennedy by marriage, had published several books by and about John Kennedy. Members of the firm were themselves honorary Kennedys. Further, most of the American book royalties would have to go to the John F. Kennedy Library. Manchester was, in the Kennedys' eyes, being hired for a task, not contracting for a book whose reward would be his because the resources marshaled for it were his from the outset. He signed an agreement which stated that "the final text shall not be published unless and until approved" by Robert and Jacqueline Kennedy.

It would seem that Robert Kennedy had covered every contingency, binding his author down to an official account of his brother's death. But each effort he made at a totality of control became self-defeating. Kennedy wanted to maintain good relations with President Johnson, and the book became a sore point between them just as the 1968 campaign was taking shape. He wanted to keep the book out of electoral politics — it was not to appear until the end of November in 1968, after the votes were in — but it came out, to sounds of controversy, in 1967. He wanted a dignified account, and was drawn into a sordid squabble. He wanted to protect the President's widow, and the book affair caused the first dip in her popularity polls since the assassination. He wanted a compliant author, yet Manchester's very devotion made him protect his literary "eternal flame" to President Kennedy's memory.

Manchester, to his delight, felt promoted to the position of honorary Kennedy by the 1964 commission. He was allowed access to the family and to family retainers; was invited to social affairs with them; compared notes on "their" Kennedy books over lunches with Arthur Schlesinger. This access led to emotional identification and excess. When he turned in his manuscript, Evan Thomas had the grace to be embarrassed for the Kennedys (who had not been embarrassed by Manchester's first effort). The editor wrote to Kennedy's designated censors (Justice Department associates John Seigenthaler and Edwin Guthman) that the book turned John Kennedy into "the child of Arthur and Guinevere." Jacqueline Kennedy appears "born of elves in a fairy glade and dressed in such magic cloth of gold (chosen by Prince Jack) that the Texans in their polka dot dresses and bow ties are seen as newly arrived scum — plucked from the dung heap by magical Jack."

That last point was the crucial one. Thomas, while praising the work as potentially "a great book," wrote the Kennedys that it was "gratuitously and tastelessly insulting to Johnson," just what they wanted to avoid. On other matters Manchester had been very obliging. He understood that Robert did not welcome conspiratorial speculations about the murder, and he suggested the book's publication be moved up to counter them:

> I'm convinced that our appearance early next year [1967] will eliminate most of the problems created by irresponsible books about the tragedy. For example, Epstein's *Inquest,* a really poisonous book, needn't trouble us any longer. With the help of Dr. Burkley and Howard Willens I think I've knocked out what, at first reading, appears to be the one strong point in Epstein's version.

But on the subject of Lyndon Johnson, Manchester had absorbed all the grievances, real or imagined, of the honorary Kennedys he interviewed. Even in the earlier book, it should be remembered, his tribute to Kennedy involved a contrast with the "Hottentots" Eisenhower and Truman. In his first draft of the 1967 book, Johnson became a type of the murderous obtuseness that struck down the graceful ruler. While admitting he had gone to excess, Manchester clung to his hatred and wrote Mrs. Kennedy: "Though I tried desperately to suppress my bias against a certain eminent statesman who always reminds me of somebody in a Grade D movie on the late show, the prejudice showed through."

When various Kennedy deputies started picking at his manuscript, Manchester felt they were inexplicably whittling at the dead President, with whom he now identified his work and himself. When Robert Kennedy joined the attack, Manchester seemed to go to pieces. Evan Thomas felt the situation was getting out of control and urged Robert Kennedy to send the emotional author a telegram — which was later used to show Robert had approved the manuscript. Even after Manchester had altered many references to Johnson, and dropped things that Mrs. Kennedy said would embarrass her (like the search in a mirror for wrinkles on the day her husband was shot), various honorary Kennedys weighed in with contradictory criticisms of the book. Their loyalties were separately engaged. Arthur Schlesinger, writing his own semiauthorized book, wanted to defend its historical claims by muting any charge that Kennedys censor their authors. Richard Goodwin had first inserted himself into the process with a few minor suggestions, implying they were all that was needed; but then Mrs. Kennedy made him her agent, and he took a much harsher line on what must be altered.

The Kennedys were not used to having their courtiers rebel — and certainly not in the name of a higher loyalty to Kennedyism. The serialization of the book had been arranged in America and foreign countries — an aspect of publication that had no royalties earmarked for the Kennedy Library; so Robert accused Manchester of trying to profit from his brother's death. It was a charge as unwise as it was unfair. It convinced Manchester that Robert just did not see the issues involved. He told others, "This is not the brother of the man I knew." Manchester would have to defend the President alone, if necessary. At last he understood how the ruthless "Bobby" had set out to get Jimmy Hoffa. The old stories of federal agents knocking on newsmen's doors at night seemed confirmed when Kennedy showed up at the hotel room where Manchester was hiding under an assumed name and pounded on the door, demanding that he open it. (He didn't.) The Kennedy who had shed some of his reputation as a McCarthyite now seemed a book-burner, vindictive in the treatment of his own chosen author. Sorensen concludes: "The poisonous fallout from this controversy did more than anything else to affix the image of ruthlessness on Bob Kennedy."

Most shocking to Manchester was the way his fairy princess showed her claws. She told others she had "hired" Manchester and could fire him. She threatened him with court action, and said he had no chance against her at the peak of her postassassination popularity: "Anyone who is against me will look like a rat unless I run off with Eddie Fisher" (as Elizabeth Taylor had). *Esquire* ran on its cover a composite photo of Mrs. Kennedy carrying Fisher off on a sled. Mrs. Kennedy told her assistant that she had "the right to destroy the entire transcript" of her interviews with Manchester. She summoned Michael Cowles of *Look* magazine to Hyannis Port and told him to kill the serialization of the book. When he refused, she said, "If it's money, I'll pay you a million." When he said it was not money, she pointedly remarked, "You're sitting in the chair my late husband sat in."

The Kennedy courtiers rallied to her. Arthur Schlesinger told William Attwood of *Look,* "There will never be another Kennedy byline or my byline in *Look."* The Kennedy lawyers descended to the kind of pettiness they had exhibited against Hoffa. Mrs. Kennedy's lawyers told Manchester he could not give credit to any Kennedy people in the acknowledgments to his book — or, for that matter, to anyone else. "Not even my wife?" Manchester asked. "Not even your wife." The mobilization of high-powered lawyers and advisers — Goodwin, Sorensen, Burke Marshall — drew further attention to the conflict. The very passages marked for criticism came out isolated, harsher than in context. Rumor exaggerated the hostility to Johnson, till the book, even before publication, was known as an anti-Johnson tract. John Connally attacked it as such. Everything the Kennedys did by this time just hurt them more. The crisis management team proclaimed the importance of the crisis. It was called a literary Cuban missile affair, since so many of the same minds were at work on it. The overreaction forced Evan Thomas to defend his writer against his former patrons, causing a split with his friend Seigenthaler. As John Corry wrote, in his account of the affair, "It is a fact that a good many people who got involved in the fight on both sides had inscribed pictures of President Kennedy in their homes and offices. . . . Ultimately, the battle of the book involved only old friends and neighbors, which was inevitable since only old friends and neighbors were ever invited to participate."

This was entirely a squabble between and among honorary Kennedys — a thing that was once considered unthinkable. There were too many cadres of loyalists, with loyalties variously engaged. The Kennedys had relied on the emotions they could arouse; but emotions are often unstable. Charisma dazzles, and flashbulbs woo the lightning bolt. The whole charged circle of electric fascinations was shorting out. The honorary Kennedys, once a source of power, were becoming liabilities. There were too many of them now, and too few real Kennedys. In attempting a totality of control over the image of his brother's death, Robert Kennedy made sure that if anything went wrong, everything would. And it did.

9

The Prisoner of Family

The danger of betraying our weakness to our servants, and the impossibility of concealing it from them, may be justly considered as one motive to a regular and irreproachable life. For no condition is more hateful or despicable, than his who has put himself in the power of his servants.

— SAMUEL JOHNSON, *Rambler* No. 69

FAMILY SERVANTS BECAME honorary Kennedys of a lower sort — John Kennedy inherited his older brother's black valet from Harvard days, and acquired another black valet from Arthur Krock when he entered Congress. ("This big fat colored boy," as Krock put it in his oral history, accompanied Kennedy to the White House.) But strangers brought onto the White House staff had to be disciplined by more than loyalty: they were all required to sign a pledge not to write or give interviews about their period of service with the family. At the time this pledge became known, it was taken as evidence of the Kennedys' superior taste. There would be no undignified dog-walker's account of "John John" in cute moments. Now we know the odd living arrangements of John Kennedy had to be concealed. One way or another, hundreds of people were bound to silence around the private life of the President.

The Kennedys later thought they had bound William Manchester with a double tie, of loyalty and of legal obligation. They did not realize that the two are at odds. Loyalty truly binds only if freely given. To add the note of legality is to absolve, in some measure, from free tribute. Not that Manchester ever thought he was disloyal.

But outsiders blamed him less, the more the Kennedys relied on legal technicalities.

There is a middle echelon of Kennedy retainers that plays an important role in family history. William Douglas and James Landis were honorary Kennedys in the family patriarch's eyes. But his "Four Horsemen" — the business operatives who accompanied him — were glorified "gofers." They had a variety of roles, most of them subservient. The Blairs write: "When the Ambassador took a girl out on the town, he brought along bachelor Joe Timilty. If they were seen, the assumption was supposed to be that the girl was with Timilty." Timilty was a man whose silence did not have to be bought.

Wealthy people acquire a penumbra of errand-running "friends." They are a luxury that soon becomes a necessity. What if a wealthy young man wants to sail, and his serious contemporaries are at work, are following their own projects? It is good to have a school chum who stands by on more or less instant call to crew for him; to take the boat back when the young heir must fly to his next appointment; to supervise the boat boy's shopping for the next sail. If Jacqueline Kennedy needed an escort to the theater, it was nice to have a safe and reliable one she could call on. For years, Truman Capote served this function for New York ladies, observing the code of the attendant — not to gossip to outsiders. (Gossip within the women's own circle is one of the services he was expected to provide.) The fury of the escorted women was so intense, when he broke the code, because the code was so uniformly assumed. One reason for having elegant gofers is to keep outsiders away — just as Manchester was commissioned to keep other authors away. People with a clamorous public need buffers to protect them from paparazzi, autograph-hunters, people who might sit down at one's table or join one's walk. Designated escorts fend off competitors for the escort role. Anyone who took Mrs. Kennedy out had the undoubted virtue, in her eyes, of not being Gore Vidal.

To some extent the Secret Service performed the role of gofer for the Kennedys in office. But a Secret Service agent cannot play golf or raise a jib or join a bridge hand, and at the same time keep his eyes out for potential assassins. So, John Kennedy made his old Navy friend "Red" Fay an Undersecretary of the Navy. This brought him to Washington where he could play golf, tell jokes, and sing "Hooray for Hollywood." Ben Bradlee could not understand the endless appetite of the Kennedys for this latter distraction. But Fay had other services to perform — Kennedy made him the escort for Angie Dickinson on his inauguration night. Fay endlessly obliged, and obligingly ran a picture of himself hooraying Hollywood in his book on the Kennedy years.

Fay was regularly addressed as "Grand Old Lovable" by Kennedy, who understood instinctively how one asserts ownership over another by renaming him. Thomas Broderick told the Blairs: "Jack was always giving people nicknames. He called me Tommie or the Thin Man." To serve its purpose, the name had to be made up by Kennedy himself. Thus men normally called "Jim" by their family and friends became "Jamie" to John Kennedy. "Ben" Bradlee became "Benjy." Inga Arvad was both claimed as a lover and trivialized as one when Kennedy addressed her, invariably, as "Inga-Binga." Kennedy was a Steerforth in the way he could attract people by putting them in their place, expressing superiority and affection in a single name. Steerforth, remember, makes David Copperfield proud that the school hero is familiar enough with him to call him "Daisy." Only shrewd Miss Dartle sees how the name flatters and unmans at the same time:

> "But really, Mr. Copperfield," she asked, "is it a Nickname? And why does he give it you? Is it — eh? — because he thinks you young and innocent? I am so stupid in these things."
>
> I colored in replying that I believed it was.
>
> "Oh!" said Miss Dartle. "Now I am glad to know it. He thinks you young and innocent; and so you are his friend? Well, that's quite delightful!"

Theodore Sorensen (known as "Ted") noticed that Robert Kennedy bristled at "Bobby," yet the President kept using that name. After the assassination, a note from Robert let Sorensen know where the diminutive belonged. It began "Teddy old pal" and ended "Bob."

If the gofers of the rich are a convenience to them — someone to run into town for supplies during a party — they also demand some care and servicing. Loyalty can be presumed, but only if it is prudently re-recruited at sufficiently close intervals. Besides, real affection is normally engaged on both sides. Perhaps the gofers who most entered the Kennedy affections were Ann and Joseph Gargan, the cousins who lost their own parents in childhood. The Kennedy family nursed pious Ann through a period when she seemed to have multiple sclerosis, and she repaid their tenderness a thousandfold when she became the Ambassador's indefatigable nurse after his stroke.

Joseph Gargan went to law school, but subjected his own career to that of Edward Kennedy, with whom he grew up, an almost-brother to the youngest brother, male company to the "stranded" last Kennedy son. Gargan was always ready to clean up after a race, put the sails away — only partly a Kennedy, but a Super-Kennedy because of that. The Ambassador sent Gargan to fetch his car, and forgave him when he hit a tree with it. The father was as forgiving to him as to any of his sons — but only because he expected less of him. *Time* magazine wrote, after Chappaquiddick: "Gargan is used by [Edward] Kennedy largely as companion for carrying out miscellaneous chores — making reservations, ordering food, emptying glasses and drawing baths."

The extra thing Gargan could supply in the pell-mell world of Kennedy competition was thoughtfulness for less privileged gofers. The reminder of a birthday, the joke that deflects a quarrel, the inclusion of a forgotten retainer — it was he who smoothed the social life for his admired patrons.

[I] was amply recompensed by seeing an exact and punctilious practice of the arts of a courtier, in all the stratagems of endearment, the gradations of respect, and variations of courtesy. I remarked with what justice of distribution he divided his talk to a wide circle; with what address he offered to every man an occasion of indulging some favourite topick, or displaying some particular attainment; the judgement with which he regulated his enquiries after the absent; and the care with which he shewed all the companions of his early years how strongly they were infixed in his memory, by the mention of past incidents, and the recital of puerile kindnesses, dangers, and frolicks. (Johnson, *Rambler* No. 147)

Gargan, who shared Edward Kennedy's "puerile kindnesses, dangers, and frolicks," had also worked in the campaign of Robert Kennedy, where part of his social duty to fellow gofers led him to joke with the "boiler room girls." With his customary thoughtfulness, he did not let them go unremembered. He arranged the first party for them at Hyannis Port; and, the next summer, invited them to the Edgartown regatta. Performing such services not only benefited "the girls," but gratified him. Part of his claim to favored position was his ability to produce a Kennedy at parties where that is the ultimate distinction. And part of Kennedy's debt to this loyalest of gofers was to allow himself to be, periodically, produced.

The last Kennedy has to service all the inherited gofers as well as his own — and all the honorary Kennedys, veterans of 1960 and 1968, who suggest new campaigns, send speeches, line up supporters. These may come in handy some day — though the 1980 race proved that many old speechwriters took more time than they were worth. They all feel they have the one essential bit of advice the candidate must hear. In 1980 Edward Kennedy sought surcease from the buzz of them all by turning off his advice-receiver almost entirely. He is not good at hurting the feelings of those who have some old bond with the family. The tendered services are never entirely refusable, once he has heard them. And the demands made can become quite bizarre — one stalwart from the past even asked that Kennedy inform his own child that its mother had died. ("He is so used to dealing with sorrow.") There are endless weddings, funerals, graduations the family heir must go to, to express the family's gratitude.

That was the meaning of Chappaquiddick. Kennedy was trammeled up in other people's lives because they had suffered at his brother's death. He had to brace himself for endless reminiscings about Robert's campaign — the only thing that bound "the girls," through Gargan and his peers, to "the Senator." Popular gossip made of Chappaquiddick a kind of tawdry orgy. Actually, like many "celebrations" Kennedy is compelled to attend, it was part of his extended death watch or permanent floating Irish wake. Friends have to be sorted out according to which brother they accompanied to meet his killer.

Though Gargan could produce the Senator to awe the "girls," that did not mean he could attract any other people of consequence to this very minor entertainment. The others were friends of Gargan, fellow gofers — the Kennedy chauffeur, John Crimmins; Ray LaRosa, who also drove for Kennedy when called on; Charles Tretter, who had done advance work for the Kennedys; and Paul Markham, whom Burton Hersh calls "Joey Gargan's Gargan." Markham and Gargan went to Georgetown Prep together. Through Gargan, Markham received the Kennedy patronage that helped him become United States Attorney for the state of Massachusetts. Markham had fetched the Kennedy boat to Edgartown, where he was supposed to serve on its crew; but he banged his leg sailing there, and could not race after all. Furthermore, the Shiretown Inn was so crowded he had to give up his room to Kennedy, to stay with Crimmins and the others at the rented house on Chappaquiddick. One who rises by virtue of friendship with a gofer remains a gofer even when he holds the highest federal prosecutor's post in the state. Chappaquiddick was a roll call of the well-paid errand-runners, to honor the errand-dispatchers from campaigns past.

Crimmins, who had brought the Kennedy car over to Martha's Vineyard on the ferry, met Kennedy at the little island airport, early in the afternoon, and drove him to the hotel in Edgartown, where Kennedy dropped his luggage (and turned Markham out of a room). The men then crossed to Chappaquiddick for a swim at the beach just over Dyke Bridge. (Less than twelve hours later the same car would go off this bridge.) Then Kennedy went back to Edgartown and the regatta heat, a competitive chore when (as then) his back was hurting from fatigue and travel — the *Victura* came in ninth.

Kennedy had a postrace drink with fellow skippers and dressed for the cottage cookout; for the twilight milling of sun-dazed people at a resort town, for the maudlin laughter at campaign tales told over again, a listing of glad things remembered across an abyss of sadness. Someone always has his or her "Hooray for Hollywood" at such a gathering, and Kennedy must summon up his brothers' laughter out of the past. It was an important time for the boiler room workers, whose lives (they thought) would never again be as meaningful as when they worked for Robert Kennedy — unless they should get the opportunity, some time, to campaign for the Kennedy whose attention now flattered them. They stayed on and on — past the departure time of the last ferry. Kennedy, of course, claims that he and Mary Jo Kopechne dashed for the ferry and turned by accident onto the dirt road leading to Dyke Bridge. But his story is so unsupported, contradictory, or improbable in various of its parts, that we cannot know for sure what happened during that time for which he is the only witness.

Perhaps he does not know what happened. Fatigue, drink, panic were at work on him. Did he black out? He could have left the car before Miss Kopechne crossed the bridge, and pieced events together later (Jack Olsen's thesis). Any number of things could have happened — including the presence of another passenger in the car. Even the testimony of those left at the party is suspect. Robert Sherrill, in *The Last Kennedy,* has shown how jumbled is their account of comings and goings and mutual time-checks — though the synchronized support for Senator Kennedy's testimony about when he left (11:15) emerges with suspicious clarity from this chaos. The later silence kept by all involved does not inspire confidence. After every other scandal of this period, journalistic enterprise and checkbooks have led to interviews, books, movie or TV presentations based on at least one of the witness's accounts. There have been none out of Chappaquiddick. The loyalty of Robert's workers carried over to Edward's troubles. In the first week after the accident, Esther Newberg was deputed to give the partygoers' account of the night in two interviews. But that experience taught the Kennedy team to impose a total silence: she admitted in both interviews that she did not remember when the Senator and Ms. Kopechne left the cottage; her watch was "not working properly" — though she would later testify to the Grand Jury that she marked the time by looking at her watch. Apart from these canceled experiments in minimal candor, the coordinated testimony before the Grand Jury remains the participants' first and last public account.

Three men at the party (Gargan, Markham, and Tretter) were lawyers, and they invoked a client relationship with Kennedy to justify their silence. But there is little doubt that they would be loyal to Kennedy with their silence, even if they were not attorneys. What else are loyalists for? In fact, this episode resembles the Manchester affair as a tale of the way honorary Kennedys flock to rescue one of the family in his troubles.

If Chappaquiddick resembles the Manchester controversy in one respect, it began with a fainter but more poignant echo from another night of crisis for the family. After the interval in which something happened that led to Ms. Kopechne's death, Kennedy reappeared, but only dimly, at the rented cottage where the party's aimless milling continued after midnight. Standing by the other car the party was using, Kennedy called out softly to the one man outside the doorway, Ray LaRosa: "Ray, get me Joe." Kennedy sat inside the car waiting for Gargan — and, when he arrived, asked him to get Markham. Why had he not asked for both in the first place? Was Gargan too drunk, fuddled, or panicky at the sight of Kennedy alone? Was a cooler head needed? All we know is that the first loyalist, ever since boyhood, was turned to first — and that Gargan soon brought "Joey Gargan's Gargan" out to the car. The three went off, they say, to dive over and over into Poucha Pond trying to rescue the woman in the car.

Little over a year before this, Kennedy had awakened another loyalist with a whisper through the night — Arthur Schlesinger, sleeping at Hickory Hill where the family was locked in debate over the political future of Robert Kennedy. Then Edward went on to wake Sorensen. He had been probing around the edges of a slumbrous house to report back Eugene McCarthy's refusal to cooperate in the 1968 primaries. He came to the cottage at Chappaquiddick with more disastrous news; but very early the people he called began to consider his own future of primaries and campaigns, and how this night would affect them. The spookiest point of resemblance is that Mary Jo Kopechne had been present, hardly noticed, at Hickory Hill the night of Robert Kennedy's decision to run. She stayed late to type up Sorensen's and Schlesinger's declaration of Robert's candidacy.

Gargan and Markham, both lawyers, did not call for professional help — divers are available at a resort for rescue work, if that was their goal. Nor did they inform authorities that an accident, perhaps a crime, had occurred. They say they left the scene of the accident, drove Kennedy to the crossing for Edgartown, watched him dive into the channel and swim off into the night, then returned to the cottage and — at Kennedy's request — told the women nothing. The next morning they managed to show up at Kennedy's hotel room without being seen by the ferry operator. If all this happened as they say, the two men enter the pantheon of all official friends. And if it didn't happen that way, they ascend even higher for saying that it did. These gofers would go for a human body without complaining, though Markham thereby lost any hope for higher public office.

Kennedy could rely on such loyalty absolutely. That is why he considered for many hours whether to report the accident at all. Though we do not know for sure what happened on Chappaquiddick, there is outside testimony to his actions back at Edgartown; and, in conjunction, those actions plainly indicate that until 9:30 on the morning after the accident, Kennedy either did not know for sure about Ms. Kopechne's death, or pretended not to know. He was confident that, whatever story he told, his two confidants would support him.

Kennedy's secret return to his hotel (either by swimming, as he says, or in a borrowed boat) would allow him to claim he had left Chappaquiddick before the accident occurred, without any inconveniencing testimony from the ferry operator. Back at the inn, Kennedy was either awakened by a noisy party, or pretended to be, and let the innkeeper see him at 2:55 A.M. By 7:30 he was outside the inn, where he met the winner of the previous day's regatta heat, and accompanied him to the hotel's second-story porch where the two talked casually about upcoming races (with no indication on Kennedy's part that he would not be participating in that day's heat).

At 8:00 Gargan and Markham arrived, and went into Kennedy's room. When Charles Tretter, who had trailed Gargan and Markham back to the main island, saw the three men in heated conversation through a window, he began to enter but was waved off angrily by Kennedy. At 8:30 Kennedy went to the inn's desk, ordered the New York and Boston papers, and borrowed a dime for the public phone (Kennedys never have money on them). Gargan says he urged Kennedy to return to Chappaquiddick, where he could find a safely private telephone for the series of messages he had begun to send, calling in other loyalists to salvage the situation. The three men had reached the other side by 9:00, and Kennedy was still at the pay phone near the landing when the ferry returned to fetch the recently discovered body of Ms. Kopechne. Asked if he had heard of the accident, Kennedy said yes, and took the ferry to Edgartown, where Gargan was dispatched to the women's motel. While Gargan finally (and sketchily) told the women what had happened to their friend, Kennedy told the police there had been an accident.

Gargan and Markham, to defend their failure to inform the police earlier, claim that Kennedy assured them, before swimming off the night before, that he would report as soon as he arrived on the other shore. But the two men went back to the cottage, said nothing to the others there, and slept till dawn. They did not warn the others that police were about to descend on them with disorienting news, because — obviously — they expected no report to trigger that result. In the morning, they hurried the women back to their hotel without telling them a word. Only when Kennedy was actually walking toward the police station did Gargan let them know about the accident. Until then, all options were being maintained — including the option of denial that Kennedy had been involved at all.

One of the early theories about Chappaquiddick was invented by Jack Anderson, who supposed that Gargan was scheduled to take the blame. Whether this was seriously considered, the theory naturally arose, since those who know Gargan have little doubt that he would take the fall if asked. Such loyalty is touching, and a little scary. It gives its recipient a kind of parachute for bailing out of sticky situations. But it also tempts that recipient to take risks, on the assumption that he can always walk away untroubled. Kennedy later accused himself of inexcusable delay in reporting the death; but he could only entertain thoughts of delay because he knew the loyalists around him would not challenge him or his story, whatever that turned out to be. Once again, the sources of strength debilitated. He leaned too long on their passivity. They had nothing to offer but obsequiousness, when he needed stringency and hard talk.

Even in his panic, Kennedy knew that he needed sharper advice than Gargan could give him — or than he could give himself. One of the first phone calls he made was to Burke Marshall. Marshall had been one of Robert's shrewdest and toughest assistants in the Justice Department. Before Robert's death, Marshall was considered the leading contender for the Attorney General post in a second Kennedy administration. Burton Hersh says Marshall was known to the family as a "defuser of blockbusters." So Edward Kennedy, with three lawyers on the scene, was going for a super-lawyer — itself a signal of the danger he was in. In Hersh's words, "Importing Burke Marshall to deal with a motor vehicle code violation was tantamount to whipping frosting with the great screw propeller of the Queen Elizabeth." There was a precedent for this. John Corry says that the Manchester struggle looked serious only when Burke Marshall appeared to represent the Kennedys. Everyone knew, then, that "bigger guns had taken over."

Kennedy was busy at the telephone. He had to seek out his brother-in-law Stephen Smith, who was on vacation in Europe. Once the campaign manager was alerted, the campaigners would troop in — the old team attracted toward Hyannis Port, in the next several days, as by some magnetizing of their PT tie pins. Robert McNamara showed up, and Sorensen, and Goodwin, offering help and advice. Others had already been dispatched on cleanup chores — William vanden Heuvel to tell the Kopechnes what little he knew of their daughter's death, Dun Gifford to take away the body, an act which, as it turned out, made an immediate autopsy impossible. Gargan held the hands of other gofers. Sorensen wrote the TV defense Kennedy would make after his Grand Jury testimony. Eight lawyers were representing Kennedy by that time. Loyalists were everywhere, putting the best face they could on what had happened.

If Gargan and Markham passed the ultimate test for gofers on that muddled night, the bigger names in the Kennedy entourage performed an equivalent service in the next few weeks. It seems that Kennedy told few of them (if any) much more than he told the rest of us. They submitted to the test of silence, and rallied nonetheless. Men with their own careers, they used their reputations to cover Kennedy's shame. These were not people who could be bought or intimidated. If they helped cover up what happened, they did it out of a primal sense of loyalty, out of the honor code of honorary Kennedys.

Once again newspapers compared this convening of heavyweight talent to the time of the missile crisis. Missiles in Cuba, Manchester writing a book, Robert deciding to run, a girl dead by accident — public and private events mingle around the Kennedy reputation; perspective alters according to the engagement of the family in events that would otherwise be minor, however sad in themselves.

Each crisis is major if a Kennedy is involved; and the missile team gathers. The frightening thing is not that courtiers should assemble to help Edward Kennedy after a car accident. The frightening thing is that making Kennedys look good was no doubt an important motive for these courtiers during the missile crisis itself.

And, sure enough, the men of power and influence repaired whatever was reparable after this disaster. They soothed the Kopechnes, wooed officials, won special treatment. No autopsy was performed. No one else present has ever talked. The only charge brought against Kennedy was for leaving the scene of an accident. He bargained a plea of guilty in return for the minimum sentence, suspended. He lost his driver's license for a year. At the Grand Jury hearing, he was treated respectfully; other witnesses did not have to explain difficulties in their testimony. Despite all the damage Chappaquiddick did to Kennedy, he was reelected to the Senate, welcomed back by his colleagues, and remained a contender for the presidency. He has successfully "stonewalled" attempts to discover more about that mysterious night. William Buckley criticized the way Chappaquiddick was handled; but Sherrill considers it a masterpiece among cover-ups, one in which Kennedy was given the benefit of every legal doubt while cooperating as little as possible with the investigation.

> For the first nine hours or so after he drove the woman to her death he said nothing about the accident because, he explained later, he was out of his mind. Then for the next week he stayed in seclusion and avoided the press because, he said, he was recovering from the physical ordeal of the accident (he did break out of his hiding to attend the Kopechne funeral, but he said that was not an "appropriate" time to talk but promised to talk when the time did become "appropriate"). Not long thereafter his attorneys became engaged in a fight to block the inquest from being open, and while that was pending Kennedy excused himself from talking by saying his lawyers wouldn't let him while his case was in litigation. As soon as the inquest was launched, Kennedy had a perfectly fine reason for keeping quiet because the cooperative Judge Boyle ordered all inquest witnesses not to talk about what they had testified. That order held until the inquest transcript was released, which brings us back to the present moment when Kennedy was saying, "The facts of

this incident are now fully public, and eventual judgment and understanding rests where it belongs. For myself, I plan no further statement."

Ironically, Kennedy's very success in evading the full scrutiny and pressure of the law disqualifies him for the presidency. A man for whom other men of power and fame are already willing to stretch and bend the law, to whom they will lend the support of their reputations, should not be further raised above the law by holding the nation's highest office. Sherrill quotes, for its irony, Kennedy's later attack on President Nixon's attempted cover-up of Watergate: "If this country stands for anything, it stands for the principle that no man is above the law." No man should be given special treatment. Yet the crush of affectionate loyalists works always for such special treatment of a Kennedy.

The loyalty perdured, though some were angry at Kennedy for damaging the family prospects they all share. Sorensen, after penning Kennedy's TV defense, crossed out references to his brilliant future in a book he was completing on the Kennedy legacy. By being weak, by having to rely on them, he disillusioned his own defenders, who remained loyal to him even as they lost respect for him. Yet reliance on them had led him into this trap. Reliance on the honorary Kennedys can, after a while, sap the strength of real Kennedys. With so many "Kennedys" around, serving him and being serviced by him, he ceased to be fully one himself. In all the bumbling rush to save his reputation, the man disappeared; and people who would do anything to save the family name were, by that very willingness, tainting the name.

III

IMAGE

If you had said to a man in the Stone Age, "Ugg says Ugg makes the best stone hatchets," he would have perceived a lack of detachment and disinterestedness about the testimonial. If you had said to a mediaeval peasant, "Robert the Bowyer proclaims, with three blasts of a horn, that he makes good bows," the peasant would have said, "Well, of course he does," and thought about something more important. It is only among people whose minds have been weakened by a sort of mesmerism that so transparent a trick as that of advertisement could ever have been tried at all.

— GILBERT CHESTERTON

10

Creating the Kennedys

Promise, large promise, is the soul of an advertisement.

— SAMUEL JOHNSON, *Idler* No. 40

ONE OF JOHN KENNEDY'S BOYHOOD FRIENDS told the Blairs that he had never heard of a "PR man" till he met his schoolmate's father. Joseph Kennedy used professional public relations people; but he was his own best manager of reputations. He early learned the techniques for getting attention. In this he resembled the Hollywood "moguls" who could shape American taste though their own sense of taste was deficient. Still, what the moguls did for "starlets," Kennedy wo)ld do for his offspring.

He took great pains to have the Kennedys portrayed in public as, invariably, winners. One of the first difficulties he had to face in this project was the existence of one Kennedy who clearly seemed a loser. When his daughter Rosemary proved slow at learning, Kennedy urged her to try harder — that, after all, was how he made his sickly son John play football. As with his other children, he was tenderly compelling, but compelling. He expected results. But he got none. By the time Gloria Swanson, a believer in health foods, suggested that Rosemary try *them*, Kennedy blew up at her; told her not to tempt him with false hopes. He had faced the fact that Rosemary was a permanent loser, retarded from birth; the best doctors could do nothing for her. One of the "Four Horsemen" around Kennedy warned Ms. Swanson that the subject was too sensitive, she should not bring it up again.

But if all the Kennedys could not be winners, they could be made to appear winners. Rosemary's deficiencies were disguised as long as possible — she was even presented at the English court with the rest of the Ambassador's family. And when she went to a home for the retarded, that fact was denied for decades. At first it was said she had entered a convent to teach. When James MacGregor Burns was given access to the family for his first biography, he relayed the family line that Rosemary had a vocation to "help care for mentally retarded children." Joseph Dinneen and Joe McCarthy repeated that story in early biographies. Even when it became clear that Rosemary was not doing any teaching, her father could not confess that she was retarded from birth. He told the press that she had suffered a childhood attack of spinal meningitis. When the Kennedy Foundation was set up, and money was given Archbishop Cushing to establish a home for the retarded, the Archbishop heeded Kennedy's wishes and said the donation was for care of "poor children." Later, when the truth about Rosemary came out, the generosity of the Kennedys helped improve mental care for the handicapped. Eunice Shriver, especially, became identified with the Special Olympics. But for decades Joseph Kennedy succeeded in hiding what he obviously considered a family disgrace.

The impulse to hide weakness led to the sequestration of John Kennedy's medical records. The Blairs, in their search for doctors who had treated the young Kennedy, found it hard to document the precise time and place of various treatments. His bad back had been with him from childhood, but he told John Hersey that it originated in the strain of rescuing his comrades after his boat was sunk. (Those comrades do not remember his mentioning any back injury at the time.) The habit of covering up his multiple health problems culminated in the series of lies about his Addison's disease. When Lyndon Johnson revealed the existence of this problem in the 1960 campaign (thereby incurring Robert Kennedy's fieriest anger), the Kennedy camp issued outright denials. Its spokesmen later rationalized this by saying he did not have Addison's disease because the public wrongly thought the disease invariably fatal: so it would give a false impression to use the term, even though it was the correct one. But they not only did not use the term. They expressly denied it was applicable in any sense, and portrayed Johnson as a candidate willing to invent any lie convenient to his purposes. (The family sealing of the President's autopsy report would later fuel conspiracy theories inimical to Johnson.)

When Edward Kennedy was caught cheating at Harvard, his father took steps to cover that up, too — including the employment of the young man who had taken the exam for his son. But the patriarch's skill was more often used for enhancing the family's good points than in suppressing the truth about defects. The selling of his sons began with their Harvard careers, where he urged them on to athletic distinction. He had, from their boyhood days, introduced them to influential people who would sponsor them (later he had Justice William Douglas take Robert to Russia with him). He wanted his sons to study with famous professors — and sent Joseph, the eldest, to the London School of Economics, where Harold Laski not only instructed the boy but let him travel with him. Arthur Krock developed the family line on Laski, one that has been endlessly repeated — that the patriarch disliked Laski's Marxism but wanted his sons exposed to all views. Actually, Kennedy was a celebrity hunter; he was more interested in what a man could do for his boys than in what the man thought. Felix Frankfurter had described Laski as "the greatest teacher in the world." To be thought that by a Frankfurter was to possess power, and Kennedy meant to send his sons where the power was.

The point, in other words, was not to study with Laski, but to *have* studied with him. So, in his *Who's Who* biography, John Kennedy claimed for years that he was a "Student of London Sch. Economics, 1935–36." Actually, his health made him withdraw before he could attend any classes. Unlike his brother, he never studied under Laski, though the family worked hard to develop the impression he had — James Landis, Dean of Harvard Law School, even claimed that Kennedy got his ideas for *Why England Slept* from Laski.

The first major effort at selling John Kennedy was the Ambassador's treatment of his senior paper, which he turned into a best-selling book. Just as studying with Laski mattered less than being known for having studied with him, writing a book mattered less than being known for having written one: "You would be surprised how a book that really makes the grade with high-class people stands you in good stead for years to come. I remember that in the report you are asked to make after twenty-five years to the Committee at Harvard, one of the questions is 'What books have you written?' and there is no doubt you will have done yourself a great deal of good."

When his son's book appeared, the Ambassador sent a copy to the Royal Family, another to Churchill. Given Henry Luce's opening plug for Wendell Willkie, Kennedy was tactful enough not to send it to Roosevelt. But he did send a copy to Harold Laski, which was a mistake. Laski, with whom John Kennedy is supposed to have studied, and from whom James Landis claimed he took this very book's ideas, wrote to the doting father:

> The easy thing for me to do would be to repeat the eulogies that Krock and Harry Luce have showered on your boy's work. In fact, I choose the more difficult way of regretting deeply that you let him publish it. For while it is the book of a lad with brains, it is very immature, it has no structure, and dwells almost wholly on the surface of things. In a good university, half a hundred seniors do books like this as part of their normal work in their final year. But they don't publish them for the good reason that their importance lies solely in what they get out of doing them and not out of what they have to say. I don't honestly think any publisher would have looked at that book of Jack's if he had not been your son, and if you had not been ambassador.

Kennedy no doubt agreed that the book was published because of his position. After all, that is why he wanted such a position — to help his boys. And he was less interested in what his son had got out of the academic exercise than in what he could get out of it as a political exercise — which, it turned out, was a great deal.

It should be remembered that Laski was reading the completed book, after Arthur Krock's ministrations to its style and the Ambassador's additions to its content. The Blairs show in parallel passages how literally Kennedy copied extracts from his father's letters directly into the final text. The senior paper on which the book is based was even more ragged in structure and style. Carl Friedrich, the famous political scientist who judged it, explained why the paper should not get a *magna cum laude:* "Fundamental premise never analyzed — much too long, wordy, repetitious. Bibliography . . . spotty.

Many typographical errors. English diction repetitive. Cum laude plus."

It was unpromising material. But Joseph Kennedy was a great promoter. He had Krock rewrite the manuscript, retitle it, find it an agent. He supplied charts, statistics, and arguments himself. He arranged for Luce to introduce it, in a campaign year, by describing it as relevant to the election. Kennedy paid to send out 250 free copies, over twice the publisher's norm in those days. Thus, blessed by the New York *Times* (in the person of Krock), and the *Time-Life* organization (in Luce), the book sold 80,000 copies in America, enough to put it briefly on the best-seller list in the summer of 1940. An English edition sold well too. Beginning with a school paper that "half a hundred seniors do" every year, the elder Kennedy had created a Promising Young Thinker in the public mind. Much of the Kennedy legend would turn on his future treatment as a scholar, an historian, a writer. When the Ambassador arranged for his son to travel to useful places with press credentials, Krock celebrated him as a brilliant young journalist. Krock even claimed that Kennedy, as a journalistic stringer in England, predicted the surprise 1946 defeat of Winston Churchill, though the Blairs uncovered clip files and letters to disprove that claim. John Kennedy the writer was almost entirely the creation of Joseph Kennedy the promoter. It is significant that, when the father wanted a ghost for his own 1940 book, *Why I'm For Roosevelt,* he did not turn to "the writer" in the family, but to that writer's writer, Arthur Krock.

The next step in the selling of John Kennedy was the celebration of his wartime heroism. The heroism was real. Kennedy saved the life of Patrick McMahon. He undertook the most dangerous assignments in looking for rescuers. His physical courage can never be questioned. If anything, he took unnecessary risks. But to this basis of heroism John Kennedy added a number of legendary embellishments. He released to biographers a preliminary and inaccurate draft of the citation for his Navy and Marine Corps Medal. This citation says his boat was rammed "while attempting a torpedo attack on a Japanese destroyer" and that he "personally rescued three men." The later citation corrected the errors. The attempted torpedo attack becomes a simple "collision" there, and he is said to have "contributed to the saving of several lives." The changes were not incidental.

Kennedy had put his own men in for the Silver Star, a combat medal, and had been put in for one himself. This application was downgraded to the life-saving award given all three officers of the PT boat. (Enlisted man John Maguire assisted in the rescue too, but got no medal.)

Kennedy repeatedly tried to establish that he was on the attack when his boat was sunk. In the account he gave to John Hersey, who first wrote up his adventure for *The New Yorker,* he claimed that "Kennedy saw a shape and spun the wheel to turn for an attack." Later, when the Ambassador arranged for *Reader's Digest* to run a condensation of the *New Yorker* piece (reprints of which became campaign handouts over the years), John took special care that the phrase "turn for an attack" was retained while other sections were cut.

In fact, interviews with others on the boat make it clear that there was no attempted attack. The destroyer loomed over the idling PT boat before anyone knew it was near. This was a sore point for the crew, and even more so for its skipper. After all, two men died in the collision — was Kennedy as negligent in the Solomon Islands as his brother would be at Poucha Pond? It was fear of that charge that made Kennedy falsify the story of his boat's ramming. The event is mysterious in itself. How did a light plywood boat made for speed and maneuverability manage to get itself cut in two by a more ponderous destroyer? It had not happened before. It did not happen again. It was a mystery to Kennedy himself. Just after his rescue, a friend named William Liebenow asked, joking, "How in the world could a Jap destroyer run you down?" Kennedy replied, "Lieb, I actually do not know."

It is not clear from the accounts laboriously gathered by the Blairs whether Kennedy had shut off one or more of his boat's three motors, was idling them, or stalled them, or what watch conditions let an expected boat bear down on 109 without warning. Kennedy would cryptically tell Robert Donovan, after the Bay of Pigs invasion, "That whole story [of PT 109] was more fucked up than Cuba." And Barney Ross, of the PT crew, was astonished when the *New Yorker* account came out, showing an alert crew consciously on the attack — a story that makes the collision even harder to explain. Ross told the Blairs: "Our reaction to the 109 thing had always been that we were kind of ashamed of our performance. . . . I had always thought it was a disaster, but he [Hersey] made it sound pretty heroic, like Dunkirk."

There was nothing in the handling of PT 109 to be very proud of. Its assignment was to intercept destroyers running men and supplies through a strait; or, if they missed at the first passage, to hit the ships as they returned north before dawn. The 109 was part of a four-boat detachment whose leader spotted the Japanese and went for them, expecting the others to follow. Kennedy, for some reason, was out of touch, and did not make that initial attack. He waited for the second chance, two hours later, and was caught off guard. His boat fired none of its torpedos and spotted no enemy ship till the *Amagiri* sliced it in two.

It may be said in extenuation of Kennedy that PT boats in general were poorly equipped with navigation and radio equipment. Their record was dismal — the plywood hulls, the topheavy and unreliable torpedos, made them floating explosions waiting to happen. PT boats were romanticized in war propaganda after one took MacArthur off the Philippines. Recruiting had taken place among Ivy Leaguers and the rich — those who had sailed their own boats — and the individualism of the skippers, together with the unpredictability of the boats' performance, made some Navy officers consider them a menace to the American cause.

If, in 1944, John Hersey had tried to find out how a PT boat could be run down by a destroyer, military censorship would have blocked his effort. Inflation of heroic deeds was encouraged by the whole war atmosphere. It is typical of the "gentleman songsters" aspect of the PT command that Kennedy first told Hersey of his exploit after dining at the Stork Club and going to the theater. Hersey had married an old girl friend of Kennedy's, and the two met at social affairs before and during the war. This was one more confirmation of the Ambassador's belief that knowing the right people would pay off, down the road, in unforeseen ways. "Doing the town" while on leave, Kennedy ran across just the right celebrator of his legend.

If the Navy encouraged exaggeration of its heroes' exploits, it nonetheless downgraded the medal Kennedy was recommended for, and rewrote the citation, and delayed the bestowal for nine months — which suggests to the Blairs that there were some misgivings about the accident 109 was engaged in. Kennedy did not get his medal until his father's friend, James Forrestal, became Secretary of the Navy. From the time of the Inga Arvad affair, Joseph Kennedy had been closely engaged in the Navy's treatment of his sons. Through his lobbying, the U.S.S. *Joseph P. Kennedy, Jr.* was commissioned and cadet Robert Kennedy was assigned to serve on it. The promoter who had opposed entry into the war, and who lost a son to it, was nevertheless determined to get some mileage out of it for his other sons' careers.

So the legend was born. On his desk in the Oval Office, Kennedy kept the cocoanut shell he carved as a message to potential rescuers. In the legend, this did the trick. In fact, an Australian spotter had already arranged for the rescue before the cocoanut was received. From his first race for Congress through his entry into the White House, Kennedy used his shipmates as campaign speakers. The PT 109 tie clip became a status symbol on the New Frontier. Edward Kennedy created a sensation by giving them away in Africa. Not since Theodore Roosevelt charged up San Juan Hill with two journalists at his side had a military episode been so expertly merchandized for its political value. In the White House, Kennedy oversaw all aspects of the movie made about his adventure, approving the script and director, choosing the star, Cliff Robertson. (His first choice, Warren Beatty, turned the President down.)

In time, John Kennedy surpassed his father in skill at creating the right image for himself. Though a lackluster student at Harvard, Kennedy left school with material for a book that made him seem a promising young intellectual. He managed his congressional career the same way. While not distinguishing himself for legislation or leadership among his peers, he gave a key speech (on Algeria) and published a key book (on courage) that attracted public notice. *Profiles in Courage* was a "twofer," not only a prize-winning performance in itself, but a reminder to readers and reviewers that the war veteran knew something about courage, about the Hemingway quality of "grace under pressure" mentioned in the book's first sentence.

John Kennedy is rightly called the author of *Profiles in Courage*, as he is the author of his own inaugural address. He authorized each — was the only one who could deliver it; directed the writing; delivered nothing he did not accept; had final right to delete anything or add anything. His authority could not be overruled. It was all done in his name. But Theodore Sorensen, not the author in any of the senses used above, wrote the inaugural address. And Sorensen, along with Jules Davids and others, wrote *Profiles in Courage.*

The book was put together much like a major speech. Scholars and politicians were canvassed for suggestions. Subjects were chosen to give political balance to the book — three Senators from the South, three from the Midwest, and two Republicans were included lest the Democratic Senator from Massachusetts be accused of making courage a New England or a party monopoly. Yet the Senator from Massachusetts meant to connect himself with a noble tradition — so two Senators from Massachusetts were included in this study of eight Senate heroes. The network of honorary Kennedys was pressed into service. Dean Landis wrote a memorandum that remarkably defines the book's theme. Professors Schlesinger and Commager were asked for suggestions and read drafts. Alan Nevins wrote the introduction. Jacqueline Kennedy brought her history teacher at Georgetown — Jules Davids — into the process. Arthur Krock made suggestions to Sorensen, who was *this* book's Arthur Krock.

This kind of political production is normal, not only for an office-holder's speeches but for his books. The two categories tend, in fact, to merge when a politician is "writing." Books just collect or expand on his speeches, written by various aides. There is no deception in this, because there is no pretense that the man signing his name did all or even most of the writing. But things were complicated in Kennedy's case by the fact that Arthur Krock was lobbying to win the book a *writer's* prize, the Pulitzer.

If the Ambassador was right, if it helps to have written a well-received book, it helps immeasurably more to have received a Pulitzer Prize for having written a book. John Kennedy wanted that award, and was willing to make claims of authorship that went well beyond the political authorization involved in delivering a speech. Indeed, he made claims, and insisted on them repeatedly, that are not sustainable. When it was suggested that Kennedy had not written his own book, he showed anger and threatened suits; his father asked the FBI to investigate his accusers. The Senator displayed notes in his own hand, and dictabelt tapes of his own voice.

But those notes and tapes are now in the Kennedy Library, and

Herbert Parmet's investigation of them destroys Kennedy's claim to have written the book. The notes pertain mainly to one subject — John Quincy Adams, the Massachusetts favorite among Kennedy's chosen heroes; and even these are not drafts of a continuous text. The tapes are a jumble of quotes from secondary sources (many of them passages read straight from Margaret Coit's life of John Calhoun). There is no draft, at any stage, for the book, or for any substantial part of it. The notes show he was keeping up with the progress of the work; but Kennedy was ill, traveling, or campaigning most of the time when the book is supposed to have been composed, and Sorensen was working on it full time — sometimes for twelve hours a day — over a period of six months. Parmet leaves no doubt who did most of the work, and especially who supplied "the drama and flow that made for readability." From his first work on his senior paper at Harvard, Kennedy was never able to sustain a long passage of prose — he assembled that paper in a mad flurry of work with a team of hired secretaries to whom he dictated, pointing out passages for copying, working more as compiler than prose artist.

Sorensen follows the code of the political speechwriter in maintaining that his principal was the author of whatever he signed. Within the constraints of his craft, speaking its code as it were, Sorensen told the truth. But Jules Davids, who wrote lengthy first sketches of four chapters, told Parmet that he and Sorensen did most of the research and drafting of the book. Kennedy loyalists supported the Senator's specific claim to having written the book, though James MacGregor Burns admitted in his oral history report at the Kennedy Library: "I think Sorensen, or whoever was helping him, gave him more help on the book than you or I could get if we were doing one." The rules for Kennedys are different, that's all.

One of the books *Profiles* shoved aside for the 1957 Pulitzer was Burns's own *Roosevelt: The Lion and the Fox,* which was the second choice of the biography panel (consisting of Julian Boyd and Bernard Mayo). The first choice of the judges was Alpheus Mason's *Harlan Fiske Stone: Pillar of the Law.* Three other books were also recommended: Irving Brant's *James Madison: The President, 1809–1812,* Samuel Flagg Bemis's *John Quincy Adams and the Union,* and William N. Chambers's *Old Bullion Benton.* It would have been ridiculous to place Kennedy's work in the company of these biographies, and the two historians did not. But the Pulitzer Advisory Board has the power — and the bad habit — of overruling its own judges' recommendations, and that happened in 1957, when Arthur Krock "worked like hell" (in his own words) to get the prize for Kennedy.

The board, naturally, denied improper influence — which reduced it to the puerile explanation that the Milwaukee *Journal*'s president, J. D. Ferguson, swayed twelve grown men with the news that his twelve-year-old grandson enjoyed *Profiles in Courage*. Herbert Parmet, the best student of this whole episode, is skeptical of the board's rather humiliating explanation of its own act:

> Keeping his hands off would have been out of character for the Ambassador. Allowing the Pulitzer prize to be decided by chance would have been especially unique for a man who placed so much importance on having his son gain literary respectability en route to power, and Hohenberg [historian of the Pulitzer nominations] has admitted to Krock's visibility in the situation. Furthermore, the *Times* correspondent had been "instrumental" in deciding "several" other Pulitzer prizes. His credentials as a lobbyist within that journalism fraternity were first-rate.

Because of his book, Kennedy was chosen to chair a special Senate committee for choosing the five outstanding Senators in America's history. This committee announced its winners just one day before Kennedy won the Pulitzer. Of the five Senators chosen to be honored, three were included in Kennedy's eight "profiles," and the press treated those by referring to Kennedy's text. The book's appearance, his service on the committee, and winning the Pulitzer made up a kind of triple play for Kennedy in the spring of 1957, just as his presidential hopes were surfacing.

In 1981, shortly after a reporter for the Washington *Post* received a Pulitzer Prize, it was discovered that her account was false. In order to advance her journalistic career, she had made up a sensational story. She had to resign in disgrace, and the paper apologized for inadvertently misleading the prize committee. The Pulitzer Prize is given for reporting and writing. The book award is given and accepted on the assumption that the writer's skill is at issue, not the patron's office. In taking the prize, Kennedy falsified the facts of the book's production; and he spent all his remaining years covering up that falsification. He lied to the nation, and conscripted various honorary Kennedys in perpetuating his image as a prize-winning author and historian. This aided his career in many ways. For instance, when he wanted the Republican Robert McNamara, who had just taken over the Ford Company, to come to Washington as his Secretary of Defense, McNamara — who had read and been impressed by *Profiles in Courage* — asked him directly if he had really written it. Kennedy solemnly assured him that he had.

So, a woman tried to advance her career, and is ruined. A student tries to pass Spanish, has a friend take his exam for him, and is kicked out of Harvard. But a Senator claims that he wrote what he did not, and goes blithely on to the presidency. This would pose an ethical problem for a man who did not separate his "image" so clearly from any concern for truth. Putting the best face on one's performance is a fundamental political skill; and it was for Joseph and John Kennedy an imperative of family life. Creating the Kennedy "image" was a basic drive for both men. Sometimes this meant exaggerating what was, admittedly, a heroic episode. Sometimes it meant asserting a nonexistent role as writer. It seems unlikely that either man could distinguish between the two exercises in self-promotion.

The woman reporter who lost her Pulitzer had given herself false credentials when applying for the Washington *Post* job — she claimed to be a Vassar graduate. John Kennedy gave himself false credentials in his *Who's Who* entry — a nonexistent year of study at the London School of Economics. He gave biographers false credentials for his war medal. It was not enough to save one man, at the risk of his own life. He had to save three. The incremental touches of glamour were always sought. The unflattering notes were censored. The collision became an attack. The flattering *New Yorker* article became a Kennedy panegyric when tailored for *Reader's Digest* — and that in turn became a campaign document (and, later on, a movie). Reality was all a matter of arranging appearances for the electorate.

The senior Kennedy had forged a separate world for his children. It hovered above ordinary life. It created reality, as Hollywood renamed starlets and gave them more interesting biographies. Glamour was something other people yearned for; the Kennedys could supply it. An appetite was satisfied on both sides. War propaganda did for heroes what Hollywood promotion did for stars. The super-human does not just happen. It must be contrived. For a time, that master contriver of images, Joseph Kennedy, would see his family outshine any star in the fan magazines, any heroic astronaut on the cover of *Life,* any popular professor on the Harvard campus. In this world, you were whatever you could make people think you were. In that sense, John Kennedy was the writer of *Profiles in Courage.*

11

Style

Summoning artists to participate
in the august occasions of the state
Seems something artists ought to celebrate.

— ROBERT FROST, 1961 Inauguration

WASHINGTON POSITIVELY FIZZED in 1961. Kennedy had assembled a cabinet of all the talents. Brilliant people circulated, telling each other how brilliant they were. As Arthur Schlesinger remembers it:

> Washington seemed engaged in a collective effort to make itself brighter, gayer, more intellectual, more resolute. It was a golden interlude. . . . One's life seemed almost to pass in review as one encountered Harvard classmates, wartime associates, faces seen after the war in ADA conventions, workers in Stevenson campaigns, academic colleagues, all united in a surge of hope and possibility.

Both Schlesinger and Sorensen proudly count up the Rhodes Scholars riding the New Frontier.

These "eggheads" boasted of their worldliness. Harvard professors, moving south, shed weight and wives, changed eyeglasses for contact lenses, worked hard and played hard. Schlesinger delights in the fact that Kenneth Galbraith not only wrote economic tomes but satiric essays in *Esquire* (Schlesinger was writing movie reviews for *Show* while serving in the White House). In describing Richard Goodwin as "the archetypal New Frontiersman," Schlesinger includes among his credentials "dining with Jean Seberg." Sorensen gives the President's friendship with Frank Sinatra as proof of his "range." The crush of intellectuals around Marilyn Monroe, at the President's birthday party, became a favorite memory. Schlesinger included it in his book on Robert:

> Adlai Stevenson wrote a friend about his "perilous encounters" that evening with Marilyn, "dressed in what she calls 'skin and beads.' I didn't see the beads! My encounters, however, were only after breaking through the strong defenses established by Robert Kennedy, who was dodging around her like a moth around the flame." We were all moths around the flame that night. I wrote: "I do not think I have seen anyone so beautiful; I was enchanted by her manner and her wit, at once so masked, so ingenuous and so penetrating. But one felt a terrible unreality about her — as if talking to someone under water. Bobby and I engaged in mock competition for her; she was most agreeable to him and pleasant to me — but then she receded into her own glittering mist."

Other women were more accessible than Marilyn — Myra McPherson interviewed one such "Kennedy girl" for her book *The Power Lovers*. She remembered: "Kennedy set the example. Anyone in his following had to have his doxy." As Graham Greene wrote of Rochester: "He had such an art in gilding his failures that it was hard not to love his faults. . . ."

Harvard's urge toward Washington was so intense that it carried the professors halfway to Hollywood. At the Kennedy Library, the symbol of White House culture is the legendary night Pablo Casals played in the East Room. But Kennedy himself showed more interest in the planning and performances of his own birthday salutes — the first in Madison Square Garden, the second in Washington's National Guard Armory. Richard Adler, who wrote the musicals *Pajama Game* and *Damn Yankees,* was "master of revels" at these parties. For the first one, Adler brought in Marilyn Monroe to croon happy birthday for the President. And he topped himself the next year:

> I directed operations from the balcony through phones to the lighting and sound men, the conductor in the pit and the stage manager backstage. Everybody was in the Armory, waiting. And when the President made his entrance and began to walk to the

Presidential box, I pinned him with a spot and cued six trumpets for "Ruffles and Flourishes." You know: "Tum-ta-ta, tum-ta-ta, tum-ta-ta." I tell you, it was terrific! A Roman emperor entering the Colosseum wouldn't have been more dramatic! Such a roar went up from the crowd. And right away we went into "Hail to the Chief." It was fantastic! Then we give the press boys one and a half minutes for pictures, they like it, and also it adds to the excitement. Meanwhile we are lowering the lights, and I have a drum roll going, and as each group of lights goes out and the drums get louder and louder until finally they are *very* loud, and then the orchestra breaks into the National Anthem, very loud, and at that point I have two flags up high above the stage, and there are fans behind them, and the flags are picked up by spots and they billow out and I had a great singer, John Reardon, to sing the National Anthem, which is usually dull in a show. Well, I want to say that the minute the National Anthem started and those flags lit up, the crowd was on its feet, applauding (did you ever see that before?), and after Reardon finished singing he took a bow, which nobody has ever done before, and they gave him a wonderful reception. . . . We never had a President like this.

Mr. Adler knew how to please his patron: "This was the President's party, not one of those culture-vulture programs." It was a giddy time. Remembering an early White House party for the Radziwills, Schlesinger writes in *A Thousand Days:* "Never had girls seemed so pretty, tunes so melodious, an evening so blithe and unconstrained."

Even international fashions seemed to resonate to the anglophile and "swinging" tastes of Kennedy. Mary Quant's London became the center of "the action," and Americans itched outward to Petula Clark's "rhythms of the gentle bossa nova." Schlesinger raved in *Show* about Julie Christie, Peter Sellers, and (of course) the Beatles: "They are the timeless essences of the adolescent effort to deal with the absurdities of an adult world." *Real* culture was not safe, not dull and respectable like Eisenhower's early-to-bed shows. It was frisky, and risqué.

Yet elegant, too: "In an Executive Mansion where Fred Waring once flourished, one now finds Isaac Stern, Pablo Casals, and the Stratford Players," Schlesinger assured us. Mrs. Kennedy — whose next husband would decorate in whale testicles — became the very embodiment of Culture. For the best and the brightest, attracted to her husband, she personified all that was most beautiful. She defied the rule that political wives must wear American clothes and drink American wines. But that, too, separated her husband's White House from the Fred Waring days. Schlesinger approved:

> The things people had once held against her — the unconventional beauty, the un-American elegance, a taste for French clothes and French food — were suddenly no longer liabilities but assets. She represented all at once not a negation of her country but a possible fulfillment of it, a dream of civilization and beauty, a suggestion that America was not to be trapped forever in the bourgeois ideal.

So glittering did the Kennedy style appear that some accused the President of being all style, no substance. Schlesinger answered that such style was itself a political act of substantial import: "His 'coolness' was itself a new frontier. It meant freedom from the stereotyped response of the past. . . . His personality was the most potent instrument he had to awaken a national desire for something new and better." When one man's personality is an administration's most potent tool, then efficient use of resources dictates a cult of that personality. A shrewd administrator must, to achieve his policy goals, maximize the impact of the leader's charm — must, that is, join in the contriving of images to celebrate the prince. Honorary Kennedys had always tended the family image. Now an entire administration would be recruited to that task.

Sorensen's book tells us how carefully Kennedy crafted his symbols. When his back troubles forced him to use crutches, these signs of weakness were abandoned whenever he moved into an area of the White House where he could be seen. On the other hand, his rocking chair was an acceptable sign of relaxation. Even the chair had its carefully chosen "image," making it "a nationally recognized symbol of the traditional values, reflective patience, and practical informality prevailing in the White House." Hugh Sidey called Kennedy's chair "a symbol of him and his administration," with "the full status of F.D.R.'s cigarette holder."

The chair stood for relaxation, not weakness. The President declared the need for "vigah," and sent his "frontiersmen" off on fifty-mile hikes. He cut back on his own golfing, and avoided photographers when he did indulge the sport — he did not want to be compared with grandfatherly Eisenhower at this retirement sport. The putting green on the White House lawn, Ike's spike marks on the Oval Office floor, became objects of ridicule. Yet, away from cameras, Kennedy drove golf balls toward the Washington Monument, and bet "Red" Fay he could not send a drive over the Ellipse fence.

Many of Kennedy's initial moves were planned to provide dramatic contrast with his predecessor's style. No more Fred Waring. No more "Hottentot" taste in the arts. Sorensen's book reveals that the inaugural address was expressly framed to dramatize this difference:

> Few will forget the striking contrast presented by the outgoing and incoming Presidents. One was the likable, dedicated product of the rural Midwest and the Military Academy. The other was the urbane product of the urban East. Both had spent their entire adult careers in the service of their country, yet they were vastly different, not only in age, religion and political philosophy, but in their views of politics as a profession and the Presidency as power. Every eye watched them take their places, the oldest man ever to serve in the office of the Presidency and the youngest man ever elected to it. . . . Their contrast lent added meaning to the phrase: "Let the word go forth from this time and place, to friend and foe alike, that the torch has been passed to a new generation of Americans. . . ."

Sorensen's book breaks off the quote there. But his text, read on that day, continued: "born in this century. . . ." Eisenhower was born in 1890.

Kennedy's task, according to his followers, was to combat the national enervation caused by Eisenhower. If the country had to get "moving again," it was because Eisenhower had brought it to such a total standstill. In this view, presidential style not only establishes an agenda for politics but determines the tone of national life. The image projected by the President becomes the country's self-image, sets the expectations to which it lives up or down. This was the reading of history that made style equal substance; and the Kennedy transition seemed to confirm the reading. If Kennedy could suddenly energize the press, the academy, and the arts, it was because

Eisenhower had previously narcotized them. Only the vigor projected by a President can animate the citizenry.

The canonical first statement of this thesis was Mailer's *Esquire* article on Kennedy as a true hero come to rescue us from Eisenhower "the anti-hero, the regulator." Arthur Schlesinger quotes that article with approval in his history of the Kennedy administration. Mailer had grasped the essential point, according to Schlesinger — that Kennedy's style was changing the very national identity, freeing the country from its past (boring) self: "There can be no doubt that Kennedy's magic was not alone that of wealth and youth and good looks, or even of all these things joined to intelligence and will. It was, more than this, the hope that he could redeem American politics by releasing American life from its various bondages to orthodoxy." For Mailer, Kennedy was ending the era of the small town. Like Sorensen, he saw the contrast with Eisenhower in terms of a new urbanity:

> The need of the city is to accelerate growth; the pride of the small town is to retard it. But since America has been passing through a period of enormous expansion since the war, the double-four years of Dwight Eisenhower could not retard the expansion, it could only denude it of color, character, and the development of novelty. The small-town mind is rooted — it is rooted in the small town — and when it attempts to direct history the results are disastrously colorless because the instrument of world power which is used by the small-town mind is the committee. Committees do not create, they merely proliferate, and the incredible dullness wreaked upon the American landscape in Eisenhower's eight years has been the triumph of the corporation.

Electing Kennedy would be an adventure, an existential act, reminding us that "violence was locked with creativity, and adventure was the secret of love." We would at last shake off the Eisenhower spell, the deadening "benevolence without leadership" that had made the nation sluggish — its architecture empty, its manners sexless, its goals tame: "The life of politics and the life of myth had diverged too far, and the energies of the people one knew everywhere had slowed down."

The cultural revolution Mailer anticipated was, in fact, accomplished, according to President Kennedy's biographers. Yet what was this declaration of the new freedom but an abject profession of servility to the one man — whatever man — sitting in the White House? The apparent compliment to the life of the mind was in fact a profound insult. Those who could only act free with a Kennedy to inspire them confessed that they had been cowed by the mere presence of Eisenhower in the Oval Office.

What, after all, in Ike's avuncular image automatically turned off thought? On the night he was elected, did his stealthy minions, some guardian angels of boredom, slip into newspaper rooms and faculty offices, to stuff invisible pillows in the typewriters? Did they proscribe the reading of philosophy? If so, how was the proscription enforced? Did a painter wake up, late one November morning in 1952, and decide he must pack his brushes away for at least four years? Conversely, did Kennedy's election make a philosopher wake up, look at his morning paper, and say, "At last I can start thinking again?"

Put this way, it seems an absurd claim. Yet that is what Schlesinger and others believed. The appearance of Pablo Casals in the White House became for them a signal that America had adopted art as a national purpose, even as part of the Cold War: "I would hope that we will not leave it to the Soviet Union to uncover the Van Cliburns of the future," Schlesinger wrote. Poor dumb Eisenhower — he not only lost Cuba; he lost Cliburn. He created the pianist gap.

What was the political meaning of Casals (rather than Waring) in the White House? It provided John Kennedy his first opportunity to hear the cellist — and late education is better than none; though there is no evidence that the evening made Kennedy give up his show tunes for Bach. Did Casals need the boost? Hardly. Some of the Harvard faculty types coming to Washington had, no doubt, listened to Casals before; those who had not were as little likely as Kennedy himself to become addicted after this one exposure. Did the "unwashed" make a run for Casals records? If they did, the fad can hardly have lasted very long. Those who listen to Casals because the President endured one night of him will soon, I would bet, backslide in Fred Waring's direction.

What was the result of that fabled night, then? The ones who got most benefit were those who had listened to Casals all along. He did not play better, after that, or Bach sound better; but these listeners felt better — felt bigger. They had been endorsed. Listening to Bach received a presidential seal of approval. The obverse of this is that these people felt smaller under Eisenhower. Their Bach did not have that extra ingredient which can make all the difference — the President was not noticing the listeners as they listened.

This view of things gives to the President a stunning power — to bestow or withhold pleasure in Bach. But he can do this only if those craving for presidential approval have debilitated themselves — have given a ridiculous importance to their own pose as Listeners. David Halberstam argues that "the best and the brightest" were self-corrupting in their confidence — in their assurance that rational gifts and expertise and toughness can set the world straight. But there was a deep sense of social and cultural inferiority under the tough outer whir of analysis and blur of activity. These best and the brightest felt intimidated by the suspicion that Americans consider art and culture "sissy stuff." Yet here was a war-hero President saying it was all right to listen to Bach, to like art and French wines. The embarrassing gush of gratitude for this largesse infects Schlesinger's and Sorensen's books as much as Manchester's. The gratitude is expressed with varying degrees of sophistication, but it is essentially the same in all three men.

Blessed with the approval of this macho President, the cultural monitors would prove that he was not mistaken, that they were not sissies, by taking on Kennedy's own worldly and fast-living air. They would wink at his secret parties in the White House and think that the proper underside of aristocratic graces. The results of this in policy were a "frontier" love of guerrilla boldness, a contempt for dithering Adlai Stevenson and courtly Dean Rusk and moralizing Chester Bowles. Style meant that the President — and those who now dressed like him and spoke like him — did not want to be bored. They talked in wisecracks; wrote witty verse at cabinet meetings; used the code of a superior set. According to Harris Wofford, this style forbade the raising of some questions, the expression of "square" inhibitions, of "preachy" concerns. Chester Bowles was resented for having been right about the Bay of Pigs; but he was exiled from the State Department, not because he was right, but because he was dull. It was every man's duty, around Kennedy, to sound brilliant.

The pursuit of style as if it were substance leaches vitality from the style itself. The Kennedy rhetoric sounds flashy now; raises snickers. This is not simply a matter of passing time and changing fashions. Dr. King's sermons retain their power to move us — but of course they were overtly preachy, moral and old-fashioned. Arthur Schlesinger hailed a cultural revolution, and gave up his monumental work on the Roosevelt years to suppress a report on the Bay of Pigs project at the *New Republic,* to mislead Adlai Stevenson during the missile crisis, to browbeat William Attwood at *Look,* and (in the words of Murray Kempton) "to fall upon William Manchester in the alleys of the American Historical Association." Kennedy did not liberate the intellectuals who praised him; he subverted them. He played to all that was weakest and worst in them. It became apparent that they did not simply want a President who praised them for listening to Bach; they wanted a President who would listen to them, and they were willing to say whatever "played" with him. National purpose would compensate for private failure, would fill with public rhetoric the empty places in them where poetry should have been breeding. Men rose up from the ruins of their family to redeem their country; or preached the comity of nations because they could not abide the members of their own university department.

Benefactors of mankind may start tending to the world, at least in part, to get out of the house. But artists and academicians, writers and the privileged jounalists seem to feel a special responsibility for what goes on in Washington, a personal guilt when things go badly. They are prominent among those who make the threat that they will leave the country if so-and-so gets elected. This threat is not very terrifying, since its auditors would think it a blessing if fulfilled. And I do not personally know any intellectual who has missed a meal, or been put significantly off his feed, by the victory of an unpalatable candidate. But they undoubtedly think they should feel sad, and that the untoward election has blunted their creativity if not their appetite. One catches in faculty gossip about politicians the note of housewives wrapped up in soap operas — the note of a substitute vitality, shared artificial crises that alleviate the speaker's own problems. They may not agree on the merits of a "minimester," but they

all hated Nixon. More important, they all agreed to love Prince
Charming. We mainly spread havoc under Presidents we love. Camelot was the opium of the intellectuals.

Later, under the dreaded Nixon, celebrators of the New Frontier
began to express misgivings about the Imperial Presidency. Schlesinger himself then traced the growth of presidential power, admitting faults in his heroes, Jackson and Roosevelt and Kennedy. But
Kennedy's short time in office was not just an acceleration of prior
trends. It added something new — not so much the Imperial Presidency as the Appearances Presidency. The man's very looks thrilled
people like Mailer: "If the nation voted to improve its face, what an
impetus might be given to the arts, to the practices, to the lives and
to the imagination of the American." Kennedy was able to take the
short cuts he did, command support for rash acts, because he controlled the images that controlled the professional critics of our society. They had been recruited beforehand on minor points of style.
He was not Eisenhower — and that was sufficient achievement for
the "eggheads" who had been mocking Eisenhower for years. Kennedy was a Steerforth who flattered and tamed the schoolboys by
standing up to their master. He was their surrogate, their dream-self,
what all the old second lieutenants from World War II wished they
had become. Through him they escaped their humdrum lives at the
typewriter, on the newspaper, in the classroom. From OSS to MLA
is a rude descent.

None of this just happened, of course. Kennedy was a shrewd manipulator of his own appearance and impact. He crafted his non-
Eisenhower persona expertly. He monitored reviews of it. He censored undesired impressions. He thought always in terms of public
relations, and of managing the press. It was soon discovered that he
kept the New York *Times* and *New Republic* from reporting the prep-
arations of a Cuban invasion. But the way he intertwined policy and
image-making was not fully revealed until 1974, when a note in
Kennedy's hand was found in the Kennedy Library. Written just
before the invasion, it says, "Is there a plan to brief and brainwash
key press within 12 hours or so?" Those who should be brainwashed
are then listed: the New York *Times,* Walter Lippmann, Marquis
Child, and Joseph Alsop. After the invasion, Kennedy sent Maxwell
Taylor to brief and brainwash *Time-Life* editors on the disaster. The

President sent a covering letter to Henry Luce asking that the meeting be kept secret. The President said he must "emphasize the need for keeping the fact that this discussion has even taken place completely in the bosom of your official family." He claimed to be giving the editors more information than Congress had received, and that favor should be repaid.

Kennedy was admired by liberals for his nonsentimental realism. He always said ADA types made him uncomfortable. He was "beyond ideology." This calculating approach thrilled the ideologues themselves. Schlesinger said it best: his coolness *was* a new frontier. But few intellectuals saw the contempt mixed with his coolness when it came to manipulating them. When Kennedy suggested that Walter Lippmann be offered an ambassadorship, Schlesinger replied that he might do the administration more good as a columnist. Kennedy worked always to turn journalists into unofficial spokesmen for his administration, and he succeeded with a great many of them. They were there to help him arrange reality, to make style become substance, to define power as the contriving of appearances.

But Kennedy could not have shaped his dazzling facade of style unless he had a genuine feel for many of its components. He liked the kind of glamour he was now in a position to dispense. The largely imaginary English society he had read about was his to "recreate," given all the resources of the White House. The very thinness of his grasp upon Regency England helped him enact a simulacrum of it, without regard for recalcitrant historical particulars. His imagined England was a world of playboy-statesmen, and America's more purchasable intellectuals wanted nothing better. They lined up to celebrate the second coming of a secondhand Lord Melbourne.

12

The Prisoner of Image

Arm, arm, my name!
— SHAKESPEARE, *Richard II*

ROGER MUDD WAS A REGULAR GUEST at Kennedy house parties. Robert Kennedy filmed a relaxed interview with Mudd in the 1968 campaign. It seeemed inevitable that Mudd would interview Edward Kennedy if he ran for President. But Kennedy tried to put it off. All through the summer of 1979, he had been feeding speculation while dodging questions on his future. He hoped to keep the matter buttoned up until October 20, when he had to appear with President Carter at the dedication of the Kennedy Library. But Tom Southwick, his young press secretary, thought it best to get the (presumably sympathetic) session with Mudd out of the way before a heavy schedule of actual campaigning began. On September 29, Mudd was in Hyannis Port to tape what Kennedy thought would be a genial discussion of the nation's plight. Still not an announced candidate, Kennedy planned to repeat his offered-in-sadness strictures on President Carter's competence.

But Mudd, like many reporters who had been close to the Kennedys, had to prove he was not their minion. Edward must submit to the scrutiny his elders evaded. The very charm of John Kennedy, the intensity of Robert, worked against Edward. Their success at contriving appearances now put journalists on guard, made them adopt a compensatory harshness. Defenders of Richard Nixon rightly complained that their man received a ferocious coverage from which Kennedys had largely been exempt. After Watergate, it was a point of pride for journalists to exhibit omnidirectional skepticism.

And so, as Burton Hersh says, "Mudd set Kennedy up." He bore in with personal questions. What was the state of his marriage? Why did he need so many advisers to help him tell the story of Chappaquiddick? What of reports linking him with other women? How does he differ from his brothers? Why did he say he looked at a clock in the car, after fetching Gargan, when there was no clock in the car? Mudd even took on a dramatic role to ask one question in the most offensive manner: "What happens, Senator, if some heckler stands up at a rally, a Kennedy rally, and says, you know, in the loud voice, red-faced, he's angry at you, and he says, 'Kennedy, you know you were drinking, you lied, and you covered up.' What — what are you going to tell him in a situation like that?"

Kennedy was clearly disconcerted at being heckled in his own home by a man he thought his friend. With the cameras turning, he stumbled backward, verbally off-balance and finding no firm ground beneath him. Even when Mudd returned to questions Kennedy had been expecting, he was disoriented, still, and inarticulate:

> MUDD: What would you do different from Carter?
> KENNEDY: Well, in which particular areas?
> MUDD: Well, just take the — the question of — of leadership.
> KENNEDY: Well, it's a — on — on what — on — you know, you have to come to grips with the — the different issues that we're — we're facing. I mean, we can — we have to deal with each of the various questions that we're — we're talking about, whether it's in the questions of the economy, whether it's in — in the areas of energy.

Mudd's editing and later commentary were deftly hostile; they made Kennedy look even more dithery, as his weak answers were distributed throughout the hour show. In his added remarks Mudd said Kennedy's marriage existed "only on selected occasions," and called the Senator a "captive of his bushy-tailed staff." Mudd used shots of the Chappaquiddick scene to back up this judgment: "It is now obvious that Kennedy and his advisers plan to volunteer nothing more on Chappaquiddick, or make any attempt to clear away the lingering contradictions."

All the images of the past were there — the compound at Hyannis Port, scenes of the family clustering around its matriarch, a Kennedy on the hustings, shots of the crowd — but here they were arranged as in a nightmare-reversal of the old iconography of Kennedy brains and bravery. The brothers had lived by expert contriving of appearances; but their survivor was being dismantled, aspect by aspect, in terms of the old impressions. Kennedys were by definition bright and glib — but this one stammered incoherently. Kennedys were tough and took the initiative — but this one collapsed under questioning. Kennedys used TV to create desired impressions — but this one was being destroyed by TV, before our eyes.

Not quite before our eyes, though. CBS, defying Kennedy's wishes, ran the documentary three days before he announced his campaign; but did it on the same night that a rival network ran the movie *Jaws*. The audience for Mudd's show was small; but even that became a disadvantage for Kennedy. Various journalists had received a transcript of the show, and leaked it ahead of schedule, most of them to ridicule it in print. It would have been better for people to see Kennedy than to read the excerpts treated, later, with derision by those who had been friendly to the Kennedys, people like Jimmy Breslin and Mary McGrory. Rambling sentences, spoken, get tied together by inflections, by the tonal trajectory of a thought. Even John Kennedy's expert performance at press conferences left behind a printed record of incomplete, interrupted, circumlocutious answers. For that matter, Mudd was less than word-perfect in *his* performance. One question read in its entirety: "You were not aware — did not — you did not figure that the — that the main road ..." Asked what, precisely, he wanted to know about Chappaquiddick, Mudd had at first no specific question to offer, then fumbled his way into one: "When you came back to the cottage, after your car had left the bridge, and you got Mr. Markham and Mr. Gargan to go with you, you noticed that the time was approximately 2:15 — 2:20, 12:15 ..." These things are less noticeable as conversation weaves them into inflected continuities; but Kennedy did not get the benefit of that fact as his more garbled answers were reprinted and made fun of in column after column.

Kennedy not only looked bad in his own right; he was made to look even worse by contrast with exaggerated memories of his brothers' wit and verbal presence of mind. And he was clearly not in charge of the *way* he was portrayed. President Kennedy managed to appear where and how he liked on television. He used the medium; it did not use him. He once rebuked his brother Robert for bringing in a camera crew without preparing him; sent Kenneth O'Donnell to view the film; decided it was not flattering; and had the network kill it. The Kennedy skill at charming or coercing reporters had developed early — John Kennedy had a reference to his father's anti-Semitism taken out of the Dinneen biography. At the Justice Department, Robert Kennedy's agents investigated Victor Lasky for publishing an unfavorable book about his brother. Jacqueline Kennedy was as concerned with the proper control of journalists as any of the family she married into. When the White House staff was sworn to secrecy about its years of service, Maude Shaw had been overlooked. Perhaps, as a British nanny, she was considered discreet by type; or, as a noncitizen, less easily bound to silence. When she published an adoring memoir of her time in the White House, Mrs. Kennedy deeply resented it — perhaps for revealing that she, Maude, had been the first to tell Caroline about her father's death. Mrs. Kennedy asked that this detail be removed from Manchester's book — which shows that she was not merely concerned with accuracy, but with making sure that she was seen in the best light. Mrs. Kennedy was also bitter about "Red" Fay's harmless and playful memoir, perhaps because he mentioned the gossip about rifts in the Kennedy marriage:

> A marriage between a beautiful, enamored young lady and a worldly public figure in his mid-thirties is not as simple a matter as the union of a teen-age boy with the girl next door. . . . There is no question that the demands of public life placed an unusual strain on the marriage of these two bright, attractive young people. Gossip mongers wanted to interpret the slightest deviation from what "newly married Town Square U.S.A." would do as a telltale sign of unrest. . . . With Jack's candidacy for the Democratic nomination now widely recognized, there were persistent idle rumors that Jack and Jacqueline were suffering marital differences.

It was not enough to deny such rumors; one had to pretend they did not exist, erase them from the record entirely.

Edward Kennedy was always the least manipulative of the Kennedy brothers, the most candid and outgoing, the one little given to posing or appearances. When Senator John Kennedy underwent back surgery, he used this moment of apparent weakness to project an image of strength — he was writing a book flat on his back, turning adversity into opportunity. When Senator Edward Kennedy had back surgery following his plane crash, he asked the family's academic courtiers to give him a seminar on political and economic matters. He was not the teacher, but still a pupil. The tame professors came, and performed; but the contrast with Sorensen's use of such men during John's illness was striking.

Eventually, of course, Edward had to come out with his own campaign books; but he simply went through the motions. His brothers planned books to support their political careers in multiple ways. John's theme of courage prompted most reviewers to remind their audience of the author's war record; his concentration on the Senate made him a candidate for the next profile in courage. Robert's *The Enemy Within* gave a "law and order" justification to the author's reputed ruthlessness — people want cops to be tough. That newspapers noticed these books helped their authors. But it has been largely a blessing for Edward that few can remember his books.

In 1968, just after Robert published a collection of speeches to help his campaign (*To Seek a Newer World*), Edward came out with his own collection, *Decisions for a Decade*. It was foolish to publish similar volumes so close together, since the younger brother had to be careful not to outshine the older. Beyond that, however, he succeeded in embarrassing them both by demonstrating that they used the same speechwriters (or writers who cribbed from each other). Peter Lucas, in *The Reporter,* listed eight interchangeable passages from the two books.

Here, for instance, is Robert: "One Latin American President told me succinctly: 'If you want a government that says always "yes, yes, yes," you will soon have to deal with a government that says "no, no, no." ' "

And Edward: "As a Latin American president once said to an American official: 'If you demand a government which says "yes, yes, yes," you may finally get one that says "no, no, no." ' "

Or Robert on local government: "To meet the problem, Jefferson urged the division of the nation, within each state and community, into what he called 'republics of the wards.' "

And Edward: "What we need, in a favorite phrase of Thomas Jefferson, is to 'divide the counties into wards,' creating small units of government." And so on.

The younger brother's lackluster performance may have been expected while older brothers were still around to shine, to get first crack at the best writers, at their brightest phrases. But even after the death of both brothers, on the eve of his own first run for President, Edward issued a book more damaging than helpful to him. *Our Day and Generation* (1979) is a collection of rhetorical snippets from Kennedy speeches interspersed with "family of man" pictures, visual and verbal clichés juxtaposed within wide margins as if to emphasize the poverty of thought.

Naturally, the tame professors paid homage. But this time they gave the game away. Henry Steele Commager took blame for assembling the book, and pretended in the introduction to derive "a consistent philosophy" from the tags and campaign sentences he calls "observations and admonitions." Then, to complete the humiliation of attendants, Archibald MacLeish contributed a foreword that claims more can be learned from these Kennedy "papers" than from "professional pollsters or propagandists."

Trying to use the Kennedy image, Edward has constantly been undone by it. Tricks that worked twice all seem to fail on the third try. Dramatic touches from the older brothers' repertoire become mere bathos when Edward invokes them.

Roger Mudd, in his TV interview, made a sardonic reference to Kennedy's Chappaquiddick speech, forcing the Senator renounce one of its weepier claims:

> MUDD: Senator, when you gave your television — televised speech after Chappaquiddick, you mentioned thinking that there was some awful curse that was hanging over the Kennedy family. Do you still think that?
>
> KENNEDY: Well, I don't — I don't think so any more. I mean, there were a sudden series of circumstances which happened in fairly rapid sequence at that time, which I think probably helped me to reach that — that observation. In the period of the last ten years, I — I think life has been — been much more probably nor-

mal in — by general standards, and it's been — been able to reach a
sense of — of perspective of life on it, which I — I wouldn't say
that that viewpoint is — is mine any — any longer.

This last of the glamorous Kennedys, pleading to be treated as "normal," has traveled far from the memories of Camelot.

The worst blow came when commentators like John Chancellor
compared the Chappaquiddick talk to Nixon's Checkers speech.
That had always been a symbol, for Kennedy admirers, of the contrast between their man and the Republican he defeated. Nixon had
"no class," as John Kennedy put it; no taste, no sense of style. He
crawled and whined his way back onto the ticket with Eisenhower in
1952, making an emotional appeal to the public to let him run despite rumors about a "slush fund." He invoked his dog. Now it was
a Kennedy's turn to plead that constituents would keep him in the
Senate. He invoked his curse. *Life* magazine treated Kennedy as a
bumbling contriver of appearances, one who not only did not con-
trive what he wanted, but was caught trying to: "He was simply
hustling heartstrings, using words, cashing in on the family credibility." John Chancellor said that Nixon at least had the excuse of a
presidential campaign's pressures — an excuse Kennedy lacked. It is
the ultimate betrayal of Kennedy appearances to come off second
best to Richard Nixon. Theodore Sorensen, the verbal cosmetician,
labored hard on the hopeless assignment Edward gave him. But
everything he did just made things worse. Quoting himself, Sorensen had Edward recite the closing paragraph of *Profiles in Courage.*
Life observed: "There was also some decidedly awkward talk of mo-
rality and courage, including an eloquent passage from his brother's
book, which Teddy recited as though oblivious to the way the
meaning rebuked him."

Each time he evokes his brothers, he seems to dwindle beside the
shadowy evocations. Yet he must go on evoking them. He is a prisoner of his brothers' charm, which he must trade in even as he seems
to cheapen it. It was regard for the family name, and a sense of the
family power, that made him seek Kennedys first, not the police, at
Chappaquiddick. And it was that very delay that made him, and the
family, look so bad. And having relied on the image while trying to
preserve it, he had to keep using it to rescue him from the trap it had

led him into. All the ghosts had to be summoned now. Only if people were bowing to the ghosts could he hope to slip by the constable. He was using the Kennedy name, but using it up. The Kennedy loyalists came and served, but they looked ridiculous doing it — like the professors who bowed to his speechwriters' platitudes. Other people gave in, one more time, to the Kennedy influence; but grumbled as they did so. The whole point of being a Kennedy was, in the father's scheme of things, to look good. But now being a Kennedy meant looking bad, and making others look bad, even as the Kennedy name won a series of dim little victories over minor officials. At least seven people had to be distracted by what remained of the Kennedy dazzle:

1. Edgartown Police Chief Dominick Arena, watching the recovery of Ms. Kopechne's body, was told that Senator Kennedy wanted him back at the police station. Arena did not have Kennedy brought to him, to the radio car which was the sole communications center of his police force. He left the car with the divers, crossed on the ferry, and heard Kennedy's admission of involvement. He asked for a statement, and left the Senator alone with Gargan to confect it. Gargan took down the minimal statement. Arena then typed it; Kennedy was not even asked to sign it. Arena demanded no expansion on the statement, and therefore did not learn about others on the island — which meant that the partygoers slipped away, to be asked no official questions for six months. Then Arena let the body be removed without an autopsy. He did not cite Kennedy for leaving the scene of an accident until pressured by journalists' questioning. He felt obliged to be cooperative, even to the point of personal risk, when dealing with a Kennedy. "I've been so cooperative that they're going to put me on the stand and make a jackass of me."

2. Dr. Donald Mills, the substitute medical examiner, did not give the body an external observation. He did not turn it over. He pulled down Ms. Kopechne's slacks only far enough to feel her "tummy" (his word). He sent the body to the mortuary expecting an autopsy, but was flustered into signing a release when a man came to him speaking for Senator Kennedy. "I was almost pushed to the point of irrationality and blackout as I did my best to answer the barrage of questions." The doctor's reward for being impressed by "the Kennedy man" (as he called Dun Gifford) was, he later said, to

live with accusations that he had been bought by Kennedy money. The power of the Kennedys is precisely that they do not need to buy deference.

3. Dukes County Special Prosecutor Walter Steele led reporters away from any gossip about the party, and carpentered the minor charge which Kennedy plea-bargained with Steele's support.

4. District Attorney Edmund Dinis kept the case away from the Grand Jury as long as possible. Dinis asked for a Pennsylvania court to exhume the body for an autopsy, but had too little information to support his request. Three months after the accident, he had not talked to any of the partygoers.

5. Judge Bernard C. Bronminski, who presided over the exhumation hearing in Pennsylvania, was facing reelection in a heavily Catholic district, and delayed his finding until after the election. Then he decided against exhumation, since fuller medical evidence might lead to "speculation" — as if slimmer evidence *reduced* ill-grounded speculation.

6. Judge Wilfred Paquet brought in a priest to pray for the Grand Jury when he addressed it, and counseled inaction.

7. Judge James Boyle put on the strangest performance. He (a) presided at the leaving-of-the-scene hearing, and volunteered that Kennedy had been punished enough, a statement that should have disqualified him from (b) presiding over the later inquest on Ms. Kopechne's death where (c) he blocked, directed, or took over the questioning process, defending Kennedy before (d) accusing Kennedy of perjury, after which, as he later admitted, (e) he was required by law to issue an arrest warrant, though (f) he didn't. Judge Boyle is the best example of the way men of independent standing react to the aura of power around a Kennedy, even while they resent or belittle that aura. It is Edward Kennedy's fate to be treated in terms of an image he is felt not to have earned. The image by which he is judged may have been false or hollow from the outset; but that does not help him. If for no other purpose, it remains valid for one — to tie his actions to stylistic claims he can neither fully embody nor entirely relinquish.

IV

CHARISMA

What a strange Nemesis lurks in the felicities of men! In thy mouth it shall be sweet as honey, in thy belly it shall be bitter as gall! Some weakly organized individual, we will say at the age of five-and-twenty, whose main or whole talent rests on some prurient susceptivity, and nothing under it but shallowness and vacuum, is clutched hold of by the general imagination, is whirled aloft to the giddy height; and taught to believe the divine-seeming message that he is a great man: such individual seems the luckiest of men: and, alas, is he not the unluckiest?

— THOMAS CARLYLE

13

Counterinsurgency at Home

Eisenhower embodied half the needs of the nation, the needs of the timid, the petrified, the sanctimonious, and the sluggish. What was even worse, he did not divide the nation as a hero might (with a dramatic dialogue as the result); he merely excluded one part of the nation from the other. The result was an alienation of the best minds and the bravest impulses from the faltering history which was made. America's need in those years was to take an existential turn, to walk into the nightmare, to face into that terrible logic of history which demanded that the country and its people must become more extraordinary and more adventurous, or else perish.

— NORMAN MAILER, "Superman Comes to the Supermarket"

PRESIDENT EISENHOWER'S CRIME, in Norman Mailer's eyes, was a government by committee. Committees are not creative. They stifle originality, impose conformity. Eisenhower had let problems go untended in order to preserve the country's (and his own) tranquillity. An "existential" leadership would dare to go "outside channels," to confront the unexpected with a resourceful poise of improvisation.

Schlesinger and Sorensen, official historians, portray their leader as just the "existential" hero Mailer pined for. His first job was to dismantle the protective procedures Eisenhower had woven around the presidency. Kennedy wanted to be exposed, not shielded — out on the battlements, scanning all horizons, not seated in his chamber sifting documents. His ideal was the Franklin Roosevelt celebrated by Schlesinger and Burns and Neustadt. Richard Neustadt's 1960 book, *Presidential Power,* became the "hot" item of the transition. In it, Roosevelt and Eisenhower were contrasted — Roosevelt as a man free from procedural entanglements, Eisenhower as the slave of them:

> Where Roosevelt let his channels and advisers become orderly he acted out of character. With Eisenhower, seemingly, the case is quite the opposite. Apparently he had a sense of power and a source of confidence as unlike Roosevelt's as were the two men's methods. For Eisenhower the promotion of disorder was distinctly out of character. When he could not work through a set procedure, or when channels failed him, or when his associates quarreled openly, he grew either disheartened or enraged. . . . Eisenhower has been a sort of Roosevelt in reverse.

Which meant that Kennedy, to imitate Roosevelt, had to become a sort of Eisenhower in reverse.

Neustadt, who had been appointed during the 1960 campaign to prepare for the transition, turned in his first report to the candidate on his airplane:

> After a time, Archibald Cox, who was aboard, said that the Senator was ready to see him but cautioned against conversation; "he's saving his voice for Chicago." Neustadt, going back to Kennedy, handed him a bundle of memoranda and said, "You don't have to say anything — here are the memoranda — don't bother with them till after the election." One memorandum listed priority actions from election to Thanksgiving. Another dealt with cabinet posts. Another was called "Staffing the President-Elect"; sensing Kennedy's affinities, Neustadt added to this appendixes discussing Roosevelt's approach to White House staffing and to the Bureau of the Budget. Half an hour later Kennedy bounded out of his compartment in search of Neustadt. Finding him, he said, "That Roosevelt stuff is fascinating." Neustadt said, "You're not supposed to read it now." Kennedy repeated, "It's fascinating."

At his first session with Kennedy after the election, Neustadt gave him a copy of *Presidential Power* and recommended that he read chapters three and seven. Schlesinger continues: "Kennedy, almost as if surprised at the limited assignment, said, 'I will read the whole book.' When he did, he found an abundance of evidence and analysis to support his predilections toward a fluid presidency."

There would be no Sherman Adams in Kennedy's White House. The President would direct his own operation. All bottlenecks to fluidity had to be broken up. The National Security Council, for one. Under Eisenhower, this was a coordinator of information coming to the President. Kennedy meant for it to be his own arm reaching out — through, over, or around the government — to get things done. Schlesinger applauded the birth of what became the Vietnam-planning organ of government:

> Mac [Bundy] was presently engaged in dismantling the elaborate national security apparatus built up by the Eisenhower administration.... Richard Neustadt had taken great pleasure during the interregnum in introducing Bundy to the Eisenhower White House as the equivalent of five officers on the Eisenhower staff. Bundy promptly slaughtered committees right and left and collapsed what was left of the inherited apparatus into a compact and flexible National Security Council staff. With Walt Rostow as his deputy and Bromley Smith, a remarkable civil servant, as the NSC's secretary, he was shaping a supple instrument to meet the new President's distinctive needs.

A pattern was being set, by which the President's special teams actively took on an adversary role toward the rest of the executive branch.

Kennedy's appointments reflected his sense of priorities. Dean Rusk, a southern gentleman acclimated to Eastern Establishment ways as head of the Rockefeller Foundation, would be custodian of the State Department's traditional duties toward other countries. But McGeorge Bundy would supply the ideas on foreign policy, from his office in the White House. Schlesinger felt that Washington could pose no difficulty too great for a man who had been king of the hill in Cambridge: "Bundy possessed dazzling clarity and speed of mind — Kennedy told friends that, next to David Ormsby Gore, Bundy was the brightest man he had ever known — as well as great distinction of manner and unlimited self-confidence. I had seen him learn how to dominate the faculty of Harvard University, a throng of intelligent and temperamental men; after that training, one could hardly doubt his capacity to deal with Washington bureaucrats." It is an interesting psychological point — and typical of the time — that Schlesinger considers the enemy to be dealt with, not as hostile foreign powers, but as the bureaucracy.

Dean Rusk soon became the butt of jokes emanating from Bundy's circle of bright men at the White House. David Halberstam describes Rusk's patience during this ordeal: "He resisted the impulse to react to stories being told about him, but at times the anger and irritation would flash through. 'It isn't worth being Secretary of State,' he once told Dick Goodwin, 'if you have a Carl Kaysen at the White House.' Substitute for the name Kaysen the name Bundy." Rusk, it was said with condescension, actually liked to attend meetings. It was a point of pride at the White House not to hold meetings. Sorensen boasts: "Not one staff meeting was ever held, with or without the President." The few meetings the President had to call were shams: "He never altered his view that any meeting larger than necessary was less flexible, less secret and less hard-hitting. . . . No decisions of importance were made at Kennedy's Cabinet meetings and few subjects of importance, particularly in foreign affairs, were ever seriously discussed. The Cabinet as a body was convened largely as a symbol, to be informed, not consulted."

Kennedy's men felt they had broken the logjam caused by Eisenhower's committee approach to government. Sorensen describes his leader's attitude this way:

He ignored Eisenhower's farewell recommendation to create a First Secretary of the Government to oversee all foreign affairs agencies. He abandoned the practice of the Cabinet's and the National Security Council's making group decisions like corporate boards of directors. He abolished the practice of White House staff meetings and weekly Cabinet meetings. He abolished the pyramid structure of the White House staff, the Assistant President–Sherman-Adams-type job, the Staff Secretary, the Cabinet Secretary, the NSC Planning Board and the Operations Coordinating Board, which imposed, in his view, needless paperwork and machinery between the President and his responsible officers. He abolished several dozen interdepartmental committees which specialized in group recommendations on outmoded problems. He paid little attention to organization charts and chains of command which diluted and distributed his authority. He was not interested in unanimous committee recommendations which stifled alternatives to find the lowest common denominator of compromise.

The Kennedy teams lived on the move, calling signals to each other in the thick of the action — as Sorensen put it, like basketball players developing plays while the game moved on; not, like Eisenhower's people, withdrawing into football huddles after every play. In his 1963 book on Kennedy, Hugh Sidey celebrated the escape from Eisenhower: "John Kennedy, it is clear, recaptured all the power and more which Dwight Eisenhower ladled out to his Cabinet officers. In fact, Kennedy in the first weeks nearly put the Cabinet on the shelf as far as being a force in policy matters, and he rarely bothered to dust it off. His government became a government by function, not by organizational chart."

If Kennedy thought the State Department was not his to be used, but an alien thing to be tamed, he was bound to feel the same way about the Defense Department. It, after all, bore much of the blame for letting a missile gap develop. Eisenhower had won election with a promise that he would go to Korea. Kennedy had promised, in effect, that he would go to the Pentagon — and he did so in the person of Robert McNamara. A product of the Harvard Business School, McNamara had been part of a team that planned the expansion of the Air Force during World War II, a team (known as the Whiz Kids) that went intact to the Ford Motor Company after the war. McNamara had just become the president of Ford (the first one not to bear the family name) when Kennedy called him to Washington. This intellectual-as-manager would assert civilian control over a Pentagon in love with the giant implements of massive retaliation. And, having done that, he would be called on for advice in every area of government. Sorensen describes the man's extraordinary impact on the President:

> The Secretary of Defense, Robert McNamara, was clearly the star and the strong man among the newcomers in the Kennedy team. His own staff and subordinates ranked with Bob Kennedy's and Douglas Dillon's as the best in Washington and possibly in history. . . . In eleven years with Kennedy I never saw him develop admiration and personal regard for another man as quickly as he did with Robert McNamara, enabling the McNamaras to be excepted

from the general Kennedy rule of keeping official and social friendships separate.

Kennedy's successor in the presidency would be equally impressed by
McNamara's brains and discipline. For years, intelligent men re-
mained convinced that the Vietnam war could be won, because
McNamara told them so, and McNamara always delivered.

A President who treated his own executive branch as something
to be raided, prodded, or ignored was bound to deal with Congress
as an adversary. Kennedy's own lackluster performance as a Representative and Senator derived in large part from his sense that real
power lay with the executive branch (if only a non-Eisenhower
would come along to energize it). Congress was, in his mind, the
epitome of government by committee. Its principal power was to
obstruct, to "deadlock" the system (as James MacGregor Burns argued in an influential book of the period). A strong President was
needed to use all his power against the recalcitrant legislative branch.

The President early decided to take on the committee system at its
strongest node, that obstacle to all legislation, "Judge" Howard
Smith's House Rules Committee. Kennedy packed the committee,
with Speaker Sam Rayburn's help, but this was a pyrrhic victory.
Schlesinger admits: "It was a close and bitter business, and the memory of the fight laid a restraining hand on the administration's
priorities for some time to come." This assertion of power had
drained power away — something that did not fit the Neustadt conception of power; but the lesson was lost on Kennedy.

Instead, Kennedy concluded that, if outright confrontation failed,
then circumvention of the process must be relied on — executive
orders instead of legislation, extensions of authority for the team
players, isolation of the less responsive parts of government. Let the
uncooperative agencies atrophy, while a few vigorous men took on
more and more general tasks. Sorensen describes the process: "It was
largely through the President's confidence in McNamara's competence that the Department of Defense began to play a far greater role
in areas in which other agencies were concerned: civil rights, defense,
space, intelligence, paramilitary operations, foreign aid and foreign
policy in general." A small band of likeminded men, in conferences
that were "flexible, secret, and hard-hitting," might save the sluggish

democracy despite itself. This "happy band of brothers" came straight from the pages of John Buchan. Kennedy's fascination with counterinsurgency in other countries is well known. More important is the extent to which he viewed his own administration as a raid of mobile "outsiders" on the settled government of America. He had assembled a hit-and-run team to cut through enemy resistance, go outside channels, forgo meetings, subvert committees, dismantle structures. Democracies need such strong (and often secret) leadership by an enlightened few pitted against the many dullards of the bureaucracy.

Kennedy had been encouraged by his father to despise professional diplomats. As Ambassador, Joseph Kennedy mocked the "striped-pants set," and carved his way to a controversial independence in England — hoping to save his country from war, to shock those at home with the hard facts of England's demise. The tough realism of that posture, the cutting through "crap," came naturally to the man who was a loner in the business world, carrying out a series of raids, at odds with his fellow entrepreneurs' corporate routines. Both father and son believed in inspired amateurs, in the gentlemen saviors of their country.

As President, Kennedy conveyed his lack of respect for the State Department in many ways, once calling it "a bowl of jelly." Schlesinger, by 1978, had come to see some flaws in this contemptuous attitude:

> The Kennedys had a romantic view of the possibilities of diplomacy. They wanted to replace protocol-minded, striped-pants officials by reform-minded missionaries of democracy who mixed with the people, spoke the native dialects, ate the food, and involved themselves in local struggles against ignorance and want. This view had its most genial expression in the Peace Corps, its most corrupt in the mystique of counterinsurgency. The gospel of activism became the New Frontier's challenge to the cautious, painstaking, spectatorial methods of the old diplomacy.

Abroad, counterinsurgency meant that a regime like Diem's could not fight off insurgents alone; it was too mired in the past, too crippled by old compromises with the colonial power. But a team without such ties, a fresh force with clean hands, could purge and reform the administration while propping it up. It could fend off insurgents *and* alter the Vietnamese establishment. The assignment at home was not very different. In order to get the country "moving again," make it clean and tough enough to confront the Russians, crisis teams would have to save the bureaucracy from itself, take over its duties, force it to join the successful operation of the outsiders. Henry Fairlie rightly called this a vision of "guerrilla government."

That ideal gives its real meaning to a term that became popular in and around the Kennedy presidency. James David Barber claims that *charisma* was "a much pawed-over concept Kennedy brought back to clarity." But that was hardly the case. Kennedy's admirers stretched and cheapened the sociological term adopted, half a century earlier, by Max Weber. Yet there was an unnoticed justice in the application of this word to the New Frontier. Weber distinguished three kinds of authority — traditional, relying on the inertia of sacred custom; legal, based on contractual ties; and charismatic, based on the special gifts of a single ruler. Charismatic leadership is transitory — the "grace" is attached to one person, who must constantly revalidate it in action ("existentially," according to the sixties jargon). It serves, amid the collapse of order or old ways, to bind together a new effort — the embodiment of a cause in George Washington or Mao Zedong. The founders of states, or of religious orders (a favorite Weber illustration), have to exert *personal* authority, since they have no preexisting majesty of office or sanction of law to draw upon.

In Kennedy's case, personalized leadership consciously distanced itself from the "traditional" father-king role of Eisenhower and the "legal" order of bureaucratic committees. Power came from Kennedy's person, according to Schlesinger, which had to be displayed, deployed, brought to bear. His "cool" was his program, style and vigor his credentials. Kennedy's term in office was later studied as just one more stage in the development of an Imperial Presidency. But his own followers saw it as a radical break with the institutional passivity of the post-Roosevelt presidency. They were returning to the last President who had been charismatic in Weber's sense. Franklin Roosevelt, given special powers to deal with the crisis of the Depression, broke free of tradition, defied the two-term rule, took on himself the sacred mantle of war leader, and made policy by sheer personal fiat. Aspiring to a Rooseveltian presidency, Kennedy hoped, without benefit of depression or war, to assume emergency powers and assert a ruling charisma. Thus point after point in Reinhard Bendix's analysis of Weber's concept has its application to the New Frontier (a term which was itself intended to cut the new administration free of settled ways). In *Max Weber: An Intellectual Portrait,* Bendix articulates the different aspects of charismatic authority.

1. Charismatic leadership is "the product of crisis and enthusiasm"; it has an "emergency character." The pressure of danger makes followers look to the single hero who is fearless and can save them. Accounts by New Frontiersmen make it sound as if the Kennedy presidency was just one crisis-meeting after another. Some of these crises were undoubtedly posed by circumstances beyond the team's control. But there was a tendency to court new crises (e.g., the U.S. Steel confrontation) or sharpen them once they occurred (e.g., the imposition of a deadline for removing the Cuban missiles). Kennedy tried to instill a sense of crisis during his campaign by exaggerating the slim (and, it turned out, erroneous) evidence of a "missile gap" that put America in imminent danger of destruction.

Sorensen's account of the administration is gleefully crisis-oriented. He admiringly counts sixteen of them in Kennedy's first eight months as President. The atmosphere is perfectly caught by Halberstam: Kennedy bequeathed to Johnson "crisis-mentality men, men who delighted in the great international crisis because it centered the action right there in the White House — the meetings, the decisions, the tensions, the power, *they* were movers and activists, and this was what they had come to Washington for, to meet these challenges." Kennedy had come to office sounding the alarm over a missile-gap crisis — as he had sounded the alarm in 1940 over England's airplane-gap crisis at the beginning of World War II. (A. J. P. Taylor has demonstrated that the first gap was no more real than the later one.) In his inaugural address he asked the nation to welcome "the role of defending freedom at its maximum hour of danger." In his first State of the Union address he said: "Before my term has ended we shall have to test again whether a nation organized and governed such as ours can endure. The outcome is by no means certain." To convey a sense of crisis over Cuba, he risked alerting Castro to the Bay of Pigs invasion by saying, in a TV interview just before the landing: "If we don't move now, Mr. Castro may become a much greater danger than he is now." He tried to "jolt the democracy" (as his 1940 book recommended) by calling up the spectre of a civil-defense gap. Sorensen admits that Kennedy was just trying to lend urgency to the Berlin crisis: "The President's aim was to bestir a still slumbering public; and he succeeded beyond his own expectations and desire." Debate over who would be saved in the bomb shelters became hysterical, with talk of shooting neighbors who tried to crowd in. "The confusion and panic were aggravated by the Kennedy administration's lack of a comprehensive shelter program, a clear-cut shelter policy or even an authoritative voice placing the whole program in perspective." Kennedy meant to frighten people a little so they would flock toward him. Since the charismatic leader's special powers grow from special dangers, the two feed on each other. For some crises to be overcome, they must first be created.

2. "The charismatic leader is always a radical who challenges established practice by going to 'the root of the matter.' He dominates men by virtue of qualities inaccessible to others and incompatible with the rules of thought and action that govern everyday life." Many people have noticed the way Kennedy, without being radical himself, seemed to inspire a wave of radical action, from the freedom rides to the Free Speech movement. He sent out young people in the Peace Corps to be missionaries for American values; but many seemed to catch the values of the countries they went to. This was not his intent; but the very act of sending them out was radicalizing — it was adventurous, and it reflected the contemptuous attitude Kennedy's people had for older means of diplomatic suasion and propaganda. Insofar as the charismatic leader asserts an entirely personal authority, he *delegitimates* the traditional and legal authorities. Attempting to prop up the Saigon regime, Kennedy's Vietnamese ambassadors and advisers actually called its slim claims further into question. And the same was true, in less degree, of the bureaus and agencies at home. While deferring to the FBI himself, Robert Kennedy made clear to others that it could not be relied on in the protection of civil rights workers. While expressing formal regard for "Secretary Rusk" (never, even in private, was it "Dean"), the President made clear his slight regard for the State Department.

By relying on a few "generalists" Kennedy signaled the lack of authority in most branches of his own administration.

Charismatic authority is constructive only when it builds order from chaos. When it tries to supersede continuing forms of authority, it destabilizes despite itself. The more insistent became Kennedy's personal call to follow him, the less compelling was any order that did not issue directly from him. The nontransferability of such personal authority was evident in the refusal of many Kennedy followers to treat President Johnson as fully legitimate. Johnson's authority came from procedures and legal precedent, not from the personal charisma of his predecessor.

3. Charismatic leadership works through "a loose organizational structure." Criticism of Eisenhower's "structures" was endlessly repeated among Kennedy's followers. When authority flows from a *person,* that authority cannot be delegated. The magic touch must be bestowed by the ruler himself. He must go out among the people, lead the action. Everything must be referred to him, decided by him, must bear his mark, embody his style. He must be in constant touch with everything that goes on. As Hugh Sidey wrote of Kennedy: "He wanted all the lines to lead to the White House, he wanted to be the single nerve center." And when he cannot act personally, he must do so through a personal emissary created ad hoc, not through official, impersonal machinery.

4. Thus, though the organizational structure of charismatic leadership is loose, it calls up "disciples, chosen for their qualifications, who constitute a charismatic aristocracy within the wider group of followers." The power of these aristocrats does not come from their office but from their proximity to the person of the ruler. Members of his family are especially valued carriers of the charisma. The creation of "honorary Kennedys" was thus an instrument of rule, not only in the Justice Department but in the White House itself. In order to speak for the "graced" ruler one must, in some measure, *be* the ruler, be merged in his auriole. Sorensen rejoiced in being thought of as Kennedy's alter ego or second self, and many other people tried to win that distinction.

5. In economic as in other ways, charismatic leadership does not rest on settled modes, but prefers "risky financial transactions. . . . Such economic activities are worlds apart from the methodical man-

agement of a large-scale corporation, in which success depends upon professional competence and an everyday steadiness in the conduct of affairs that is incompatible with the indispensability of any individual and the sporadic character of very risky transactions." Though the nation's economy was less porous to Kennedy's guerrilla raids than was the bureaucracy, his model for political action was the jolly piratical creed of his predator father. When the Cubans captured at the Bay of Pigs needed ransom money, the Attorney General went outside governmental channels, used family charisma for remedial action. He did the same thing, as Senator, in setting up his own social program for Bedford Stuyvesant. These "raids" for political action and advantage were privately financed — like the Kennedy campaign itself, for which the elder Kennedy bought his son his very own airplane, the *Caroline.* And once in office, that son's foreign moves took on "the sporadic character of very risky transactions."

When John Kennedy reached the White House, his father retired gracefully into the background. Schlesinger and others saw in this a demonstration that all fears of his father's influence were groundless. But the father did not have to speak or be present to have an effect on the President. Joseph Kennedy had labored to create a separate world for his family, an aristocracy floating free of lesser ties, where image and power would be controllable, resources instantly mobilizable for the family's advantage. John Kennedy, by his personalization of the authority of the President, simply drew up the United States government — or as much of it as could be lifted — into that encapsulated world of charmed Kennedy power, of charisma.

14

Enjoy! Enjoy!

[Theodore White observes] his rule that there is something improper about disliking a politician.

— MURRAY KEMPTON

THE PRESIDENCY OF DWIGHT EISENHOWER was such an ordeal for American liberals because they had been excited by the prospect of having Adlai Stevenson in office. Stevenson first promised intellectuals the sense of belonging that they came to experience, at last, with Kennedy. In fact, it was a profound mystery to most intellectuals that the American people had been able to reject their hero in 1952. This so disillusioned Murray Kempton that he swore never to vote again in a presidential election. The idea that the "best man" could win in that forum was dashed forever in the anguish of Adlai's loss. John Kenneth Galbraith writes of that election: "It would be hard for the young to understand not only our surprise but our shock at the outcome . . . we learned that the natural order had come to an end."

Richard Neustadt felt the shock, and noticed the even greater scandal — that some *intellectuals* supported Eisenhower:

> The striking thing about our national elections in the Fifties was not Eisenhower's personal popularity; it was the genuine approval of his candidacy by informed Americans whom [sic] one might have supposed would know better. . . . To place him in the White House without losing him as hero seems both reasonable and prudent on the part of average citizens, no matter what their general

view of politics or Presidents. The same thing can be said of the Republican professionals who managed Eisenhower's nomination in 1952; their action appears reasonable and prudent in *their* terms. They twice had tried a leading politician [Dewey] as their candidate; this time they wanted most of all to win. But when it comes to journalists, and government officials, and business leaders, and professors, who joined in the parade or urged it on, one deals with a phenomenon decidedly less reasonable.... When one finds attitudes of this sort in the circle of articulate observers one wonders at the meaning for American society.

For such people, the choice of Eisenhower over Stevenson was an affront to reason sufficient to shake one's faith in democracy. If the people could be so manifestly wrong, maybe they were incapable of self-government after all. McCarthyism had been scary enough — for a while the Senator from Wisconsin had commanded majority support in the polls. But the passing sway of a demagogue could be weathered. Eisenhower posed a more serious problem. He was not a demagogue, in the Neustadt view of things; just a dope. But dopes, if they last in government, may be even more serious threats to democratic values than impassioned fanatics who quickly burn themselves out. Dopes not only have personal durability; under their prolonged sway the nation can lapse into narcolepsy, let all its problems breed in the darkness, storing up trouble.

For John Kennedy, who had taken his view of democracy from John Buchan, the choice of Eisenhower was no mystery. He knew, and had written in *Why England Slept,* that democracies like to take the easy way, to avoid looking at problems until it is too late. That is why they need strong leaders, willing to administer timely jolts to the people as a form of therapy. But this did not fit well with an older American liberalism, which feared power and trusted the people — the liberalism for which Adlai Stevenson spoke when he asked that the "cup" of power pass him by. Friends of Kennedy laughed at the mere idea of his asking to be spared the cup of power.

What Neustadt's book signified was the willingness of American liberals to confess that the older liberalism could not cope, it must be jettisoned. There should be an "end of ideology" in the name of "existential" leaders — Schlesinger instanced Hemingway and Camus — for whom "authenticity" in action was the test, a sense of one's own will to deal with life. Neustadt's Roosevelt was seen through such postwar filters of existential leadership. He was a manipulative man, a tough pragmatist experimenting, one who did not go by the rules but imposed his will. There would be no more talk of fearing power. The brave man must take up power as a joyful encounter with reality. The failure to do that was, in fact, Eisenhower's greatest flaw:

> Eisenhower also lacked Roosevelt's enjoyment. At least until his seventh year the politics of power in the Presidency never was his sport; not recreation for him; certainly not fun. . . . What kept experience from sharpening his sense of power and his taste for it? . . . He wanted to be arbiter, not master. His love was not for power but for duty.

The mood of the time can be seen in the fact that the very terms Neustadt uses to criticize Eisenhower would once have been terms of praise. And that fact becomes more interesting when we realize that every criticism directed at Eisenhower could be doubled upon Adlai Stevenson. Stevenson was even *less* the jolly warrior, the master manipulator, the seizer and user of power. Truman had called him a "Hamlet." The Kennedy people learned to despise him for wanting things he would not openly work to win. They mistreated him and he came back for more. In moving from Stevenson to Kennedy, liberals had not — as Eleanor Roosevelt feared — given up their principles; they had finally seen the solution to the Eisenhower problem. They had gone back to the true sense of power exemplified by Mrs. Roosevelt's husband.

Neustadt's was just the first in a series of books that told Presidents they must, above all else, love power and seek it with unbounded gusto. The theme of them all was "Enjoy! Enjoy!" Neustadt led off:

> Roosevelt's methods were the product of his insights, his incentive and his confidence. No President in this century has had a sharper sense of personal power, a sense of what it is and where it comes from; none has had more hunger for it, few have had more use for it, and only one or two could match his faith in his own competence to use it. Perception and desire and self-confidence, combined,

produced their own reward. No modern President has been more nearly master in the White House. Roosevelt had a love affair with power in that place. It was an early romance and it lasted all his life.... For Roosevelt, this was fun.

From now on, having fun in the White House would be a presidential task. It was his duty not to be merely dutiful. Lack of enjoyment was of itself a disqualification for office. Vigor can emanate only from the President's own appetite for the life of power: "The more determinedly a President seeks power, the more he will be likely to bring vigor to his clerkship. As he does so he contributes to the energy of government." A long literature of common sense had taught men to suspect power and the men who thirst for it. Now that literature would be turned on its head. The man who is suspect is the one who shows any suspicion over power and its uses. The old view had been discredited in the deadening Eisenhower days: "His virtue was supposed to be that he was above politics, and disenchantment with him rarely seems a disenchantment with this odd criterion. Instead it is all Eisenhower's fault that he is not what temperament and training never equipped him to be."

Theodore White, in his first *Making of the President* volume, took up the theme of power as a beneficial intoxicant:

> [Theodore and Franklin Roosevelt] not only understood the *use* of power; they knew the *enjoyment* of power, too. And that is the important thing. Whether a man is burned by power or enjoys power, whether he is trapped by responsibility or made free by it; whether he is moved by other people and outer forces or moves them — this is the essence of leadership. John F. Kennedy had known much of the quality of leadership in American life long before he became President in 1960 — the legends, delights, songs, deals and reach of power.

Needless to say, the official Kennedy literature is drearily joyful in repeating how much fun Kennedy had being President. Schlesinger sang along: "Not since Franklin Roosevelt had there been a President who so plainly delighted in innovation and leadership." Sorensen too: "John F. Kennedy was a happy president.... He liked the job, he thrived on its pressures.

Since it was a President's duty to seek all the power he could get, and our duty to choose men with this appetite, it was clearly our duty to relinquish the power — to be as glad that he seized it as he was in the act of seizure. He ennobled us by instilling awe for his office. Sorensen put this creation of awe among the great human achievements of all time:

> One of John Kennedy's most important contributions to the human spirit was his concept of the office of the Presidency. His philosophy of government was keyed to power, not as a matter of personal ambition but of national obligation; the primacy of the White House within the Executive Branch and of the Executive Branch within the Federal Government, the leadership of the Federal Government within the United States and of the United States within the community of nations.

The founders of this nation would have been surprised to hear that executive supremacy is a noble cause; and other nations might wonder at the elevation of American power over all other countries as a contribution to the human spirit. But I suppose we are lucky Sorensen did not make his pyramid of power — America over all, the executive over America, the President over the executive — culminate in the title he celebrated while writing Kennedy's campaign speeches: the Commander-in-Chief. During the Watergate days, Alexander Haig was mocked for telling William Ruckelshaus, in the Special Prosecutor's office, that his Commander-in-Chief had given him an order. The President is the Commander-in-Chief of the Armed Forces, not of the citizenry at large. But in his 1960 campaign Kennedy assured us that the American people yearn for leadership: "They want to know what is needed — they want to be led by the Commander-in-Chief." And the President was not only the Commander-in-Chief of all American people but of the whole free world — he must be "a man capable of acting as the Commander-in-Chief of the grand alliance." Hugh Sidey significantly called his chapter on counterinsurgent warfare in other people's countries "Commander in Chief." Needless to say, the Constitution did not set up military titles for foreigners to obey. But Kennedy-Sorensen was convinced that all the world's free people yearned for a leader who enjoyed the widest powers he could lay claim to. Thus was "the human spirit" itself vindicated.

The new awe for the presidential role rubbed off on the President's very working space:

> The whole White House crackled with excitement under John Kennedy, but the soundproof oval office, the very center and stimulant of all the action, symbolized his own peace of mind. The tall French windows opened onto the completely renovated flower garden of which he was inordinately proud. Even on gloomy days the light pouring in through those windows on the blue rug and freshly painted cream-colored walls bathed his ash splint rocking chair and two beige couches, brought in for more friendly talks, in a quiet glow.

Breathless description of that office became a set piece in post-Kennedy hymns to the presidency. In his later book, *The Kennedy Legacy,* Sorensen said that the Nixon people first began to use capital letters for the Oval Office. He forgot Theodore White's 1961 book:

> But the exercise of the President's power must be framed by reason, by the analysis of reality as it can only be seen from the President's desk — and by leading other men to see this reality as he alone perceives it. A hush, an entirely personal hush, surrounds this kind of power, and the hush is deepest in the Oval Office of the West Wing of the White House, where the President, however many his advisers, must sit alone. The Oval Office, thirty-five feet long by twenty-eight feet, four inches wide, is almost too peaceful and luminous a place to echo to the ominous concerns that weigh upon the man who occupies it. Its great French windows, eleven and a half feet high, flood it with light, so that even on somber days it is never dark. From the south windows the President can, in leafless winter, see through the trees all the way to the Washington Monument and beyond; he can, by craning, see west to the Memorial where Lincoln broods. The three windows on the east open out on the lawn, on the rose garden and the brilliance of flowers in spring and summer; when he chooses the President can enter or leave the Oval Office by one of these east windows, which opens as a door, going to or from his private dwelling place in the heart of the White House. The tones of the room are as perfect as its proportions. The

gray green expanse of carpeting, into which is woven the Great Seal of the United States, is keyed to the same pastel tonality as the cream-beige walls and the beige drapery. The room changes somewhat from President to President, as it has changed from Eisenhower to Kennedy. Where in Eisenhower's time the room possessed an uncluttered, almost overpowering openness as one approached the seven-foot, four-inch dark walnut desk at which Eisenhower (as all other Presidents since 1902) sat, it has been softened now with two new curving cream-white sofas before the fireplace that invite the visitor to a respectful closeness with the President.

There is more — much more — of the description; pages more. It culminates at the principal cult object within the shrine, the Presidential Telephone: "The telephone is silent — it rings with few or no incoming messages, it quivers, generally, only as he exerts his will through it."

Hugh Sidey, in his 1963 book on John Kennedy, called the last chapter "The Oval Office":

> There was an awesome presence in that Oval Chamber which was then quiet, cool, sunlit — the very heart of this nation's meaning, the very core of freedom, thirty-five feet long by twenty-eight feet, four inches wide. To an outsider the feeling of awe is always there — any man who walks into that office senses it. I wondered if the President ever got used to it, and then I decided that he never does either.

Earlier Sidey had described it as "the biggest office in the world," and in his book on President Ford he would call it "the epicenter of power." But the prize for bedazzlement by the room goes to John Hersey, in the book he wrote about his old Yale football coach, Gerald Ford:

> This room was an egg of light. I had seen that each person who came into it was lit up in two senses: bathed in brightness and a bit high. I had clearly seen each face, to the very pores, in a flood of indirect candlepower that rained down from a pure-white ceiling onto the curving off-white walls and pale-yellow rug and bright

furnishings in shades of gold, green, and salmon. But there were also dazzling parabolas of power here; authority seemed to be diffused as an aspect of the artificial light in the room, and each person who came into this heady glow seemed to be rendered ever so slightly tipsy in it and by it — people familiar with the room far less so, of course, than first-time visitors, some of whom visibly goggled and staggered and held on tight as they made their appeals; but even the old hands, even the President's closest friends, and even the President himself, sitting in a bundle of light behind the desk of the chief, seemed to me to take on a barely perceptible extra shine in the ambiguous radiant energy that filled the room.

Hersey takes us on tour, as others have, but spares us the dimensions-down-to-inches. He likes the furniture, especially a grandfather clock whose "forceful ticking inexorably marked the moments of history — and of nonhistory — in this room of light." The office itself was now a superhuman dwelling place, as Theodore White made embarrassingly clear in his genuflections at the shrine: "For the laws of Congress cannot define, nor can custom anticipate, the unknown — and this is where the great Presidents must live, *observant of the law yet beyond the law, Chief Executive and High Priest of American life at once.*" (Italics added)

Charisma, in the Weberian sense, is not transferable — even to members of the "graced" leader's own family. But later Presidents would be measured by the expectations Kennedy raised. He did not so much elevate the office as cripple those who held it after him. His legend has haunted them; his light has cast them in shadow. For the cult of power launched by Neustadt continued into the seventies. The "in" book on the presidency during that decade was James David Barber's *Presidential Character* (1972); and no work better illustrates how the fads of an academician's graduate school days remain his dogmas in later life. His first scholarly work is the outgrowth of those fads, and he is inclined to defend that work against later evidence. Barber tests presidential character entirely by Neustadt's norms, and especially by the capacity to *enjoy* the exercise of power. The subchapter on Roosevelt's character is titled, "Franklin's Growth to Joy in Work." We are told that his upbringing gave him the self-confidence that led to a "hunger for results." This makes for contrast with Eisenhower and Coolidge, who are "guardians of the proper system," working through channels. Barber's Eisenhower fails, like Neustadt's, by the dutiful rather than joyful exercise of power: "Why then did Eisenhower bother to become President? Why did he answer those phone calls on the golf links [those symbolic golf links]? Because he thought he ought to. He was a sucker for duty, and he always had been. Dutiful sentiments which would sound false coming from most political leaders ring true from Eisenhower." The Coolidge-Eisenhower type is not result-oriented: "Its political weakness is its inability to produce, though it may contribute by preventing." Nonetheless the nation's "unfinished business" accumulates under this type. So: "Eventually some leader ready to shove as well as to stand fast, someone who enjoys the great game of politics, will have to pick up the pieces."

Another leftover of the sixties was Arthur Schlesinger's claim that John Kennedy was a late developer, but one who showed great capacity for growth through experience, making him an "existential" leader who learned by doing. All these notes are struck in the Barber sections on Kennedy. The Roosevelt-Kennedy type has a "sense of the self as developing, demonstrated externally in evidence of openness, experiment, flexibility, and growth." Though Kennedy did not develop during his congressional years, his response to the Bay of Pigs and the missile crisis showed that he was capable of growth in office. "Along the way he discovered what he believed." He demonstrated "the capacity to incorporate experience." Thus "the inner confidence he had acquired as a youth freed him to grow as President, through one crisis after another, to a grasp of the full potentialities of the office." Naturally, those potentialities involved a sense of enjoyment in power, one radiated to others: "Jack left people feeling they could do better and enjoy it. . . . He found Earth an exciting place to live, and said so. His emphasis on arousing democracy to action is obvious from 'Ask not. . . .' "

Barber's addition to the Neustadt-Schlesinger cult of enjoyed power was the set of four categories he set up for "typing" modern Presidents. This was meant to be a predictive tool, though Barber's later use of it for that purpose has been wrong when not hedged. Jimmy Carter read the Barber book on the way to the presidency, and felt he could be the type implicitly praised throughout, the "active-positive" Roosevelt-Kennedy type; and Barber gave cautious support to that expectation. Jody Powell, Carter's press secretary, dutifully reported that the President enjoyed his time in the White House.

Barber does not say where he picked up his four categories. One would think his scientific claims called for methodological explicitness. But he just posits the types by fiat. True, one of the "baselines," as he calls it, was almost a given at the time he wrote:

> The second baseline is positive-negative effect toward one's activity — that is, how he feels about what he does. Relatively speaking, does he seem to experience his political life as happy or sad, enjoyable or discouraging, positive or negative in its main effect. The feeling I am after here is not grim satisfaction in a job well done, not some philosophical conclusion. The idea is this: is he someone who, on the surfaces we can see, gives forth the feeling that he has fun in political life?

At this point, presumably by some mixing of his file cards, Barber attributes to Henry Stimson the quote I gave above on page 178 from Theodore White, on the enjoyment of power as the test of a leader. Aside from that mixup, Barber's "baseline" is pure Neustadtism.

Barber might have graded all Presidents along this single line, as a continuum; in fact, he ends up doing that. But he has methodological aspirations that require the creation of separate boxes, so this baseline must be intersected at right angles with another, the "active-passive" one that grades a man on his energy or lack of it, depending on his "stance toward environment." It might seem that the two things run parallel rather than at right angles. After all, the enjoyment of power and the exercise of it are naturally concomitant; and one who dislikes it will not be active in using it. But the actual cases Barber discusses suggest that he is distinguishing self-image from reciprocal expectations of others. That is made clear in the psychobiographical episodes Barber uses — which, in turn, reveal that another sixties fad has been taken over for pseudo-scientific exploitation. Positive or negative attitude toward oneself, positive-negative attitude toward one's environment — what are they but the two basic attitudes, yielding four "life positions," of Transactional Analysis as that was popularized in Eric Berne's *Games People Play*

(1964) and Thomas Harris's *I'm OK — You're OK* (1967). Though Barber pretends not to be judgmental in ranking his four types, he clearly sees them in the order of preference set by Berne and Harris. The person who "feels good about himself and others" is the adult. The other types are deficient.

Harris's "I'm Not OK — You're OK" is the child's world, of low self-esteem and high regard for others. In Barber that becomes the active-negative presidency of Richard Nixon or Lyndon Johnson, where there is active striving to win approval, but the very striving tends to defeat its object: "Active-negative types pour energy into the political system, but it is an energy distorted from within."

Harris's "I'm Not OK — You're Not OK" is the adolescent's disillusioned state, tending toward withdrawal if not autism. This becomes Barber's passive-negative (or Coolidge-Eisenhower) type, which "does little in politics and enjoys it less" because of "low self-esteem based on a sense of uselessness." Presidents of this type tend "to withdraw, to escape from the conflict and uncertainty of politics by emphasizing vague principles (especially prohibitions) and procedural arrangements" — all those damn Eisenhower *committees.*

Harris's "I'm OK — You're Not OK" is the rebellious adolescent stage tending toward crime. Whom could Barber put here? Not Richard Nixon, who committed crimes in office — he has already been slotted as a childish "active-negative." Actually, no Presidents really fit this slot, so Barber pulls a fast one on us, tacitly redefining his norms rather than spoil the quadripartite symmetry of his scheme. He puts Taft and Harding in this category because they had "low self-esteem (on grounds of being unlovable, unattractive)." That should make them *negative* types, not positive — but he introduces a second note to keep them from slipping over to keep company with Eisenhower and Coolidge. He says they have a "superficial optimism" that somehow survives the low self-image. In other words, they have high expectation of others — which should, by parallel with the other types, put them in the active as well as the positive category! They are being forced into the mold, to keep the mold intact.

Harris's "I'm OK — You're OK" is the healthy adult world in which people joyfully take up "the wager of action." That obviously is Barber's ideal — the Roosevelt-Kennedy "active-positive" presidency combining "high self-esteem and relative success in relating to the environment." The whole rickety structure was put together to give a quasi-systematic justification for the Neustadt presidency: "The man shows an orientation toward productiveness as a value and ability to use his styles flexibly, adaptively, suiting the dance to the music. He sees himself as developing over time toward relatively well defined personal goals — growing toward his image of himself as he might yet be."

What is consistent in Barber's analysis comes from the Neustadt continuum. What is inconsistent comes from the Berne-Harris categories. Even Neustadt, in a later edition of his *Presidential Power,* finds it useless to consider Johnson and Nixon along with Wilson and Hoover as exemplars of a single type: "I admire but am doubtful of a scheme that crowds these four into a single square." He would doubt more, probably, if he reflected that Barber also put John Adams in that square. The differences are so much more important than the similarities that the grid becomes distortive, even if one assumes that Barber has "correctly" assigned people by his own norms. Yet even that assumption is dubious. Barber has clearly read the biographical evidence with a bias toward "typing" people. Intimates of Dwight Eisenhower would be amused to learn he had a low self-esteem; yet that is what is called for, if he is to fit Barber's purposes, so that is what he acquires. The man condemned for being dutiful is given the duty of fitting in. He might comfort himself with the fact that he shares room in this low category with that other President who lacked self-esteem, George Washington.

All this might be dismissed as games academics play, except for the fact that Barber's book was taken fully as seriously as Neustadt's — testimony to an intellectual need for the glorification of Kennedy (and power) at the expense of both Eisenhower *and Stevenson.* What Stevenson lacked was the "balls" (in Joseph Alsop's words) to shake the nation out of Eisenhower's lethargic grip. It was not enough for Neustadt's liberals to be liberal. They had to be liberals in love with power. To suspect power was to doubt oneself; and self-doubt reduced a man to Adlai helplessness.

Barber's book is just one vivid example of the way the Kennedy appetite for power was used to grade all subsequent Presidents, none of whom has earned the "A" rating of active-positive. A contributing reason for their failure may be the very establishment of such a grading system.

15

Delegitimation

The White House is small, but if you're not at the center it seems enormous. You get the feeling that there are all sorts of meetings going on without you, all sorts of people clustered in small groups, whispering, always whispering.

— LBJ TO DORIS KEARNS

"CAMELOT" ENDED in November of 1963. But its effects were just beginning to be felt. The Kennedys have been a presence in the White House ever since, bedeviling later occupants. Charisma, the uniquely *personal* power, delegitimates *institutions*. Rule by dazzlement cannot be succeeded by mere constitutional procedure. Reinhard Bendix states the problem: "Such a transformation from charismatic leadership to traditional domination occurs most frequently when the problem of succession must be solved. In a strict sense that problem is insoluble, for charisma is an inimitable quality that some higher power is believed to have bestowed upon one person. Consequently a successor cannot be chosen at all. Instead, the followers wait in the hope that another leader will appear who will manifest his own charismatic qualification."

No sooner was President Kennedy dead than his followers began to think and speak of a restoration. Lyndon Johnson was at best an interlude, at worst a usurper — intrusive, in any case; out of the proper order of things. The loonier Left tried to involve Johnson in the assassination itself. Others more vaguely blamed Texas for the President's death, and made the Texan successor guilty by association. For some, Johnson had murdered, if nothing else, a style. For

William Manchester, it was an abomination to have a vulgarian inside that magic egg of blinding whiteness, John Kennedy's Oval Office.

Awareness of these criticisms dulled the political instincts of Lyndon Johnson. A man as large as Paul Bunyan in the Senate had been pre-shrunk in a White House where Kennedy aides snickered at him. And even when he came to power, he could take no revenge upon them. In fact, he had to woo them, ask for their help, try to maintain a continuity of authority. And the more he tried to do this, the less could he be his own uninhibited self. His salty style had to be toned down. He tried to assume an alien dignity that came across, on TV, as acute discomfort. His insecurities were exposed by this situation, as by no other. George Ball rightly observed of him, ringed by Kennedy's Rhodes Scholars, that Johnson did not suffer from the lack of a good education but from his sense of lacking a good education.

The true wound inflicted on Johnson was not that the Kennedys considered him a usurper but that they came, in time, to make him feel like one himself. The Kennedys, he complained, would never let him rule in his own right. The more he deferred to them, the more they made his White House theirs, even before he had left it. This odd personal struggle between two shadow-presidents reached its climax in 1966 when Robert Kennedy returned from a Paris meeting with peace negotiators. A garbled leak had the Senator from New York carrying on negotiations for the United States. When Kennedy visited Johnson, he was attacked for releasing such a story. "I think the leak came from someone in your State Department," Robert told the President. "It's not my State Department," Johnson thundered at him. "It's *your* State Department."

Johnson was President in name only, or President only for taking blame. All the credit for his own initiatives in civil rights or the poverty program seemed to go to the Kennedys. He was President only over things that went wrong. No wonder he confided to Doris Kearns:

> It would have been hard on me to watch Bobby march to "Hail to the Chief," but I almost wish he had become President so the country could finally see a flesh-and-blood Kennedy grappling with the

daily work of the Presidency and all the inevitable disappointments, instead of their storybook image of great heroes who, because they were dead, could make anything anyone wanted happen.

From the very moment he took office, Robert Kennedy became an obsession to him. Eric Goldman said he spent more time and energy on "the Bobby threat" than on any other matter in those early days. He relived those days for Kearns:

> Every day as I opened the papers or turned on the television, there was something about Bobby Kennedy; there was some person or group talking about what a great Vice President he'd make. Somehow it just didn't seem fair. I'd given three years of loyal service to Jack Kennedy. During all that time I'd willingly stayed in the background; I knew that it was *his* Presidency, not mine. If I disagreed with him, I did it in private, not in public. And then Kennedy was killed and I became the custodian of his will, I became the President. But none of this seemed to register with Bobby Kennedy, who acted like he was the custodian of the Kennedy dream, some kind of rightful heir to the throne. It just didn't seem fair. I'd waited for my turn. Bobby should've waited for his. But he and the Kennedy people wanted it now.

Even the Kennedy people who worked energetically for Johnson remained suspect; and if they began to express any doubts about policy, that was taken as a defection to the Kennedy government in exile. Robert McNamara prosecuted the war in Vietnam more vigorously than anyone in Johnson's administration. But when he began to sense the futility of his own efforts, he could not make a case for withdrawal to Johnson. The President saw this as a Kennedy plot. The Kennedys had got him into this war; now they would tell him to get out; and he would look the fool either way:

> McNamara's problem was that he began to feel a division in his loyalties. He had always loved and admired the Kennedys; he was more their cup of tea, but he also admired and respected the Presidency. Then, when he came to work for me, I believed he developed a deep affection for me as well, not so deep as the one he held for the Kennedys but deep enough, combined with his feelings about

the office itself, to keep him completely loyal for three long years. Then he got surrounded by Paul Warnke, Adam Yarmolinsky, and Alain Enthoven; they excited him with their brilliance, all the same cup of tea, all came to the same conclusion after old man Galbraith. Then the Kennedys began pushing him harder and harder. Every day Bobby would call up McNamara, telling him that the war was terrible and immoral and that he had to leave.

The same course of suspicion darkened Johnson's relations with McGeorge Bundy, and George Ball, and Bill Moyers. His circle of power shrank, by voluntary withdrawal or suspicious expulsion. He became a man exposed, at odds with his own government, sensing enmity everywhere.

The impact of "Camelot" on what followed was profound; but I think it has often been misunderstood, or inadequately stated, because of the trivialization of the word "charisma" during the sixties. It is said that Johnson's problem was his lack of charisma as mere glamour, mere sophisticated ease of manner; that John Kennedy had created an appetite for such points of style and Johnson could not satisfy that yearning; that the New Frontier had inflated expectations of the presidential office in a way that enabled Johnson to launch ambitious programs without having the flair to bring them off. But if we take charisma in its sociological sense, of a *personal* rule pitted against traditional and legal procedures, Johnson was forced to take up a charismatic role. He could not rest in the office he held on such tenuous terms, in a government establishment he felt disloyal to him. He tried to use his Senate skills and a few cronies to conduct his own kind of "guerrilla government," defiant of Georgetown, the press, the bureaucracy. He reverted to Texas hyperbole and a personal war waged from his ranch as much as from the White House — "Son," as he told a military aide gesturing toward his presidential helicopter at an Army camp, "they are all my helicopters." *His* war, waged almost as much against its critics at home — even those in his own government — as against the far-off shadowy enemy. The real impact of Kennedy on his successors was not so much an inflation of the office they succeeded to, but the doomed way they imitated his attempt to rule *against* the government. Inheriting a delegitimated set of procedures, they were compelled to go outside the procedures too — further delegitimating the very office they held.

This was most apparent in the administration of Richard Nixon. Narrowly defeated by Kennedy in 1960, Nixon was mesmerized by Kennedys. Even during that first race, Nixon's attacks on Kennedy seemed half-envious, never contemptuous. Murray Kempton observed at the time: "Mr. Nixon is cursed by the illusion that he is playing dirty with his betters." Like Johnson, Nixon felt compelled to mimic where he could not scorn — the Nixon inaugural address was slavishly imitative of Kennedy's more successful one. Yet he also felt an urgency to defile what he aspired to. As soon as he was in the White House, Nixon acquired a team of "gumshoes" to smear his foes. Their first assignment, during Nixon's first summer in office, was Chappaquiddick. Tony Ulascewicz's team was dispatched to Martha's Vineyard, not as law enforcement officers, but to dig up further scandal for Nixon's private use. The same team followed Kennedy, questioned his associates, planned at one point seduction of putative "girl friends" who might be blackmailed to inform against him. It was the sordid beginning to all Nixon's later "dirty tricks" — the break-ins, the name-blackenings, all that scurrying in back alleys to bring down the shining Kennedy name. Charles Colson, who knew what would please his master, had Howard Hunt forge cables that would link Kennedy directly to the assassination of Ngo Dinh Diem. (Johnson, too, dwelt at times on the gruesomely satisfying thought that Kennedy might have assassinated another ruler just before his own assassination.) Nixon was at least as obsessed with Kennedys as Johnson had been.

And, like Johnson's, Nixon's admiring resentment of the Kennedys combined with earlier grievances against "the establishment" and various aspects of Washington. Nixon's service under Eisenhower had been a demeaning one. Respectable Republicans treated the Vice-President's "low road" tactics as a homeopathic medicine against McCarthyism's deadlier poisons. Washington circles were Nixon's feared enemies long before he reached the White House. Later, his defenders would say he resorted to private teams of lawbreakers because the official lawbreakers — the FBI, the CIA — had resisted his attempts to use them. But H. R. Haldeman hired private "investigators" just after the inauguration — long before there was a chance for the bureaucracy to oppose his master. Nonetheless, it is fitting that Haldeman — and brighter observers as well, like Nicholas von Hoffmann — should think the CIA, which overthrew foreign governments, overthrew Nixon's as well. He was governing *against* the government from the outset.

Nixon's inability to trust even his own government became a kind of blessing for the nation. He was brought down by his own drive to supplement the government's illegal taps and bugs, break-ins and smear operations. He felt more embattled in office than Johnson had, a counterinsurgent President distrusted by the establishment and under siege from the counterculture. He governed from a mental foxhole, with official enemies at his back as well as hostile "kids" out front. His attitude was expressed in the odd outburst he allowed himself when Charles Manson was on trial for the cult murder of Sharon Tate and others. Speaking extemporaneously in Denver, on the way back from his summer White House, Nixon denounced the press for glamorizing a mass murder, and contrasted this with the values in a John Wayne movie he had seen the night before (*Chisum*), where Wayne took the law into his own hands and rid the community of undesirables.

To be a hired gun for good, to ride in and rescue where there is no sheriff — that is the outsider's dream. But Nixon was the appointed sheriff when he reveled in that dream. And he was not talking of a man who "got away with" murder. Manson had been apprehended, and was standing trial as Nixon spoke. (Manson's lawyers moved for a mistrial when the President called their man guilty before his conviction.) Manson would be legally convicted. But that did not seem enough for Nixon. The hatred of the lawbreakers had not been expressed vigorously or directly enough by the press. The head of lawful government publicly entertained the desire for remedies outside the law, for a press lynching — the very thing sheriffs are supposed to prevent. (Earlier that summer, Nixon had spoken well of Lieutenant Calley, another mass murderer, because he was a lyncher of sorts, not a potential lynchee.)

Nixon fascinated the press and others by his ability to reveal his fantasy life so directly. At the time he launched the Cambodian invasion, he watched the movie *Patton* several times, but not to indulge vicarious bloodthirstiness. *Patton* was not about male aggression satisfied, but about the baffling of a good man's energies — and by Eisenhower! Nixon was not bracing himself with vicarious aggression, but with shared rejection. He was stiffening his spine with the surest medicines for it — resentment of his critics, and self-pity. Even as he wheeled vast forces of destruction to their work half a world away, he was the outsider, the despised one. The loyalty of his followers, their protectiveness, came from this vulnerability of the man hastening to hurt because he had been so deeply hurt himself. Nixon's was called an Imperial Presidency; but it was a backstairs presidency. He plotted against his own throne, and brought it down. Hating John Kennedy even more than Lyndon Johnson had, he felt even less worthy of that man's oval office, and carried on a personal guerrilla campaign against the traditional and legal governments of Washington.

Gerald Ford, it is true, did not seem obsessed with the golden family. But the acting president for foreign affairs during Ford's administration, Henry Kissinger, had been rejected by his Harvard peers of Camelot, and adopted many of Nixon's devices of secret government — tapping his own underlings, leaking, manipulating the press, governing *against* the State Department from the White House and by a purely personal reign when he went over to State. He believed in "back channels," and resented the bureaucracy.

Jimmy Carter ran more openly "against Washington" than any candidate before Ronald Reagan. The Hamilton Jordan memorandum of 1972, which planned the campaign of 1976, established Carter's basic theme: "Perhaps the strongest feeling in this country today is the general distrust of government and politicians at all levels." By riding that feeling into power, Carter confirmed and amplified it, denigrating the very power he had won. Arrived at the summit, he could not let himself be contaminated by close relations with the rest of his administration. Hoping to bestow decency on the presidential office from his own store of personal integrity, he forswore the trappings of office, and asked to be thought of as President *Carter* not *President* Carter. He was insistent on his personal concern, outrunning mere obligations of place. He encouraged people to think that one could be a good man only by keeping his personal characteristics daintily aloof from the dirtied center of power.

In fashioning a charismatic countergovernment, Carter — the student of James David Barber — absorbed the State Department not only into the White House but into his own person. Anwar Sadat and Menachim Begin were invited to Camp David, where the President shuttled back and forth between them, praying with each, assuring them he loved them. The Camp David Accords were hatched in his very own nest, under his warming breast. When Carter could not go to others in person, he sent surrogates, friends who would express his esteem — Andrew Young to African nations, Rosalynn Carter to speak Spanish to Latinos, Hamilton Jordan to meet with Omar Torrijos over the Panama Canal treaties or with Sadegh Ghobtzadeh over the Iranian hostages. Like other critics of the bureaucracy, Carter tended to *add* special envoys or experts to the "useless" machinery — a new office for Alfred Kahn to cope with inflation, a special Mideast mission for Sol Linowitz. And, all the while, distrust of official Washington led to disproportionate reliance on a "Georgia Mafia" — Charles Kirbo, Bertram Lance, Hamilton Jordan, Jody Powell — whose only credentials were their proximity to Carter and their total dedication to him.

Like other charismatic leaders, Carter found crisis necessary to enhance "emergency" powers. When he sank to a record low in public opinion polls during the summer of 1979, he withdrew into a ten-day retreat at Camp David, canceling speeches and summoning spiritual as well as political leaders to meetings shrouded in mystery. When he came down from the mountain, it was to proclaim a national affliction with "malaise," a moral and spiritual "crisis of confidence," for which the solution was announced: "We simply must have faith in each other." This meant: Have faith in me to lead you out of this newly discovered darkness. Carter reached for the emphases of the "active-positive" Roosevelt type in his speech of July 15: "And above all I will act . . . I will listen and I will act."

It didn't work. The machinery for cranking up the artificial crisis was too visible. Carter's real problem was too obviously his own slippage. The polls continued unfavorable, and Kennedy entered the race. But then national trouble became a political blessing. The capture of diplomats in Iran gave Carter a real crisis, one he nurtured for months, exploiting it all through the primary season, fashioning a "Rose Garden strategy" which kept him off the campaign trail tending a crisis too dangerous to be left alone for a single minute. If this mood could have been sustained for a whole year, Carter might have been reelected on the strength of it. But as urgency was dissipated, month after month, so were Carter's powers.

Like other successors to John Kennedy, Carter fashioned his charismatic presidency as a fearful attack on the former President's family. His most significant departure from the Jordan memo of 1972 was his failure to cultivate Edward Kennedy. On the contrary, he took the occasion of a 1974 Law Day address in Georgia to upstage and alienate Kennedy. When the family heir removed himself from the 1976 race, Carter wrote to let him know this was no relief to him: "Let me say quite frankly that as one who has considered becoming a candidate myself, I've always viewed you as a formidable opponent . . . and I certainly take no pleasure from your withdrawal." During the campaign he boasted that he did not have to "kiss Kennedy's ass" in order to win. Once in office, Carter showed no favor toward one of the most powerful Senators of his own party. On the contrary, he failed to consult him, gratuitously insulted him by omission (e.g., from the first invitations to a party at the Kennedy Center for representatives of the People's Republic of China), treated with suspicion such friends of his as Joseph Califano, and made sure that the newspapers carried his boast, on the day after Kennedy announced his own health plan, that he would "whip his ass" if Kennedy ran in 1980. It would have been easy for Carter to forestall any Kennedy race that year, simply by recruiting him to his own administration's efforts early on. But he sought an opportunity for defeating Kennedy. Later Presidents have not considered themselves fully legitimate until they prove they can deal with the heir presumptive.

Perhaps Ronald Reagan has broken the Kennedy spell over the White House — he awarded the medal Congress had struck in Robert Kennedy's honor and President Carter had "sat on." Of course, Reagan won in a year when Edward Kennedy finally did run. And he was not awed by the fake-Hollywood glamour of the Kennedys — he is (as they say) "real tinsel." Also, as the last of the Roosevelt-era politicians to win the presidency, he had a very different view of Neustadt's and Schlesinger's hero. His views were formed before "Camelot" occurred. Though he has been hailed as introducing a new politics to the White House, he is still fighting our century's oldest electoral battle, the fight over the New Deal.

Time plays tricks on us all. Reagan as the oldest President to be elected, and Kennedy as the youngest, will be frozen in their images, ages apart. Yet they were born only six years from each other. If Kennedy had lived, he would have been sixty-three when the sixty-nine-year-old Reagan was sworn into office. It is odd to remember now, but Kennedy was also speaking for Army Lieutenant Ronald Reagan when, at his inauguration, he said that "the torch has been passed to a new generation of Americans, born in this century, tempered by war, disciplined by a hard and bitter peace, proud of our ancient heritage, and unwilling to witness or permit the slow undoing of those human rights to which this nation has always been committed, and to which we are committed today at home and abroad." In one sense, Reagan just came to fulfill that messianic view of America's place in the world.

With the exception of Jimmy Carter's short intrusion, America has been ruled for nearly four decades by politicians who served in World War II. The men who appeared in a long succession had been rivals and contemporaries. Kennedy, Nixon, and Johnson fought over the prize in 1960. Reagan entered the fray in 1968, just as Johnson dropped out. After Eisenhower, our last President born in the nineteenth century, the new generation came onstage represented by its youngest member, then its oldest — first Kennedy, then Johnson (born three years before Reagan). Nixon (born two years after Reagan) and Ford (Nixon's exact contemporary) preceded Carter, the exception — the first President in almost half a century not to have seen active military duty in the war (he was still at Annapolis when it ended).

So, even if Reagan has escaped the Kennedy obsession, it is not surprising that he retains a fondness for the war President, Roosevelt, on whom Kennedy tried to model his performance. It has been considered odd for a right-wing Republican, the enemy of "big government," to admire the New Deal President. But if that is strange, it should be put beside its sister paradox, that Kennedy, who considered himself the successor to Roosevelt, was also scathing in his criticism of "the bureaucracy," of big government as a set of procedures resisting the will of a great leader. Ronald Reagan's promise to "get the government off the backs of the American people" is a culmination of the anti-Washington "counterinsurgent" tendency that was launched by Kennedy and continued by his rival-imitators. The puzzle in both Reagan's and Kennedy's attitude is this: How could they admire so heartily a man who, more than any other, helped create the huge bureaucracy both men expressed such contempt for?

Roosevelt presided over the two-stage "takeoff" of big government in America. The first stage, the New Deal, doubled the government's budget over a period of eight years. This is the achievement the right wing has always criticized. It does not seem bothered by a second stage, though it was more important in bureaucratic terms. After the nascent welfare state had doubled the size of government in eight years, the warfare state doubled that larger government in half the time. In both cases, the expansion responded to emergency; and in both cases it refused to go away when the emergency had been met. Roosevelt built in terms of long-term size and continuing expansion. He did not see big government as a necessary evil. If anything, the emergencies supplied an opportunity for developments desirable in themselves. Yet those who admired this man had become, by 1960, critics of the large structure that was his most lasting bequest to the nation. In the eyes of Neustadt and Kennedy, the vigor of Roosevelt's will somehow discredited the sluggish huge bodies that will had called into being. It is hard for charismatic leadership to prolong itself, even in its own most intimate products.

16

Veralltäglichung

FRANKLIN ROOSEVELT HIMSELF could not have been a post-Rooseveltian President. Those who wanted to apply his techniques to a world which those techniques had shaped were mistaking their own and Roosevelt's historic moments. Neustadt tried to teach Kennedy how Roosevelt had circumvented the bureaucracy. But Roosevelt did not circumvent that apparatus; he invented it in the first place.

Presidents since Kennedy have conceived their task as a David-and-Goliath struggle with the vast machinery of government. Control from within of all those cogs and wheels is impossible — they would just churn the President up. So a series of raids from the outside was called for, hit-and-run tactics, guerrilla government. But Roosevelt had been Goliath, not David, proliferating agencies outward from him, not sending raiders against them. The initiator of programs is not a prisoner of their past record, of precedent and procedure. He controls them by setting their goals, choosing their first personnel, presiding over their authorization. All new systems have energy and focus, from the very effort that brought them into being. The dead hand of the past is not yet felt, since the new department has no past, just a bright unindictable future.

The very pressure of events gave the early welfare state and warfare state sharp definition. Roosevelt did not have to induce a sense of crisis to get his programs accepted. The Depression was real enough; Congress begged the President for *more* bills during the busy first three months of his administration. People yearned for him to do something, anything, to meet the crisis — and the demands of that crisis, rather than any ideological program, dictated what measures were taken. Some of these were makeshift, some mistaken, some illegal; but all were aimed, supported, desired. Spontaneity and resourcefulness were given a free hand — but only to create measures soon translated into programs, with set procedures.

There was the same virtue of definition in war measures. Roosevelt was free to override not only ordinary procedures but basic rights. The public supported the most irregular means of guaranteeing national security — a secret decision like that to build nuclear weapons, or an arbitrary punishment like the imprisoning of Japanese-Americans, or unilateral fiat like the unconditional surrender demand. The Manhattan Project was a spectacular success because, in time of peril, the President could commandeer men and talent, site and materials; he could assign tasks, and cloak the whole matter in secrecy, and use the weapons without consulting the citizenry. In all these ways, war gave Roosevelt quasi-charismatic powers —powers most Americans would shudder to see granted in peacetime. After the war, the spontaneous and arbitrary yielded to settled ways again. Security procedures, for instance, may have been unfair after the war, but they were not arbitrary and secret — Congress reviewed and regularized them. If agencies called up in wartime were to justify their continued existence, they had to do so by standards different from those applied at their inception. The one great exception was the CIA, whose funding was kept unconstitutionally secret, and whose mandate had a wartime character. It is no accident that the presidential itch to use charismatic power to overthrow foreign governments, or spy on Americans, or come up with criminal weapons, found its readiest outlet in the CIA's activities.

Crisis enables the charismatic leader to launch, unchallenged, projects that must *meet* challenge in a postcrisis atmosphere. Charisma, that is, must give its own products continuity by submitting to an "everydayizing" of its claims (*Veralltäglichung* in Weber, normally translated "routinizing"). The successful routinizer of charisma solves the successor problem by presiding over the dissolution of his own unique first claim. Thus George Washington's authority was lent, in diluted and diffused manner, to the constitutional procedures he affirmed by his resignation of power. The alternative to this is a jealous retention of crisis powers when the crisis is abating. Then the charismatic leader will not surrender his reign to anyone else, nor submit to the least cutback in his authority — the course of Napoleon, of Stalin, of Mao. The problem of routinizing charisma is presented, in parable form, by the formulaic Western movie. A gunfighter is called in to handle problems too great for the doddering sheriff. If the gunfighter, having got rid of the evil gang, tries to stay on and rule the town with his gun, then getting rid of *him* becomes the problem. Nixon's extraordinary musings on the movie *Chisum* show that he conceived his own task as charismatic, not regular — as the gunfighter's, not the sheriff's. If bureaucratic "big government" gets defined, permanently, as a doddering old sheriff, then each presidential election becomes a call for some new gunfighter to face the problems "government" cannot solve.

Kennedy's successors have drifted, steadily, toward this conception of their role. But their appeal to Roosevelt as a model is unjustified. It is true that crises gave Roosevelt quasi-dictatorial power, and that dictatorship in the old Roman sense became respectable again in the thirties. A widespread disillusionment with parliamentary procedures, combined with a fear of the radical Left and with economic breakdown, led to the call for strong leaders — for Hitler and Mussolini, Franco and Salazar. This mood even gave a momentary glamour of menace to American figures like Huey Long and Father Coughlin or an Englishman like Sir Oswald Mosley. But Roosevelt's achievement, like Washington's, was to channel his own authority into programs and institutions. In that sense, Roosevelt resisted even while exercising "charisma," *re*legitimating institutions at a time when other strong leaders were *de*legitimating them. This made Roosevelt differ not only in historical moment from the Kennedy period, but even more basically from Kennedy's conception of power. Theorists of "deadlock" in the Eisenhower fifties felt that the lethargy of the public, the obstructionism of Congress, the external menace of communism made it imperative for a President to seize every margin of power available to him: he was facing so many hostile power centers that only the glad embrace of every opportunity could promise him success. No internal check upon one's appetite for power was needed; the external checks were sufficient — were *overwhelming,* in fact, unless the President became single-minded in his pursuit of power. But Roosevelt did not have this ambition of seizing power to be used against his own government. He sought power *for* that government, and set up the very agencies and departments that Neustadt and his followers resented. He created subordinate power centers, lending them his own authority. He began that process of "routinizing" crisis powers that is the long-range meaning of the New Deal. There is something perverse about the "liberal" attack on Eisenhower's bureaucracy in the nineteen-fifties, which simply revived the Republicans' first response to the New Deal.

For Max Weber, charismatic power must always yield in time, either gracefully or by violence, to the everyday order of kingship (traditional rule) or contractual "modern" government (legal rule). And if the course taken is toward *legal* rule, then it will tend, of necessity, toward bureaucracy, toward patterns of accountability, predictability, oversight, and record-keeping. By contrast with a swift and arbitrary charismatic rule, this kind of government will seem to many "inefficient." In the same way, due process in criminal law is slower than arbitrary justice. But, outside crisis circumstances, the arbitrary soon becomes indefensible. Everyday conditions call for a regularization of procedures. Reinhard Bendix breaks down Weber's concept of bureaucracy into five main notes.

1. *Continuity.* Crisis-oriented government assembles itself for the moment; and, between crises, tends to dissolve. Its actions are sporadic, ad hoc, responsive to immediate challenge, following the leader's "inspiration." A bureaucracy, by contrast, assembles itself, nine to five, every working day. Its normal arena is the normal; it resists crisis-mobilization. This is a fatal reduction if, in fact, apocalypse is just around the corner. But the opposite error is to inflate every apparent crisis into the apocalypse, to think the continuing mandate of government is, as Kennedy said at his inauguration, "the role of defending freedom in its hour of maximum danger." Kennedy's indictment of Eisenhower was that he treated the Soviet

menace as a new form of the old struggle between nations, not as a "twilight struggle" with the enemy of all freedom everywhere. Others think that was Eisenhower's best contribution to a nation he took over at the height of its McCarthyite Cold War period.

2. *Regularity.* The charismatic leader is not bound by precedent, informed by meetings, submissive to advisers. But the bureaucracy works on lines set by "what we have always done." This blunts initiative, though it lets people know, whenever they enter a program, what lies down the road for them in future years. New Deal programs like Social Security gave much of the population an "entitlement" over society's future resources, and that limits the society's freedom of maneuver. The government is tied down by long-term commitments, which check the hand of those who want to refashion government from administration to administration. But the same bonds *free* the "entitled" from uncertainty about what is owed them. Daniel Patrick Moynihan, of New York, sidling over toward Richard Nixon in 1968, attacked "big government" this way: "The next President of the United States, as I write, will not be Lyndon Johnson [who had just withdrawn from the 1968 race]. It could be George C. Wallace. How much public money would American liberals be willing to see President Wallace expend for the purposes of increasing the participation in public affairs of those elements in the population he regards as simultaneously deprived and underorganized?" But the discretionary funds of one President are severely limited — precisely the complaint of activist Presidents like Kennedy. The truly "big government" spending is on entitled programs, passed by Congress, that are hard for Presidents to cancel or curtail (a fact of life Ronald Reagan had to learn in the White House). A society becomes unwieldy to the extent that it lays itself open to lasting claims from its subjects. In that sense, "big government" is not despotic, not Big Brother free to do what it likes with the populace. It is not "innovative" to the extent that it has ceased to be arbitrary. Mere size does not make for "inefficiency." Accountability does.

3. *Delegation* of authority. Bureaucracy sets up many loci of authority relatively impervious to a single superintending will. In a bureaucratic order, large government is by definition *not* centralized government. Thus when Kennedy sent his managers out to tame the

bureaucracy, they often found the only way to assert their will was to create new programs responsive to new needs, programs that were superimposed on the old, and became a further obstruction to Kennedy's successors. Robert McNamara is the finest example of this process. Appointed to whip the military into line, he doubled the military budget in seven years, created counterinsurgency teams that drew the regular army into Vietnam, then departed from government horrified at what he had accomplished.

McNamara resembled many of Kennedy's people, and Kennedy himself, in having been formed during the war years of governmental expansion. That was a time of administrative creativity, when McNamara's planning group multiplied exponentially the production of American airplanes. But such freedom to create left a cumbrous legacy behind, an air force so large that it sought separate status and, by its very extent and expense, limited the choices for a nuclear strategy in the postwar period. By that time McNamara and his Whiz Kids had moved on to the Ford Motor Company, where, again, they were given a comparatively free hand at a time of massive postwar conversion to peacetime production. The opportunity would not easily (if ever) come again for "starting over." The responsiveness of the entire company to his hand on the tiller called up illusions of control that only McNamara's second time of Pentagon service would dispel, at great cost to him and to the nation. The man Kennedy praised for "controlling" the Pentagon at last embraced a war that controlled — and broke — him.

In other areas of government, a similar tale unfolded itself. For special reasons, Robert Kennedy could not control J. Edgar Hoover, and so he built a separate investigative and enforcement machinery at Justice, adding to the bureaucracy rather than "taming" it. The New Frontier's National Security Council became a second State Department, which clashed with the original one throughout Kennedy's and subsequent presidencies. The civil rights and poverty initiatives left behind a machinery of "affirmative action" that became a target for later critics of regulation. In all these cases, the refusal to delegate just created further centers of delegated authority. Unwilling or unable to use what was at hand, Kennedy thought he could avoid procedure by using special teams — but each special team created a whole new book of procedures. The Peace Corps, born as a brilliant improvisation, soon had to cope with rules and was mired in its own bureaucratic battles.

4. *Separation of office from the person of its holder.* The charismatic ruler must act directly on all parts of his government — or act, at the least, through surrogates who have a close personal tie with him. In a bureaucracy, by contrast, job security is defined irrespective of the particular jobholders. This involves a loss of the personal touch, a loss regretted, for instance, in the contrast between bureaucratic social services and the ministration of personal "bosses" in the city machines. But this loss is balanced by a freedom from whimsical directives not subject to appeal. A bureaucracy carries to its logical extreme the principle of "a government of laws and not of men." It would reduce even the highest officeholder to powers granted *all* Presidents. Its emphasis lies on the title: *President* Kennedy, not President *Kennedy*. The Neustadt school maintained that the presidency is only what each President makes it, that the office is defined by the man, not vice versa. This has led to the intense personalization of the institution. We talk of the Kennedy years, the Johnson era, the Nixon regime in a way that people did not think of the Coolidge era or the Wilson years. This personalization creates charismatic expectations in noncharismatic times, to be followed by inevitable disappointment.

5. *Documentary record.* The bureaucracy, in the accusatory phrase, "shuffles paper." It leaves an inky trail. Bureaucrats, according to their critics, build a record "to protect their ass." If they did not act with greater resourcefulness, it was because a *regulation* (proper number supplied here) did not admit personal initiative. This aspect of bureaucracy especially galls those who see attractive shortcuts toward an immediate goal. The awareness of always acting "on the record" limits the bargains that can be struck, the informal arrangements that break logjams. For Presidents in the Kennedy mood, the CIA became the most appealing arm of action precisely because it keeps no public record (and, in the person of Director Richard Helms, destroyed much even of the secret record).

Both Kennedy and Reagan, from their different vantage points, won applause with their attacks on governmental obstructionism and bureaucracy. Both were praised as raiders against big and unresponsive governmental structures. There is a nostalgic streak in

American history that makes its citizens want to run a large empire on the values of the small town. Even as its citizens ask for security, in the sense of guaranteed status, they hymn unconfined opportunity. The market myth makes us think that spontaneity will sort out things according to their merits, without the need for planning and regulation. The individual is supposed to forge his or her own "environment," unfettered by prior social arrangements. More and more the governmental workings of America have come to reflect the necessities of national size and ambition, while the Presidents express a romantic rejection of that machinery, a denial of the rule of necessity, a promise to escape "back" toward remembered freedoms. For Kennedy's managers, these freedoms were the take-off opportunities of a burgeoning military establishment in World War II. For Ronald Reagan, the freedoms are those of the Chamber of Commerce's imagined past, when "enterprise" built character. With both men, however, there was a business model for the resentment toward big government. Kennedy's ideal was the raider style of his freewheeling father's rise. For Reagan, it is the corporate talk of opportunity within the confines of "big business." This lends a different tone and style to the Kennedy Democrats and Reagan Republicans; but this should not hide from us how they both betray the hero they appeal to. They delegitimate government in different ways — but each way is far removed from Roosevelt's gift for legitimating government by routinizing charisma.

17

The Prisoner of Charisma

As a principle of domination, familial charisma has generic problems of its own, especially in regard to succession. . . . In any case, the whole meaning of charisma is changed in the process. From a quality that authenticates and ennobles a person through his own actions, charisma becomes an attribute of the forefathers through whose deeds a man's authority and privileges become legitimate.

— RHEINHOLD BENDIX

LYNDON JOHNSON THOUGHT he had a legitimacy problem with respect to Robert Kennedy. But Robert had an even more acute problem of succession. As the designated heir, he had to demonstrate charisma in revalidating exercises, day by day. The more charismatic have expectations become, the more difficult is the problem of succession, even within the family. For charisma cannot simply be handed on to a successor, for the same reason that it cannot be fully delegated to a subordinate. It is a unique power to handle crises, and both power and crisis must be fitted to each other, repeatedly, by the original charismatic figure — and even more urgently, against the disappointments of substitution, by any successor.

Johnson tried to solve his legitimacy problem by developing his own "countergovernment" of cronies, to defeat the obstruction of Kennedy loyalists. Robert Kennedy had to move even farther out from "everyday" government to make new charismatic claims. His was not only a government in exile, but also a kind of revolution in the hills, his own personal Sierra Maestra. John Kennedy had radicalized others inadvertently; Robert Kennedy had to keep up with the forces his brother had loosed.

Civil rights was a prime example. During the 1960 campaign Kennedy criticized the President for failing to move aggressively in this area — though Eisenhower had passed the first civil rights bill since Reconstruction, and backed up the school desegregation decision with bayonets in Arkansas. Kennedy helped free Dr. King from jail during the race, and he promised to move around congressional obstruction by executive order. He would, for instance, desegregate government housing "with the stroke of a pen." But, once in office, he delayed that move for nine months, while civil rights leaders vainly sent him pen after pen for the magic stroke. Kennedy was wooing Congress after his disabling "victory" over Judge Smith's Rules Committee.

The difference between Eisenhower and Kennedy was less one of private disposition than of the stages of black militancy. Kennedy came to office as the movement was accelerating. He asked Dr. King to call off the freedom rides; the Attorney General said protection could not be provided unless a "cooling off period" intervened. King said no, which so angered Robert Kennedy that he telephoned Harris Wofford, asking him to intervene and end the rides: "This is too much! I wonder whether they have the best interest of their country at heart. Do you know that one of them is against the atom bomb — yes, he even picketed against it in jail! The President is going abroad and this is all embarrassing him." At this point in his own development, Robert Kennedy not only identified the good of the country with his brother's reputation but with the sanctity of nuclear weapons.

Robert Kennedy also considered the Civil Rights Commission, chaired by the Reverend Theodore Hesburgh, too activist; it would cause political trouble for his brother in the South. "You're second-guessers," he told the commission. "I am the one who has to get the job done." When the commission planned hearings in Louisiana and Mississippi, Kennedy called Berl Bernhard of the staff and told him to call them off, without letting anyone know he had made the demand. "Remember you never talked to me." In all this, Robert was following the lead of his brother, who had earlier told Wofford to end the freedom rides: "Stop them! Get your friends off those buses!" The President's insensitivity to black problems astounded Wofford. When the first Peace Corps class was being sent off to foreign countries, Warren Wiggins briefed the President before he addressed the group in the Rose Garden. In that conversation Kennedy casually assumed that black people in the corps had been trained at Howard Universtiy — i.e., that young people sent out to cross cultural and national boundaries had begun their government training in segregated facilities! Kennedy also astonished Angier Biddle Duke, the head of protocol, who was disturbed at the refusal of restaurants on the highway between New York and Washington to serve UN diplomats from Africa. Kennedy's solution: "Can't you tell these African ambassadors not to drive on Route 40? It's a hell of a road — I used to drive it years ago, but why would anyone want to drive it today when you can fly? Tell these ambassadors I wouldn't think of driving from New York to Washington. Tell them to fly!"

Kennedy's encouragement of the civil rights activists was largely inadvertent, when it was not the result of good public relations work by people like Wofford. The administration tried to cancel the 1963 March on Washington; when that failed, the White House took charge of the arrangements to keep them peaceful (and screened speeches to make sure they were not too militant). The government that tried to stop the march received credit for being its sponsor.

But Robert Kennedy's slow entanglement in the civil rights cause became a serious commitment by the time of his brother's death. At first he was forced to create special squads to protect federal marshals in the South, and then to protect the two students he could not warn away from the universities of Mississippi and Alabama. (In the early stages, he was naive enough to think pro quarterback Chuck Conerly, who had starred at Ole Miss, could walk James Meredith into the university). But as he gained experience of southern justice, Kennedy's first hopes hardened into grim skepticism. He began to understand black militancy, and knew why Dr. King had been unable to call off rides and marches — he had to work to maintain his credibility with younger SNCC types becoming angrier every day. Soon Kennedy was in the same position, running to keep up with the rhetoric his brother had loosed on the nation. But Robert came to feel the bitterness himself, and was criticized for saying that he would be a rebel too if he were a black. At the outset, like his brother, he had just opposed "the system" of lawmaking and bureau- cratic administration as narrow and obstructive, not as malevolent. But by the time he reached the Senate, he listened respectfully to those who hated the system because they felt it was out to kill them.

Wofford, who helped Sargent Shriver set up the Peace Corps, tells how they worked to keep the President from turning it into an anti- Communist propaganda operation. Their resistance to this heavy- handed approach (meant to disarm congressional objections to the program) finally made Kennedy tell his own policy offspring to fend for itself. At this juncture, Shriver got needed support on Capitol Hill from Vice-President Johnson, whose aide, Bill Moyers, had be- come a Peace Corps official. John Kennedy, the cool and pragmatic leader, used the young without sharing their passion. But Robert Kennedy was easily infected with it. The resistance of the young eventually did as much to change his views on Vietnam as did rever- sals on the battlefield. He sought out radical leaders in 1967 as he had cultivated black leaders five years earlier. When Jack Newfield wrote his book on Kennedy as the "existential" politician, the term was more apt than when Arthur Schlesinger used it of John Ken- nedy: "He defined and created himself in action, and learned almost everything from experience. . . . When his brother died, he passed through a night of dread and learned about the absurd. He had the capacity to trust his instincts and become authentic. He was always in a state of becoming."

Admittedly, this was "kid talk," of the sort Tom Hayden had used in his Port Huron Statement on "finding a meaning in life that is personally authentic." But the point is that Kennedy began to like, in some measure, this assessment of his later role. He was becoming a kind of genteel outlaw-rebel, giving a muted performance of the Abbie Hoffman claim: "The revolution is where my boots hit." Where his brother had been tailored and aloof, he became tousled, shirt-sleeved, surrounded by longhaired guitar-playing aides who were his liaison with the Haydens and Chavezes. These people were praising Kennedy for educating himself by acting. It was a code that Abbie Hoffman liked to quote from Ché Guevara: "The best way to educate oneself is to become part of the revolution."

There is nothing stranger in our recent history than the way this puritanical Catholic became, in his final months, a hero to people whose earlier heroes were Ho, Mao, Fidel, and Ché. To appreciate the reversal involved, we have to remember that Kennedy had dutifully read the works of Ho Chi Minh and Ché Guevara when his brother first took office. It was part of the "counterinsurgent" mania — know your enemy, the better to beat him with his own weapons. Later, after the Bay of Pigs, Fidel Castro became a personal obsession of Kennedy's — the man who had defied his brother, made him look ridiculous. The CIA plotted to humiliate Castro, to "unman" him with drugs or depilatories; at last, to kill him. Castro brought out every combative instinct of the Kennedys. He was a hero to the young and a charismatic leader in both the superficial and the profound sense. John Kennedy was attempting a "charismatic" but very limited raid on certain aspects of America's bureaucratic legal order. Castro was charismatic in the fullest, most authentic way — he overthrew the old regime entirely and instituted a revolutionary order based on his personal authority. His "little brother" Ché was a rebel himself, off in other countries fomenting revolution. They had an all-out dash and vigor the Kennedys could only imitate in covert or surreptitious ways.

But by the rule that you begin to resemble the enemies that haunt you, Robert Kennedy toward the end of his life was taking his brother's charismatic tendencies farther out from the center of government, flirting with language that was framed in the hills of Cuba, becoming a mini-Fidel. He could only solve the successor problem by being more deeply charismatic than his brother — not in the superficial sense, not as a Prince Charming, but in the Weberian sense, as a rebel against the system. The more he tried to become a successor to the charisma of his brother, the less likely became his inheritance of power in the legal order. He was being "radicalized" just as the country was showing its revulsion against campus disorders, war protest, and civil rights militancy. Some of Robert's admirers felt that he could win over the "long hairs" and get the blue collar vote as well in 1968. They relied on some polls that showed George Wallace supporters — of all people — speaking kindly of the "mean" kid brother. But that was a protest reaction that would wilt under the realities of electoral alignment.

Richard Nixon narrowly beat Hubert Humphrey in 1968, but

only because George Wallace and Curtis LeMay won thirteen percent of the electoral votes. The combined Nixon-Agnew–Wallace–LeMay vote was one for silencing "the kids." The proof of that is not only Nixon's landslide reelection of 1972 after Wallace's shooting, but the fact that Nixon, at the peak of popular dismay over Watergate, could not be impeached for his repressive acts — not for the mass arrests of May Day, the violations of civil rights, the illegal suppression of Black Panthers and "Weathermen." Those acts were still too popular for House members to include them in the articles of impeachment.

The attempt at charismatic succession within a legal order is self-defeating, a thing Lawrence O'Brien realized when he wept that Robert was senselessly killed because "he didn't have a chance." He didn't have a chance, not because he lacked his brother's charisma, but because he embodied its next stage, the only stage he could have embodied, given his place in succession and his own fierce character.

If Robert took the charismatic protest against legal system too far for the politics of the late sixties, his younger brother has always seemed to err in the opposite direction. He lives easily with the everyday. He alone of the brothers liked and worked within the Senate system. He joined the establishment; he did not make waves. He respected his elders, deferred to the rules, worked his way up. His whole Senate career has been an enacted rejection of the Neustadt scorn for governmental machinery as obstructive. In fact, by 1980 he was under attack as the last New Deal liberal, a defender of the bureaucracy his brothers derided. He represented a *Veralltäglichung* so drastic as to mean the dissipation of charisma rather than its routinization.

Yet the trappings of charisma, or residues of it, were also present. Memories of his brothers were stirred by the accent, the gestures. He presided over a large and talented staff, attracting people with the promise of his future presidency. He had to reach beyond his "ordinary" status if only to solidify that status. He was such a good Senator in large part because he was perceived as on the verge of becoming something more — this won him special treatment from his Senate peers, special attention in the press, the brightest and best speechwriters and legislative assistants. Even if he never aspired to the presidency, he had to keep up a shadow campaign for it, to remain powerful in the Senate.

And then, the worst thing of all, he had to use his charisma, his exemption from the rules, to defend the indefensible after Chappaquiddick. Those who rushed to protect the Kennedy legacy contained in his person (as in some unworthy vessel) made the maximum claim for charisma on a minimum of performance. At this stage, charisma degenerates to mere totemism, protecting the sacred object as an endangered relic, not rallying to it as a center of active leadership. The way people rushed to tend his person, to remove the evidence of any wrongdoing, to hurry the bodies away (his and Ms. Kopechne's, along with those of the partygoers) looks like a farcical replay of the Dallas tragedy. There, too, a frantic "saving" of the body made loyalists bunch around their fallen leader and defy the world of legal order. Surrounded by aliens, Kennedy's people ignored the hospital official who said they would break the chain of evidence if they removed the President's body. Dave Powers and Kenneth O'Donnell told Dr. Earl Rose to get out of their way. Dr. Rose was expressing the legal rejection of charisma: "There are state laws about removing bodies. You people from Washington can't make your own law." Manchester, who completely agreed with O'Donnell in this confrontation, tells the story:

As O'Donnell and O'Brien were shouldering their way toward Rose they were stopped by Burkley and McHugh, who proposed another solution. They explained that a local justice of the peace was present. He had the power to overrule the medical examiner. Everyone waited while the judge was summoned; then he arrived and disappointed them. He could do nothing, he said. If a JP suspected homicide, it was his duty to order an autopsy. There were plenty of grounds for suspicion here, and he couldn't overlook them. *Ergo* — he guessed the procedure wouldn't take more than three hours.

O'Donnell asked that an exception be made for President Kennedy.

Although the din was atrocious, both he and O'Brien heard the justice of the peace say, with what they regarded as a distinctly unsympathetic inflection, "It's just another homicide case as far as I'm concerned."

The effect on O'Donnell was instantaneous. He uttered a swart oath recommending monogenesis. Thrusting his head forward until their noses nearly grazed, he said, "We're leaving."

The policeman beside Rose pointed to the medical examiner and the justice of the peace and told O'Brien, "These two guys say you can't go."

"One side," Larry said cuttingly. Jerking his head, Ken said, "Get the hell over. We're getting out of here. We don't give a damn what these laws say. We're not staying here three hours or three minutes." He called to Dave, who had backed Jackie into a cubicle. "We're leaving *now.*" To Kellerman he snapped, "Wheel it out!"

At this juncture, in O'Donnell's words, "It became physical — us against them." Kellerman, who hadn't even heard Ken, had begun to pull the church truck on his own, butting flesh with his shoulders; the agents and Dugger were pushing.

There could not be a more clear-cut confrontation of the legal with the charismatic order. Law, procedure, the orderly preservation of a record, these mattered to officials, who are taught to think of each case as "just another homicide" for the record's purposes. But it was unthinkable to the Kennedy people that such orders could dictate the movement of their leader's body, which had been given into their keeping to be protected from violation by the "everyday."

Dr. Rose, as it turns out, was right. All the confusions caused by an autopsy in Washington, away from the doctors who first worked on Kennedy's body, created a disorderly record rife with targets of opportunity for conspiracy theorists. A later critic like David S. Lifton quotes Dr. Rose with approval, arguing that the chain of custody over the body *was* broken, leaving discrepancies of reporting at either end of the journey. Robert Kennedy later compounded the problem by giving the Warren Commission only limited access to the autopsy photographs, taking the photos and the medical remains (including the elusive brain) into his personal custody, allowing others to see them only after five years and then by application to the Kennedy crisis-manager Burke Marshall.

Many later misunderstandings — including the whole Manchester affair — could have been avoided if the grieving Kennedy people had not taken the presidential plane back with Lyndon Johnson. One must sympathize with the shocked mourners, whose reactions showed a charismatic set of expectations. They held on to the White House as their man's personal shrine. It is impossible to imagine them acting otherwise under the pressure of their sorrow.

The charismatic protection of Edward Kennedy at Chappaquiddick was less defensible, but also understandable. To contain problems within the family, to cover up, to arrange appearances, was the instinct built into real and honorary Kennedys. They made up, in their own minds, a world within a world, a government within (and over against) the "regular" government. The weaknesses of that position did not seem obvious while Kennedy held the presidency, or even when the life had gone out of his body. The dead end of charismatic leadership within a legal order was not finally revealed until Burke Marshall came to contain, arrange, and cover up for the least charismatic of the Kennedys, the one who most wanted to be ordinary, the man to whom loose talk of charisma has been an almost unmixed bane, not a blessing. If it is hard to be an American prince, it is even harder to be an ordinary politician treated part-time as a prince.

V
POWER

It was, after all, Greeks who pioneered the writing of history as what it has so largely remained, an exercise in political ironics — an intelligible story of how men's actions produce results other than those they intended.

—J. G. A. Pocock

18

Bulldog! Bulldog!

When the reading [of the battle plan] which lasted more than an hour was over, Langeron again brought his snuffbox to rest and, without looking at Weyrother or at anyone in particular, began to say how difficult it was to carry out such a plan in which the enemy's position was assumed to be known, whereas it was perhaps not known, since the enemy was in movement.

— *War and Peace* (the eve of Austerlitz)

MANY JOKES, and some serious comments, were devoted to the Harvard presence on Kennedy's Potomac. But the first team to move out aggressively on the New Frontier came largely from Yale. Its captain was Richard Bissell, class of 1932 — class of 1928 at Groton, where his best friend was Joseph Alsop. Bissell stayed at Yale for his doctorate, and to teach economics. Two of his students were the Bundy brothers. Two of his colleague-followers were the Rostow brothers. Walt Rostow was a teaching assistant for one of the Bissell courses McGeorge Bundy took. Even at that time, Bissell was an innovator, introducing mathematical economics to an old-fashioned department. For special students he offered an "underground" seminar — guerrilla teaching; he gave the course pacing a small room, overpowering his awed students.

Even President Kennedy felt some of that awe before his own bright aides' brightest teacher. When Chester Bowles (Yale '24) tried to recruit Bissell for the State Department, Kennedy said no — he meant to keep Bissell at the CIA, to replace Allen Dulles as its Director. Bissell had directed two of the most successful operations in CIA history — development of the U-2 reconnaissance plane and launching of the "spy satellite" in space. Now he was working on a plan worthy of the legendary Dulles himself; and his deputy on this project was Tracy Barnes, who had followed a year behind him at Groton and Yale. Great excitement traveled through what Peter Wyden calls "the Yale-OSS-old-boy-network connection between the holdover CIA operators and many of the incoming New Frontiersmen."

Bissell had not shared the OSS experience of Dulles and other old-timers — including Barnes, who observed Dulles directing resistance inside Hitler's Germany from the famed house in Berne, Switzerland. But Dulles, who knew of Bissell's brilliant record in running Marshall Plan programs, recruited him in 1953 to save, if that was possible, resistance-building behind the Iron Curtain. In 1947, as soon as the CIA came into existence, its covert action counterpart — euphemistically named the Office of Policy Coordination — began to drop agents, supplies, and weapons in countries occupied by Russia after the war. Frank Wisner, who had worked with Dulles during the occupation, getting German intelligence on the Russians, ran the new resistance, recruiting heavily in refugee camps, spreading American money around to make up for a late start in the intelligence game.

The massive recruiting alerted Russian agents and developed what Thomas Powers calls a whole new class of espionage entrepreneurs. The supply of money created a demand for resistance centers and proliferating governments in exile. Guerrillas equipped with American gadgets were dropped into the waiting arms of Russian agents in Albania ("killed or arrested with eerie efficiency," says Powers), the Ukraine, Georgia, Yugoslavia, Poland. One of the most promising programs was the Home Army in Poland, which sent back encouraging reports as supply drops increased. But then, in 1952, General Eisenhower was elected; so Russian intelligence officers, afraid that a Republican might believe his own party's propaganda about freeing the captive nations, revealed that they had been running the fictitious Home Army all along. Eisenhower folded the resistance-building program his first year in office.

Allen Dulles hoped something could be salvaged from the scheme. What, after all, was America to do when exiles and refugees came to them bringing information, promising contacts behind the Iron Curtain? Even if most of the agents were sent to their death, resistance networks of any sort could be a nuisance to Russia when World War III broke out (as Dulles was expecting it to), and then they might breed *true* resisters of the sort Dulles used in World War II. Dulles would like to find some scaled-back way of continuing the work for resistance centers. Bissell was brought in as an outside efficiency expert to study the program. It was Bissell's first experience with the CIA, with the dream of running far-flung governments-within-governments. While going over the records, he came upon a plan for escalating guerrilla war in Albania to the point where a full invasion could be supported from within that country. He concluded that America could never mount a secret assault halfway around the world; but the plan bears a striking resemblance to one he came up with, seven years later, for invading a country in our own hemisphere.

After finishing his report, Bissell joined the CIA and, at once, had his first experience in overthrowing a government. Frank Wisner, who ran the unsuccessful operations Bissell had been studying, made the Guatemalan coup look easy. Bissell would later use directors of its various parts to help him overthrow Castro — Tracy Barnes, for instance, and David Phillips, and E. Howard Hunt. In Guatemala, Jacobo Arbenz had been accepting Soviet support, so the CIA came up with a handpicked successor for him, one trained like other Latin American military men at Fort Leavenworth, Kansas — Colonel Carlos Castillo Armas, who was given a little army in Honduras, provided with American air cover, and hailed as Guatemala's savior from radio stations at fake exile centers. Arbenz, uncertainly supported, grounded his whole air force after one pilot defected. Listening to CIA broadcasts as a nonexistent uprising tightened around his capital city, Arbenz resigned in panic before the broken-down trucks of Castillo Armas could drive all the way to Guatemala City.

Coming soon after the 1953 coup that returned the Shah of Iran to the Peacock Throne, Guatemala bred in the CIA an illusion that it could make and unmake governments around the globe. Even the coldly efficient Bissell, who as a child made toy and imaginary trains run accurately on complex schedules, shared this exhilaration. The beauty of the coup in Guatemala was that it could be held so secret.

No great army had to be recruited; no exile communities tingled with rumors; no governments in exile competed for future leadership. The "bugs" of the resistance movement in Europe had been eliminated. An operation could be improved as it was trimmed back. Less was more. "Psywar" had replaced real war. Armies could be routed with radios expertly used. Modern technology and expertise could undo fumbling large administrations, brains defeating brawn.

These were the lessons Bissell took to heart. He ran his own major projects for the CIA — the U-2 and the spy satellite — out of his own hat. Secrecy became his passion; no other parts of the CIA itself should know what he was up to — or as few as possible. He was beginning to run a secret government within the secret government, a guerrilla intelligence force in the counterguerrilla service. Sticklers for orderly procedure — mainly Richard Helms — resented the way Bissell cut them out of his growing personal sphere. Even before Kennedy arrived on the scene, Bissell had created a proto–New Frontier operation — relying on the intelligent shortcut, on impatience with bureaucracy, on the brilliance of a few amateurs and "generalists," on contempt for company men and committees and the military.

And so the Bay of Pigs was born. Kennedy legend put this failure down to the incompetence of Kennedy's predecessor. Nothing could be farther from the truth. Neither the military nor the bureaucracy misled Kennedy into the invasion of Cuba. Bissell cut all of them out, and convinced Kennedy *because* he embodied the ideals of the new administration. Bissell was proposing just what Kennedy had dreamed of doing from the White House. Peter Wyden describes early days on the New Frontier:

> Soon Mac Bundy told [Robert] Amory that the President had said, "By gosh, I don't care what it is, but if I need some material or an idea fast, CIA is the place I have to go. The State Department takes four or five days to answer a simple yes or no." This was music to the ears of Amory and his [CIA] colleagues, and they reciprocated: "People were willing to come in at three o'clock in the morning, because they knew damn well that what they produced was read personally by the President immediately." Eisenhower's cumbersome coordinating committees were scrapped. The intelligence business was fun again. And for Bissell, in particular, the stakes

were suddenly soaring. . . . Unlike the military and the State Department, the CIA got things done without so many committees,
concurrences and pyramiding delays. It did not shirk tricky, nasty
jobs. It didn't bellyache and constantly say that something was too
audacious or couldn't be done.

The distinctive note of the Bay of Pigs invasion was that it was a
military operation run *without* the military's control, an invasion
force created specially by the CIA itself, a combination of every
weapon in Bissell's private arsenal — assassination of a leader, propaganda war, guerrilla uprising, and coup from outside. Its success depended on a coordination of all these things in the mind of the master train-scheduler. Later, the plan would look so crazy that people
could not credit its acceptance in the first place. But it made sense to
a James Bond fan.

The origins were comparatively simple. Emigrés from Cuba presented the CIA with the same set of problems and opportunities that
European refugees had. Some exiles brought valuable information
about the Castro regime; rumors of resistance had to be confirmed;
agents planted by Castro in Miami had to be smoked out. Hotheads
needed controlling — the men who wanted to rent a single fishing
boat and "invade" their homeland. The wilder sort could make more
trouble for America if left alone than if the CIA harnessed their energies to some larger purpose. Howard Hunt, who thought that anything opposed to Castro must be praiseworthy, regretted the CIA effort to check extremists: "Jimmy [pseudonym for an agent] charged
the Cubans with being inefficient and insecure, said giving them
boats and ordnance was tantamount to letting them kill themselves.
I replied that much as he might be right, our policy was to help the
exiles do what they thought they themselves could do. Jimmy said
the exiles were needed in the training camps, not floundering around
in the Florida Straits."

Bissell's job, then, was to take a situation like that which led to
the inefficient resistance-building program in Europe and turn it into
another Guatemala. No long buildup of internal resistance could be
attempted; Castro would track agents down and kill them as the Al-
banians had. A short quick elimination of the whole regime was
called for, using surgical tools of modern psywar. Bissell was engag-

ing Fidel Castro in a mental game of chess, a test of comparative so-
phistications. That is why the first thing Bissell asked for was propaganda experts. Radios send out the first waves of attack in a modern
war of the minds.

Since David Phillips had run the Guatemalan radios, he was called
in, during the spring of 1960, to set up a studio for bringing down
Castro. A fifty-kilowatt transmitter was rushed from Germany to
Swan Island, off Honduras, for this purpose. Forty Cubans were
trained as radio operators, twenty at Useppa Island off the Florida
coast and twenty on the plantation of Robert Alejos in Guatemala — the plantation that would become a training camp for the
invading army.

The propagandists began with great confidence, and expended sophisticated hours making the project look unsophisticated enough
to be authentic — they removed rugs from the Great Swan studio so
chairs could be heard scraping the floor, as in some crude hideout. A
Madison Avenue advertising firm was hired to produce mimeo-
graphed releases with an amateur look. While this elaborate playact-
ing went on in Phillips's Washington apartment and New York offices, Castro's own propaganda operation ridiculed the American
tricks. This was just one of the differences between the Cuban and
the Guatemalan projects, differences the CIA resolutely ignored.
Propaganda unbalanced Jacobo Arbenz because he was teetering already. Not a revolutionary, Arbenz was a reformist trying to keep his
original military backing — the arms he got from the Soviets had to
be wielded, after all, by rightist colonels in his own country. Working to placate both sides, he formed no comprehensive program or
aggressive propaganda of his own; the distrust among his own followers could be exploited. But Castro was the master of a revolutionary regime with its own propaganda strength. Phillips did not
radio his "disinforming" messages into a vacuum but into a country
with the high morale of a revolution in its moment of success,
where resistance was easily branded as treason (when genuine), or as
United States aggression (when false).

In such a situation, the American propaganda operation's only
success was in persuading itself that resistance to Castro existed on a
scale sufficient to cause an uprising with only a little encouragement
from the outside. That is always the danger with propaganda, that it

becomes at last more credible to its disseminators than to its targets. This was increasingly true of the Cuban effort, as handling the fractious exiles became more difficult. The propaganda was used to convince the refugees, though the refugees were supposed to be the operation's own source of information! Exiles and agents drifted, without realizing it, into a relationship that involved constant fooling of each other — a pattern that would be repeated, up the rungs, into the White House itself.

If Cuba was not Guatemala, Castro was even more emphatically not an Arbenz. Eisenhower approved the Guatemalan operation when he was convinced that Arbenz was weak and could easily be toppled. But the CIA put Castro in its sights precisely because he was strong; he had not only created a discipline for Cuba, but had revived the failed hopes of Latin American Communists for a wider revolution. The campaign against Cuba was personal from the outset. Castro's jaunty defiance of the United States had made him a great villain to the American public — more resented, according to the polls, than Khrushchev himself. When Howard Hunt went to Havana to scout the possibilities of a coup, he came back with one overriding recommendation: the revolution was Castro, so Castro must be removed. Hunt later chafed and fumed that his recommendation was being neglected. But it wasn't. Acting on a suggestion from Colonel J. C. King, Bissell and Barnes made their first overture to potential assassins in July of 1960. When that failed, they got Colonel Sheffield Evans to approach underworld figures as "hit men." Meanwhile, the CIA's technicians were working on strange new devices to humiliate Castro if they could not kill him — make his beard fall out or garble his speech. Sophisticated "psywar" was the magic new destroyer of the opposition's chessmen.

Allen Dulles was relying on the power of such dirty tricks when he approached Eisenhower on the subject of Cuba. In February of 1960, early in the primary season of that election year, he suggested that Castro's sugar crop be sabotaged. Eisenhower, as usual, wanted a "program" within which such isolated acts could be judged; so the CIA framed one in a matter of weeks. On March 10, the President approved a four-point program setting up a government in exile (Eisenhower's own first priority — a moderate leadership was to be found, excluding veterans of Castro's revolution *and* Batista's regime), launching a propaganda campaign (the CIA's darling scheme), encouraging internal resistance, and training guerrillas outside American territory.

This initial agreement was rich with possibilities of future misunderstanding. The CIA was counting on its own tricks to unseat Castro before the election, despite what Bissell considered Eisenhower's lack of real interest in the plan. The President would be saved despite himself. Thus longer-range planning was given low priority; it served merely as a cover for Bissell's quick-fix approach. Two bunglers were assigned the important task of forming a government in exile: Gerry Droller (known to the exiles as Frank Bender) was a German with no sympathy for Cubans, and Howard Hunt was a right-winger with no sympathy for anti-Batista reformers. Far from seeking out moderate leadership, the two men exacerbated political conflicts in the exile community, and made noises that advertised the CIA plot. By neglecting long-range aspects of the plan he had given to Eisenhower, Bissell sabotaged his own quick "surgical" kill of Fidel.

Guerrillas were sent to the Guatemalan plantation where radio operators had been trained — first fifty, then a hundred more. While the search went on for resistance centers where they could be dropped, the secret army grew and its secrecy evaporated. Political differences among the exile fighters led to greater effort at control by the Americans, with decreasing success. Finally, when mutiny broke out and split the camp in two, the CIA rounded up a dozen "troublemakers" and held them in a prison camp till after the invasion. The political side of the operation was even messier. When Miami's Cuban leaders continued their feuding, the CIA appointed its own leaders, moved them up to New York (away from the squabbling in Miami), held them in the dark about the invasion, and issued statements in their name. If the Cubans would not act like Castillo Armas, voluntarily, they must be forced to.

By the end of the summer, it was clear that Castro would last through the American election. In August, Bissell sought authorization from Eisenhower for spending thirteen million dollars to train more guerrillas. There was still no talk of an invasion; and Peter Wyden argues, in the best history of the operation, that Eisenhower "thought the operation was in its infancy." The CIA had been disturbed all along that "Eisenhower was wary" when he was not bored: "He never gave Cuba high priority." But if Castro could not be overthrown by CIA tricks, Bissell felt sure that the next President would have the enthusiasm to give him whatever he needed. Vice-President Nixon had been the strongest supporter of the scheme within the White House, and Senator Kennedy issued a campaign statement promising support for freedom fighters in Cuba.

When John Kennedy won in November, Bissell pushed forward with his plans, certain of the support that Kennedy did, in fact, give him during the interregnum. But Bissell "sold" the plan to Kennedy by stressing its clandestine and "surgical" aspects. He was given a free hand on the assurance that a guerrilla operation would lead to a rapid coup — neither a long-run resistance, nor a full-scale invasion. The CIA had been saved from the "wariness" of Eisenhower, only to fall victim to Kennedy's romanticism about technological guerrillas. Eisenhower, the organizer of D-day, who as President approved the massive amphibious landing in Lebanon, would have put the military in charge of invasion troops — something Bissell resisted, making the whole operation depend on CIA funds and planning. But Kennedy, precisely because he wanted the plan restricted to CIA scale, cut the program back at the very time when even Bissell saw that more was needed, not less. Kennedy, unaware of the difficulties of an amphibious landing, insisted that the "raid" take place at night and in an obscure place, not at Trinidad, the obvious site for a countercapital to be set up. Kennedy was still thinking of guerrilla troops that would bring Castro down invisibly. The logic of invasion called for seizing a communications center; the logic of resistance called for secret drops that would "fade into the hills." The invasion of a remote area — the Bahia de Cochinos — fit neither scheme; it had remained remote, after all, because coral reefs and dangerous swamps made it hard to reach (or break out of) by sea or land.

Bissell was put in the position of having to expand his plan and cut it back at the same time — expand it to cope with new obstacles facing him every day, and cut it back to keep the President's support. Air cover was restricted, naval support held back from the shore. Meanwhile, striving to keep control, Bissell withheld information at the top — from the CIA's own Board of Estimates and from the

Joint Chiefs of Staff — while news of the invasion was leaking out around its periphery. Kennedy, aware only of the secrecy at the center, was taking steps to guard a secret that no longer existed. Castro knew the landing would occur; only Adlai Stevenson was kept in the dark. If the site of the invasion surprised Castro, that was only because it made no military sense.

Having denied himself the advantages of military precaution, while taking on all the dangers of a military invasion, Bissell ended up with ships crashing onto unexpected coral reefs off a lonely spot that Castro knew intimately as his favorite fishing retreat. Since control of the operation was held in Washington, reaction time to all these problems was slow — five or six hours to report the need of air support to the CIA and sue for presidential approval. Bissell's attempt at total control led to total breakdown. Not only were the military branches insufficiently informed and involved; they were not supportive, since they had been excluded from the planning. Bissell had exercised such personal control over all aspects of the U-2's construction that the resulting fleet of planes was known as the Bissell Air Force. But he could not personally check the manifests of every landing boat at the Bay of Pigs, to discover that the communications equipment was — against normal military procedure — stuffed into a single boat, which sank. Ordinary military procedure was what the CIA daredevils had transcended. That is why two hired captains of "freelance" ammunition ships fled from the shelling and had to be chased back by American planes — too late.

For many, the puzzle of the Bay of Pigs is how a brilliant planner like Bissell could have convinced himself and so many others that it would succeed. But the first thing we must remember is that "it" was never a single thing. It changed character constantly, often without Bissell himself noticing what had happened. The propaganda-cum-assassination-coup gave way, first, to a large-scale raid meant to set up a rival center of government at Trinidad. Then this was cut back to a covert raid again, but now on the scale of a small invasion. By the time this confused sequence came to the point where it must be launched or called off, Bissell seems to have taken a "cap over the wall" approach to the matter — Castro had to be attacked now, with whatever was at hand, or never. If the exile army was disbanded, to roam free telling its tale, America would lose without even trying. It would get blamed for assembling the force in the first place, and blamed even more heatedly for not using it. The Cuban political leaders would air their grievances against the CIA. Castro would have a propaganda victory fixing him more securely in the affection of his people. Russia would feel freer to move in on Latin America.

Eisenhower would have called off an amphibious invasion unless it became clear a *real* invasion was needed. But Kennedy would approve a raid on the scale of an invasion — and, having done that, Bissell thought he would have to follow up with whatever military assistance was needed to defeat Castro. The CIA would cause a crisis that America could not walk away from. In that sense, the one-man operation would succeed. A country that could not be invaded by following normal channels of military preparation *would* be invaded in order to rescue a desperate band of American-led patriots trapped on the beaches of "Pig Bay." Bissell would throw our cap over the wall, and Kennedy would have to follow. What else could a President do who had begun his reign with the promise to "pay any price, bear any burden, meet any hardship, support any friend, oppose any foe to assure the survival and the success of liberty"?

By the time of the invasion, a certitude of Kennedy's support — whatever was called for — pervaded the CIA team. Many shared Howard Hunt's feeling: "Everything seemed ready. So ready, with success so inevitable, that when President Kennedy on April 12 declared the United States would never invade Cuba my project colleagues and I did not take him seriously. The statement was, we thought, a superb effort in misdirection." The propaganda experts not only believed their own propaganda by this point, but thought the President was taking his cue from them. Clayton Lynch, the guerrilla trainer who went ashore with his Cuban pupils, could not believe it when the President canceled a second air strike — it was, he said, "like learning that Superman is a fairy." The ballsy President had betrayed the James Bonds whom he admired, and who admired him. The agents who took it as implicit that the President would back them up conveyed this certitude to the Cubans as an explicit promise — when Peter Wyden interviewed veterans of the invasion, they still felt betrayed, sold out after pledges of support.

Even Bissell had some reason to feel betrayed. If he was trying to "force the hand" of the military, draw them into a situation they would not have relished had they been given the choice, wasn't that what Kennedy's ideal of guerrilla government called for? The inventive and unorthodox agents of the President *should* cut across channels, defy normal procedure, get the bureaucracy moving despite itself; should welcome crises, not avoid them; should precipitate trouble, and then improvise; throw the cap over the wall, and then follow. That is what Kennedy had encouraged — and then, having loosed his unorthodox warriors, he failed to back them up. The President might claim he was misled into thinking this was less an invasion than a raid. But sophisticated men talked in signals, out on the Kennedy basketball court, not by way of long reports in triplicate. Bissell had only to wink among his peers, and he had taken Kennedy as a peer. How did he think a guerrilla raid in the hills could overthrow Castro in a matter of days? Kennedy had first trusted Bissell to know what he was doing; and then, at the crunch, he would not follow Bissell's recommendation to widen the war.

Kennedy apologists would later say the New Frontier was itself betrayed in this episode, misled and lied to by the government in place — overborne by the military, who took too narrow a view of the problem; awed by experts dealing with a team of novices in the fledgling administration; told that ongoing procedures could not be broken off; reminded that Eisenhower's authority stood behind the plan.

But the Taylor Report concluded, after investigating the invasion, that the military mindset was excluded from planning; that the Joint Chiefs of Staff rather acquiesced in the project than approved of it — precisely because it was kept outside their bailiwick. What was needed was more procedure and bureaucratic checking: "Top level direction was given through ad hoc meetings of senior officials without consideration of operational plans in writing and with no arrangement for recording conclusions and decisions reached." Taylor concluded that Kennedy, by instantly dismantling Eisenhower's National Security Council apparatus, removed the machinery that could and would have spotted the plan's inadequacies.

Far from being awed by military types, Kennedy trusted Bissell because he so openly expressed contempt for them. And Eisenhower's approval of the project — so far as any existed — was no recommendation to Kennedy, who tried to contrast his administration in every way possible with his predecessor's. He did not revere a man of whom he could say, when his own popularity increased after the invasion's failure: "It's just like Eisenhower, the worse I do, the more they like me." No, the Cuban invasion was taken to heart because it was so clearly marked with the new traits of Kennedy's own government. It had for its target the man who obsessed Kennedy. It had for its leader the ideal of Kennedy's "best and brightest." It was a chess game backed by daring — played mind to mind, macho to macho, charisma to charisma. It was a James Bond exploit blessed by Yale, a PT raid run by Ph.D.s. It was the very definition of the New Frontier.

19

The Midas Touch

Oh, I am fortune's fool! — *Romeo and Juliet*

A FAVORITE WORD in the Kennedy administration was "options." Eisenhower, it was contended, never heard the whole range of possible choices. By the time he was asked to decide, committees had sifted the possibilities, winnowing out the unusual or daring. Kennedy, by engaging in the decision process at every level from the outset, would consider even risky or bold new courses.

Yet it was precisely by seeking options, with regard to Cuba, that Kennedy hemmed himself in, making Schlesinger call him "a prisoner of events." Schlesinger means that there was a concatenation of pressures forcing the President toward the Bay of Pigs. Sorensen and others make Kennedy the prisoner of Eisenhower, whose plan he inherited. But Eisenhower told Maxwell Taylor, during the investigation of the Bay of Pigs disaster, that he had never even heard of an amphibious invasion of Cuba until it was in the news. What he authorized was the training of a few guerrillas, an action on the scale of Guatemala, small enough to remain covert, the kind of thing the CIA had been doing. Bissell wanted to do something much grander; and though he probably had some of the final plan shaping in his head while Eisenhower was in office, the "takeoff" in terms of scale occurred when Kennedy was elected and gave Bissell the go-ahead at a November briefing. The invading troops were almost doubled in the two months that followed, and that larger number was redoubled by the time of the landing.

It is true that Eisenhower recommended a continuation of the CIA operation against Castro; but he meant the small-scale one he had authorized. As Peter Wyden concludes: "To him, nothing called a 'program' was fully hatched. When he insisted in a September 10, 1965 interview that 'there was no tactical or operational plan even discussed' with him while he was in the White House, he was technically correct." For Eisenhower, military terms had technical meanings.

If Kennedy, inheriting an Eisenhower plan, was forced to go ahead with it despite misgivings, why did he not question Eisenhower about the operation after he took office? Make the master answer his doubts? Explore the possibilities of failure with the man who supposedly stood behind the plan? Kennedy did nothing of the sort. And even when he called Eisenhower in for a face-saving "conference" after the invasion's failure, Eisenhower noted in his diary that "the President did not ask me for any specific advice" — though Kennedy later claimed, before reporters, that he had sought Eisenhower's counsel.

When William Pawley, the conservative diplomat who had advocated an assault on Castro, gave Eisenhower some details of the operation (including the loading of the heavy signal equipment in one ship, and that ship carrying ammunition), Eisenhower wrote in his diary: "If this whole story is substantially correct, it is a very dreary account of mismanagement, indecision, and timidity at the wrong time." The right time for timidity would have been when Bissell gave the CIA the task of making an amphibious assault in force. Eisenhower was notoriously cautious when considering romantic options of that sort. Murray Kempton summed up the General's rules of action this way: "When a situation is hopeless, never listen to counsels of hope. Fold the enterprise. Do nothing unless you know exactly what you will do if it turns out to have been the wrong thing."

Before the Guatemalan coup was launched, Eisenhower asked his advisers if they were *all* absolutely *sure* it would succeed. They were. Then, when trouble developed and Allen Dulles asked for more airplanes, Eisenhower asked what were the chances of this making the difference. "About twenty percent," Dulles told him. The President later said that if Dulles had given him an inflated estimate, he would not have got the planes. For Eisenhower, only a realism verging on pessimism inspired confidence in the discussion of military matters.

By contrast, Kennedy asked his principal advisers, not if they were sure of success, but if they thought the mission worth trying. When the Joint Chiefs were asked to estimate the chances of a successful landing at Trinidad (the site chosen by the CIA before Kennedy overruled it), General David Gray wrote a report describing the chances as "fair," a term suggested by General Earl Wheeler. Wyden reports their conversation: "When they discussed what 'fair' meant, Gray said he thought the chances were thirty to seventy. 'Thirty in favor and seventy against?' asked Wheeler. 'Yes.' " Gray used no figures in his report for the White House, and President Kennedy never asked what "fair" meant. Gray thought it obvious that a "fair" rating would not imply chances were "very good" or even "good" — much less "certain." And this, remember, was the estimate for a landing site that had advantages lacking to the Bay of Pigs.

The truth is that Kennedy went ahead with the Cuban action, not to complete what he inherited from Eisenhower, but to mark his difference from Eisenhower. He would not process things through the military panels, let them penetrate Bissell's secrecy. He would be bold where he accused Eisenhower of timidity. He would not send in the Army, Navy, and Air Force, but only Bissell's raiders. In all this he was the prisoner of his own rhetoric. As Sorensen admits, "his disapproval of the plan would be a show of weakness inconsistent with his general stance."

Kennedy's campaign had promised strong action against Castro, a man, says Sorensen, who made Kennedy lose his normal "cool": "He should never have permitted his own deep feeling against Castro (unusual for him) and considerations of public opinion — specifically, his concern that he would be assailed for calling off a plan to get rid of Castro — to overcome his innate suspicions." Kennedy had "run scared" from accusations of softness on Castro in the campaign itself. When Harris Wofford was called in to produce a cam-

paign book of Kennedy speeches (*The Strategy of Peace*), he wrote
that Castro's revolution stood in the tradition of Simón Bolívar's
fight against colonialism. That passage soon came under fire, and
Kennedy told Sorensen to draft a strong statement against the
Cuban government. Richard Goodwin wrote the release, which said:
"We must attempt to strengthen the non-Batista democratic anti-
Castro forces in exile, and in Cuba itself, who offer eventual hope of
overthrowing Castro. Thus far these fighters for freedom have had
virtually no support from our government." On the eve of the Bay
of Pigs invasion, Kennedy reminded Goodwin of that statement:
"Well, Dick, we're about to put your Cuban policy into action."

Schlesinger says that Kennedy had some misgivings about taking
a hard line on Cuba and blaming its loss on Eisenhower. But campaign advantage won the day:

> Cuba, of course, was a highly tempting issue; and as the pace of the
> campaign quickened, politics began to clash with Kennedy's innate
> sense of responsibility. Once, discussing Cuba with his staff, he
> asked them, "All right, but how would we have saved Cuba if we
> had the power?" Then he paused, looked out the window and said,
> "What the hell, they never told us how they would have saved
> China." In that spirit, he began to succumb to temptation.

Began to? Adopting the method of McCarthyites in their assault on
Truman is not merely flirting with temptation. But the important
thing in this place is not the moral justification of Kennedy's campaign tactic, but the fact that his lunge toward immediate advantage
inhibited his freedom later on. He would have to live with Goodwin's language if he disbanded the freedom fighters he had called
for, had criticized Eisenhower for not raising up and "loosing" on
their homeland. He narrowed his range of future options by stigma-
tizing ahead of time the one that might prove the most sensible. A
man who has to be tough in each response is not free; his very pro-
fessions of control put the matter beyond his choice:

> Weyrother evidently felt himself to be at the head of a movement
> that had already become unrestrainable. He was like a horse run-
> ning downhill harnessed to a heavy cart. Whether he was pulling it

or being pushed by it he did not know, but rushed along at headlong speed with no time to consider what this movement might
lead to. (*War and Peace*)

As if he knew the decision was out of his hands, Kennedy cut off
criticism of the CIA's plan. Sorensen, considered "liberal" (i.e., soft)
in the early days of the administration, was not told of it; when he
heard something and sounded Kennedy out, the President quashed
any expression of disapproval by using "an earthy expression that
too many advisers seemed frightened by the prospect of a fight, and
stressed somewhat uncomfortably that he had no alternative."
Whether he had an alternative or not, he wanted to hear of none.
Wofford — whose patron, Chester Bowles, was one of those Kennedy considered "frightened by the prospect of a fight" — tells us
what "earthy expression" Kennedy was using to cut off criticism: "I
know everybody is grabbing their nuts on this."

Criticism of the plan was considered cowardice. Bowles and Rusk
and Stevenson were counted too "ladylike" to be consulted on the
manly scheme Bissell was outlining. Robert Kennedy wrote, just
after the failure: "A critical time was on D plus one, when the CIA
asked for air cover. Jack was in favor of giving it. However, Dean
Rusk was strongly against it." Maybe the "chickens" caused the failure. That is why, in the immediate aftermath of the landing, the fury
of the people responsible was directed against those who had opposed the scheme. Pierre Salinger stopped Harris Wofford in a
White House hallway and said: "That yellow-bellied friend of yours,
Chester Bowles, is leaking all over town that he was against it.
We're going to get him." Robert Kennedy confronted Bowles himself, poked his finger in his chest, and said: "So you advised against
this operation. Well, as of now you were all for it."

Despite his campaign promise to hear all sides of an issue, Kennedy showed resentment when forced to hear less than comforting
words about the future landing. After inviting Senator Fulbright to
fly with him to Florida, Kennedy read through a critique of the
CIA's plan which Fulbright brought along, put it down, and did not
discuss it with Fulbright, either on this flight or the return one.
Schlesinger was told by Robert Kennedy: "I hear you don't think
much of this business. . . . You may be right or you may be wrong,

but the President has made his mind up. Don't push it any further. Now is the time for everyone to help him all they can." It was the advice Edward Kennedy later gave Schlesinger on the subject of Robert's presidential campaign. Don't make him lose his nerve; rally round; keep up morale. The question was one of guts, and to back off was to show a lack of guts. Sorensen captures the atmosphere: "Unfortunately, among those privy to the plan in both the State Department and the White House, doubts were entertained but never pressed, partly out of fear of being labeled 'soft' or undaring in the eyes of their colleagues. . . ."

When Schlesinger took to the President a white paper he had composed on Cuba, he asked, "What do you think about this damned invasion?" Kennedy answered wryly: "I think about it as little as possible." Thinking was not the problem. Thinking might take away one's nerve. Schlesinger admits his own criticisms were checked by Kennedy's obvious unwillingness to hear counsels of caution. He tried an indirect approach when he spelled out the unpleasant tasks that would await the President if he failed:

> When lies must be told, they should be told by subordinate officials. At no point should the President be asked to lend himself to the cover operation. For this reason, there seems to be merit in Secretary Rusk's suggestion that someone other than the President make the final decision and do so in his absence — someone whose head can later be placed on the block if things go terribly wrong.

He was telling a man proud of his courage to hide, to skulk.

Kennedy was a prisoner of his own taste for crisis, for being in the midst of the action. The CIA told him he had to move fast, before Russia supplied Castro with jet planes (actually, there were already jet trainers in Cuba, which were used effectively against the invaders). Besides, the Guatemalan government wanted the growing army, whose presence was no longer a secret, moved from its territory. And the troops were anxious to go. And the rainy season was about to begin. The basketball team had to call its signals in the rush of events, if it was to keep control — which meant that events were controlling *it*. A similar taste for instant decision came into play during the missile crisis, when a dubious estimate on the arming date of Castro's missiles led Kennedy to impose a deadline on the Russians, forcing them to act in an atmosphere of panic.

The growing size of the invasion army — 1,400 men — made the administration hostage to its own agents. Their visibility made them an "asset" that had to be used immediately or moved in a way that would waste the asset. And then there was the disposal problem if they were *not* used — all those hotheads wandering around in loud denunciation of a government that promised to back them and then reneged. Once again, acquiring a "capability" chained one to its use, so that decision became a kind of resignation to the inevitable. Confronted with the "disposal problem," says Schlesinger, "Kennedy tentatively agreed that the simplest thing, after all, might be to let the Cubans go where they yearned to go — to Cuba." The simplest thing, the nondecision, was the surrender of power to one's own instruments of power. They were acquired so the President might have the option of using them; but, once acquired on this scale, he had no option *not* to use them.

The ironies multiply. Tracing the justifications for invasion, Schlesinger wrote, "If we did in the end have to send American troops to Laos to fight communism on the other side of the world, we could hardly ignore communism ninety miles off Florida." In order to have a future (hypothetical) option, one denies oneself a present (real) option. Since one *might* have to go into Laos, one *must* go into Cuba. Thus do options bind, making "freedom of maneuver" a straitjacket for the mind. The so-called domino theory, explaining enemy tactics, was — seen from the other end — an option theory, testing the will of America: if we were going to stay free to be tough anywhere else, we had to be tough everywhere. It was a hard doctrine in terms of its result — Cubans died and were imprisoned. But it was the simplest doctrine so far as decision-making goes. Every decision came, in fact, pre-decided: the "toughest" course is the only one that can be followed, unless one wants to "grab one's nuts" and look like a bum.

The last irony of all is that Kennedy failed because he had always succeeded. He was a prisoner of his own luck. As Schlesinger put it:

One further factor no doubt influenced him: the enormous confidence in his own luck. Everything had broken right for him since

1956. He had won the nomination and the election against all the odds in the book. Everyone around him thought he had the Midas touch and could not lose.

It is not mystical or perverse to say that good luck is bad luck; Machiavelli offered that as the very essence of his realism. Arguing that *fortuna* could undo even the man of greatest virtuosity (*virtù*), he gave Valentino (Cesare Borgia) as his example. Valentino was the type of *virtù* at its highest reach, a model for all who want, at once, "immunity from foes and attractiveness to friends, victory by force or stratagem, the love and the fear of one's people, the obedience and respect of one's soldiers, the destruction of those who can or might oppose one, innovative measure within an ancient system, harshness joined with charm, the disbanding of old armies to reassemble better ones, the perpetuation of friendly relations with other kings or princes, so that they welcome alliance and shy from opposition."

That sounds like a description of the Neustadt President, of the Roosevelt whom Burns called lion and fox. Such a range of skills, joined with favoring chance, would seem unbeatable. But Machiavelli lists all these skills to emphasize the fact that good luck made Valentino fail — it made his *virtù* the means of his undoing. Introduced to a spacious area of action by his papal father, Valentino both commanded and enlarged that sphere — in fact, enlarged it *in order* to command it. Only his skills could keep so many opponents off balance, and he could do that only by introducing so many new aspects to the game that his opponents were befuddled. Only by reaching for three other things could he grasp the first thing given him. But because everything depended on his superintending intelligence and will, any lapse in either of those qualities would bring the whole enterprise crashing down around him. The attempt at total control led to total collapse if one thing went wrong — in Valentino's case, an illness that immobilized him at a crucial moment. For this kind of juggler, so deftly keeping dozens of balls in the air, if one drops they all fall. Luck worked his destruction by giving him so many in the first place.

John Kennedy had neither the ruthless character nor the restless skills of a Valentino. And no President can aspire to the everyday powers of a Renaissance prince (though the modern powers of destruction far outreach anything dreamed of in the Renaissance). Nonetheless, the euphoria of the New Frontier, the ideal of the activist President always seeking more power, did make Kennedy think he could break free of normal restraints. His experience to date had been one of risks defied, of personal control, of unconventional activity backed up with the conventional might of his father's money. He was nothing if not confident — changing plans for the Bay of Pigs invasion on his personal authority, redirecting the invasion to a hidden cove, rescheduling it for night landing. He brought his own ideas to the matter, gave it his personal stamp, without seeking express military guidance from Eisenhower, from White House military experts, from the Department of Defense. He never suspected that he was out of his depth. Critics simply lacked his nerve, or were hidebound "experts," paper-shuffling "bureaucrats." They did not see how magically he had defied the odds before, how lucky he was. Wyden's interviews with participants in the control-room direction of the landing show how inadequate Kennedy was to this kind of operation:

> Fascinated, [Harlan] Cleveland watched a "stricken look" cross Admiral [Arleigh] Burke's face when the President picked up one of the little magnetic destroyer models and moved it over the horizon. It clearly pained the admiral to see the President bypass all channels of command — and all tradition. As a student of managers coping with crisis, Cleveland was chagrined to see how obvious it was that the President's only executive experience had been as commander of a PT boat.

> Throughout the day in the Cabinet Room, Kennedy did not ask enough questions, Harlan Cleveland thought. And the President failed to ask about situations in context; he would ask a "very specific question about some little piece of the jigsaw puzzle and you had to sort of guess what the rest of the jigsaw puzzle was in his mind."

> [Walt] Rostow was struck by Kennedy's deep personal concern about the fate of the men on the beaches. The President had a "small unit commander's attitude toward these people" . . . Rostow was chagrined that the President "really didn't have a very good visual picture of the whole thing."

The student of Neustadt had come to acquire power, not question it; to enjoy it, not fear it. The possibility that the very reach for power might, with luck, take one into situations beyond the measure of one's skill would not occur to a reader of Neustadt's book. James Reston rather fatuously called that book America's version of *The Prince*. But Machiavelli warns against the mindless reach for power — the victory that drains one's resources, the conquered people that are more dangerous under one's dominion than outside it, the mercenaries added to one's troops while crippling them, the added fortresses that delude a ruler with a sense of false security. For him fortune was a tricky friend when not a beguiling enemy — better held at arm's length in either case. When dealing with the subject of power, he did not say, "Enjoy! Enjoy!" but "Suspect! Suspect!" These are the real lessons to be learned from Machiavelli, and some of Kennedy's friends rejoiced that he had learned them in his bruising experience at the Bay of Pigs. But had he?

20

"Learning"

ACCOUNTS OF THE BAY OF PIGS READ like one of the "bad news, good news" jokes. The bad news is that the disaster was complete. The good news is that President Kennedy learned so much from the experience. The Kennedys, Schlesinger has been saying ever since 1960, are late learners, and we may have to pay for their education with the lives of a few hundred Cubans. Roger Hilsman put it this way:

> If some extra-galactic observer with a wisdom and insight undreamed of on earth were asked to comment on the Bay of Pigs affair, he might well say that it was through this comparatively small disaster, though disaster it clearly was, that President Kennedy learned the lessons that enabled him to avoid a much greater, nuclear disaster a year and a half later by managing the Cuban missile crisis with such a sure and steady hand. If so, the price may have been cheap.

Writers are always suspect when they introduce an imaginary being "with a wisdom and insight undreamed of on earth" to say just what the writer is saying. But many wise men on this earth have repeated this line of thought, making it a kind of orthodoxy. One of these, astonishingly, is Theodore Sorensen: "In later months, he [Kennedy] would be grateful that he had learned so many major lessons — resulting in basic changes in personnel, policy and procedures — at so relatively small and temporary a cost." I say astonishingly because, from the Sorensen account, Kennedy learned nothing at all. If the history of the invasion sounds like a "bad news, good news" joke, Sorensen's account of his learning process reads like the movie line, "Round up the usual suspects." Kennedy failed, according to Sorensen, because "John Kennedy inherited the plan." But he did not. He inherited a growing invasion force which he let grow at an even faster rate. Sorensen says the matter was out of his hands before the presidency was securely in those hands: "Unlike an inherited policy statement or Executive Order, this inheritance [of a plan] could not be simply disposed of by presidential recission or withdrawal." But presidential directive was the only thing that could stop the plan — or, for that matter, launch the invasion; and the very man Kennedy appointed to teach him the lessons of the invasion — General Maxwell Taylor — concluded that such cancellation was the proper course.

For the rest, Sorensen just repeats the Neustadt dicta. Kennedy was done in by experts and the bureaucracy. The planning "permitted bureaucratic momentum to govern instead of policy leadership. . . . He [Kennedy] did not yet feel he could trust his own instincts against the judgments of recognized experts. He had not yet geared the decision-making process to fulfill his own needs." Kennedy, who had been too confident, is called too diffident. He who broke the rules is called their victim. Is this what Kennedy learned from his own task force of postdisaster teachers?

The Taylor report has never been released; but its principal author has said enough in various places to show that the Sorensen account of Kennedy's education has little to do with that report's conclusions. General Taylor believed — and he says that his fellow investigators concurred — that it was a *lack* of bureaucratic procedure and expertise that doomed the landing. The military was blamed for an operation it did not control. It was asked to advise from the sidelines with only partial glimpses of the total plan (which Bissell kept as secret as possible from those above him, while it leaked out all over the place below him). Taylor wrote in his memoirs:

> [The Joint Chiefs of Staff] felt that they had been obliged to work under circumstances which made it very difficult to carry out even these duties. In the interest of secrecy, there was no advance agenda circulated before the meetings and no written record of decisions kept during them [only bureaucrats "shuffle paper"]. Furthermore, the plan prepared by the CIA was always in process of revision so that the Chiefs never saw it in final form until April 15, the day of the first air strike.

In a White House that was proud of its lack of structured meetings and orderly reporting, even the expressed doubts of the Joint Chiefs were either misunderstood (e.g., the rating of chances at the Trinidad landing as "fair") or did not get a hearing (e.g., the rating of chances at the Bay of Pigs as even less than fair). Taylor says:

> By mid-March, the President's growing dissatisfaction with the Trinidad plan caused the CIA authorities to propose three alternatives to the Trinidad site, one of which was the Zapata area [containing the Bay of Pigs]. Asked to comment on these alternatives, the Chiefs in a memorandum to the Secretary of Defense [McNamara] expressed a preference for Zapata from among the three but added that none of the alternatives was considered as feasible or as likely to accomplish the objective as Trinidad. Our investigation revealed the fact, never accounted for [accountability is a bureaucratic priority], that neither the Secretary of Defense nor any other senior official appeared to have been aware of this clearly stated preference and hence the views of the Chiefs never influenced the decision on this point.

Arthur Schlesinger, given access to Robert Kennedy's notes from the Cuban Study Group investigation, quotes this astonishing one: "Evidently no probability of uprisings written up or put in memo form. No formal statement of opinion was given *or asked for*" (italics added). There were many experts who could have told Kennedy that an amphibious landing is recognized, in every school of military thought, as an exceptionally difficult maneuver, and that making such a landing at night on an inadequately mapped beach would stretch the skills of a trained army properly staffed (most Cubans had been given only a few months' training). Yet Taylor found an incredible insouciance in the White House team:

> A final defect was the jerry-built organization improvised to run this complex operation extending from Washington to the beachhead. There was no permanent machinery in Washington designed to deal with such an undertaking, so one had to be improvised. When the action heated up, communications quickly broke down, and the Washington leaders were soon without the information necessary to guide their decisions.

After General Taylor submitted his report, Kennedy asked him to join the White House staff as its Military Representative, where Taylor found that the style of the Bay of Pigs operation was the style of the entire White House:

> As an old military type, I was accustomed to the support of a highly professional staff trained to prepare careful analyses of issues in advance of decisions and to take meticulous care of classified information. I was shocked at the disorderly and careless ways of the new White House staff.... I found that I could walk into almost any office, request and receive a sheaf of top secret papers, and depart without signing a receipt or making any record of the transaction. There was little perceptible method in the assignment of duties within the staff, although I had to admit that the work did get done, largely through the individual initiative of its members. When important new problems arose, they were usually assigned to ad hoc task forces with members drawn from the White House staff and other departments. These task forces did their work, filed their reports, and then dissolved into the bureaucratic limbo without leaving a trace or contributing to the permanent base of governmental experience.

This attitude toward orderly method had been derived from the President himself who, "like his subordinates, had little regard for organization and method as such." If these were the lessons Taylor was trying to teach the President, then, according to Kennedy's own alter ego, he did not learn them: Sorensen claims Kennedy went

away from the Bay of Pigs determined to push his own antibureaucratic methods even *further,* in order to protect him from the experts
(whose advice had not been solicited).

But Kennedy was not really seeking to learn new things from his
investigation of the Bay of Pigs. That is obvious both from the formal instruction he gave to the Cuba Study Group, and from the
people he appointed to that group. He wrote to General Taylor:

> It is apparent that we need to take a close look at all our practices
> and programs in the areas of military and para-military, guerrilla
> and anti-guerrilla activities which fall short of outright war. I be-
> lieve we need to strengthen our work in this area. In the course of
> your study, I hope that you will give special attention to the lessons
> which can be learned from recent events in Cuba.

Taylor himself wondered at "the almost passing mention of the Bay
of Pigs" in this plan for *expanding* guerrilla warfare, with the Bay of
Pigs used only as a cautionary tale for that purpose. An investigation
of the meaning of the Cuban invasion might have called into question the very notion of paramilitary assaults on other governments.
Kennedy's instructions precluded that. The assignment was not to
ask whether Americans should acquire a guerrilla warfare capability
but how America might do so most efficiently.

The choice of General Taylor was dictated by Kennedy's determination in this matter. Taylor had been a critic of the Eisenhower
doctrine of "massive retaliation." When he retired from office (an
act later regarded as a resignation in protest), he wrote *The Uncertain
Trumpet* to plead for a new doctrine of "flexible response," enabling
America to counter "wars of liberation" with limited-warfare tactics.
Senator Kennedy read this book during his campaign, and wrote a
letter of enthusiastic approval to its author. Theodore Sorensen
echoed one phrase from the book in the inaugural address. Taylor
concluded his argument by saying: "All the foregoing actions should
be taken to the sure notes of a certain trumpet, giving to friend and
foe alike a clear expression of our purpose and of our motives." Taylor criticized Eisenhower for cutting back military expenditures and
for allowing a missile gap to develop. All this was useful to the 1960

candidate, even though Taylor's missile gap evaporated when Secretary McNamara began looking for it.

General Taylor, despite his own minimal support of a military staffing system (certainly more orderly than Kennedy's), was also a critic of the military bureaucracy. He said: "The Joint Chiefs of Staff have all the faults of a committee in settling important controversial matters. They must consider and accommodate many divergent views before action can be taken." That was the kind of general Kennedy wanted for his Cuba Study Group — and Taylor did not disappoint. The "jerry-built" operation of the CIA was criticized only because operations of that scale should go to the Department of Defense — which, in turn, should be trained to meet paramilitary and covert-action challenges too big for the CIA to handle. Bissell's agents should be replaced with Special Forces in the Army itself — with the Green Berets. Taylor, like most critics of bureaucracy, also suggested that a new bureau be added to run the old ones — in this case, a Cold War command center. The President rejected this idea, which challenged the State Department too directly, but then set up two secret boards to perform analogous tasks; and the leading figures on these boards were the commanding personalities of the Cuba Study Group — Maxwell Taylor and Robert Kennedy.

The simplest proof that Kennedy learned nothing from the Bay of Pigs invasion is that his own solution was to make Robert Kennedy the Director of the CIA. He told Arthur Schlesinger: "I made a mistake in putting Bobby in the Justice Department. He is wasted there. Byron White could do that job perfectly well. Bobby should be in CIA. . . . It's a hell of a way to learn things, but I have learned one thing from this business — that is, that we will have to deal with CIA. McNamara has dealt with Defense; Rusk has done a lot with State; but no one has dealt with CIA." Though Robert turned down the directorship, he added the CIA's business to his crowded schedule at Justice. Robert would "deal" with the CIA, exactly as McNamara dealt with Defense. Both men spurred their organizations on to new excess.

The President did not even know the CIA well enough to realize that the best critics of the Bay of Pigs operation were within the Agency. Richard Helms, leery of covert activity anyway, resented the way Bissell had isolated himself from internal review. Robert Amory, head of the bureau's own intelligence, had been excluded from planning the invasion, along with the Agency's Bureau of Estimates. The most critical report on the Cuban performance would come from the Agency — Lyman Kirkpatrick, the Inspector General, had fought for review rights over all operations, and had won them at one of Eisenhower's regular meetings, where Dulles could not override his own Inspector General before the President. When Kirkpatrick completed his report on the Bay of Pigs, friends of Bissell considered him a traitor, much as similar agents would feel about William Colby when that Director cooperated with the Church Committee years later. Although the Inspector General's report has never been declassified, Kirkpatrick's later comments give the gist of it. Kirkpatrick not only listed technical reasons for the military operation's failure; unlike the Taylor group, he derided the whole project: "If there was a resistance to Fidel Castro, it was mostly in Miami. . . . All intelligence reports coming from allied sources [which Bissell did not consult] indicated quite clearly that he was thoroughly in command of Cuba, and was supported by most of the people who remained on the island."

Now *there* was a lesson Kennedy could have learned from the Bay of Pigs; but he made that impossible when he told his brother to "deal with CIA," since the Bay of Pigs just increased Robert Kennedy's determination to "get Castro." His emotional response to the defeat of his brother was intense. Peter Wyden describes his first reaction:

> As the planners in Washington tried to come to terms with defeat on Wednesday, Walt Rostow was concerned about Robert Kennedy, whom he hardly knew. The Attorney General, who had not attended any of the pre-invasion planning meetings, showed much more than the President how distraught he was. He refused to accept the debacle and was needlessly upsetting the other advisers. On Tuesday, RFK had warned the presidential circle harshly in the Cabinet Room that they were to make no statements that didn't back up the President's judgments all the way. In midafternoon Wednesday, with the President absent from the room for a few minutes, Robert spoke, Rostow thought, "in anguish." He called on the advisers "to act or be judged paper tigers in Moscow." They were not

just to "sit and take it." With all the famous talent around the table, somebody ought to find something to do. Everybody stared. They were "absolutely numb."

Even after the failure, Robert Kennedy thought of the Cuban problem in purely military terms; he told Taylor that "the President would have gone as far as necessary for success had he known in time what had to be done."

Robert Kennedy endorsed the Taylor group's request for a command center to wage the Cold War; and, when that was rejected, Robert became a moving force in the secret committees set up to oppose Communist-inspired regimes or rebellions. These new boards were added to a prior one, the Special Group, which oversaw covert activities. General Taylor was put in charge of this, with a mandate to turn a harsher eye on CIA proposals. The first *new* group was also chaired by Taylor, but included Robert Kennedy — Special Group CI (for counterinsurgency). This group looked to the development of guerrilla warfare skills within the Special Forces of the regular Army. The Green Berets were its pampered baby, and Vietnam is its legacy. Robert Kennedy became an ardent reader of Mao and Ho, and held seminars on guerrilla tactics at Hickory Hill. The President himself insisted on the green berets as a badge of distinction, against the Army's reluctance to set men off from others except by rank, and a green beret became a fixture on Robert's desk at the Justice Department. Whenever this President saw a wall, he started throwing caps over it.

Robert's enthusiasm for counterinsurgency made him push and prod the CI Group, enforcing his brother's belief that America's future power would depend on its guerrilla capacity. William Gaud, who served on the CI Group, said in his oral history report at the Kennedy Library that the President and Attorney General "gave a hell of an impetus to the study of counterinsurgency and to setting up schools to indoctrinate our own people in this subject. And also, as a result of what they did, our own public safety programs, police programs, have been greatly enlarged." After observing Robert at the CI meetings, Gaud said: "There wasn't any question about the depth of his interest or the depth of his understanding of the problem. He was a pretty tough customer to face if he took one point of view and you took another, or if he felt that your agency had not been doing what it should be doing in respect of some problem. I developed a very healthy respect for his ability to get things done."

The things Robert got done included training Latin American officers in methods for putting down popular unrest. Why, after all, wait till a Diem is in trouble to come to his rescue? The pro-American governments should share America's expertise in *preventing* rebellion. Though there is no evidence that torture was taught in the American schools, there is no doubt that torturers were among their alumni, further embittering some Latin Americans against the United States.

For President Kennedy, Vietnam offered an invaluable opportunity to try out counterinsurgent devices and train American personnel. According to General Taylor:

> The President repeatedly emphasized his desire to utilize the situation in Vietnam to study and test the techniques and equipment related to counterinsurgency, and hence, he insisted that we expose our most promising officers to the experience of service there. To this end he directed that Army colonels eligible for promotion to brigadier general be rotated through Vietnam on short orientation tours, and he was inclined to require evidence of specific training or experience in counterinsurgency as a prerequisite to promotion to general officer rank. He looked to the Special Group to verify compliance with his wishes in these matters, a duty which we fulfilled by means of recurrent spot checks on departmental performance.

There was no reluctance to be "drawn into" Vietnam — we welcomed it as a laboratory to test our troops for their worldwide duties.

Fort Bragg was already the center for training America's corps of antiguerrilla guerrillas. The New Frontier philosophy of counterinsurgency had been enunciated in a famous speech Walt Rostow delivered at Fort Bragg in April of 1961. Rostow's academic reputation rested on his theory of the stages of economic development. In the early stages, emerging nations are vulnerable to opportunistic "scavengers of the process" — the Communists. It was America's historical role to protect the integrity of the development process by eliminating those scavengers. The counterinsurgents were technicians of progress: "I salute you, as I would a group of doctors, teachers, economic planners, agricultural experts, civil servants, or those others who are now leading the way in the whole southern half of the globe in fashioning the new nations." America was history's midwife, nursing freedom in numberless cradles. There could be nothing more enlightened or liberal than the learning of "dirty tricks" to undo the scavengers who specialize in them. Roger Hilsman in the State Department was another enthusiast for counterinsurgency: "The way to fight the guerrilla was to adopt the tactics of the guerrilla." New Frontiersmen traded maxims from the handbooks of the twentieth-century revolutionaries, then visited Fort Bragg to see how these heroes could be undone in their own backyards. The White House press corps was taken there in October of 1961 to watch Green Berets eat snake meat, stage ambushes, skip over ponds with back-pack rockets that let men literally walk over water. The Americans were coming — savvy as the Viet Cong, and with fancier gadgets.

Robert Kennedy was ardent about the Green Beret projects of the Special Group CI; but he was even more intense in pursuing the program of the second secret body set up in the wake of the Taylor report, the Special Group Augmented (SGA). This handled high-priority plots, and the highest priority of all was given to the downfall of Castro. At the very time when General Taylor, presiding over the Special Group, was supposed to curb the CIA, the Attorney General was using the SGA to increase its anti-Castro operations. The importance of this project can be seen from the fact that Robert Kennedy commandeered for its prosecution the "star" most in demand during this high season of counterinsurgent fever. Edward Lansdale was a man of mystery and glamour on the New Frontier, the man who had taught Ramon Magsaysay and Ngo Dinh Diem how to put down rebellions against their regimes. Lansdale, who opposed the Bay of Pigs operation, was now given a textbook assignment: show the CIA how it *should* have been done. Kennedy was ready to back him up with all the resources he might need. Operation Mongoose, the anti-Castro project, became the CIA's most urgent clandestine operation. Its base in Miami was the Agency's largest, with six hundred case officers running three thousand Cuban agents, fifty business fronts, and a fleet of planes and ships operating out of the "fronts." Lansdale was told to act quickly, and he promised to bring Castro down within a year. Robert Kennedy did not want the man who had humiliated his brother to gloat long over his triumph.

Far from checking CIA excesses, Robert Kennedy forced reluctant officials to undertake things they had resisted in the past. That was signally true of Richard Helms, an espionage man who had always opposed covert activity. Only after being "chewed out" by both Kennedys for Operation Mongoose's lack of success did Helms, a man temperamentally and historically opposed to assassination, revive the plot to use Mafia hit men against Castro's life. Defenders of the Kennedys naturally deny that their heroes commissioned the assassination plots; and, naturally, there is no record of a direct order — the CIA's lack of record-keeping about "sensitive" matters was one of its attractions for the antibureaucratic Kennedys. But what else are we to make of the fact that Helms, of all people, took over the assassination plot for the first time after his meeting with the Kennedys, *and that he canceled it as soon as Johnson came into office?*

Besides, Robert Kennedy was working in the closest collaboration with Edward Lansdale all through this period, and that "enlightened" guerrilla leader asked William Harvey, who ran Task Force W (the CIA program meant to implement Operation Mongoose) to draw up papers on "liquidation of leaders" in Cuba. Harvey, a highhanded CIA veteran, told Lansdale it was stupid to put such things in writing — which does not mean that removal of it from their pages removed it from their plotting.

The evidence that the Kennedys directly ordered Castro's death is circumstantial but convincing. When Robert Kennedy was told of the Mafia's use against Castro, on May 7, 1962, he blew up at the man briefing him, but expressed neither surprise nor anger at the plot against Castro, only at the killers being used. Lawrence Houston, the CIA general counsel who briefed Robert, told Thomas Powers: "He was mad as hell. But what he objected to was the possibility it would impede prosecution against Giancana and Rosselli. He was not angry about the assassination plot, but about our involvement with the Mafia." Kennedy, who was calling CIA people at all levels to urge on Operation Mongoose, made no protest to Helms or any other CIA officer about the plan to kill Castro. That did not excite or upset him, and he did nothing — though he was by office an enforcer of the law — to make sure it was not resumed (as in fact it was). That is inconceivable unless he approved of the plan, had in fact been part of its authorization.

Lyndon Johnson, when he took office, did not continue the attempts on Castro's life. When he directly asked Helms about them and was given a full answer, Johnson was certain that President Kennedy had authorized the assassination attempts, that he was running "a damn Murder Incorporated in the Caribbean." He told Howard K. Smith: "Kennedy was trying to get Castro, but Castro got to him first." Johnson believed the gangland hit had backfired in Dallas. One does not have to accept that inference to doubt what Johnson was in the best position to know — how and whether a President directs the CIA "unofficially."

Furthermore, how did Robert Kennedy expect Lansdale to bring down Castro within a year, absent outright invasion or overt American participation, without a palace coup to go with the popular uprising? The *prevention* of palace coups had been Lansdale's specialty in the Philippines and Vietnam; he was brought in to exercise his skills in reverse, so far as Castro was concerned; and his highest contact inside Cuba had insisted that such a coup, *preceded by execution of the President,* was necessary to any plan for overthrowing the government. Rolando Cubela, a major in Castro's army, was given various weapons for killing Castro, and was actually picking up one of these in Paris on the day President Kennedy was shot. At a time when Robert Kennedy was calling Lansdale and others incessantly, charging them with inactivity, would Lansdale withhold from him the key to his whole operation? And if he did so, how could Robert, intent on discussing the "nuts and bolts" of guerrilla war, expect him to overthrow Castro? Kennedy certainly knew about various sabotage efforts — he checked frequently on the attempt to destroy the Matahambre copper mines — which involved the death of Cubans in the area. In that sense, he authorized the killing of Cuban civilians and soldiers. Why not the killing of the soldiers' commander-in-chief?

I referred earlier to Robert Kennedy's extraordinary lack of interest in the motives or mechanics of his own brother's death. This man, once the pursuer of those who merely humiliated his brother, showed no such vindictiveness, or even curiosity, about Lee Harvey Oswald (whose name he garbled in referring to him) or any accomplices Oswald might have had. Harris Wofford argues that this reluctance came from disgust over his own knowledge about the plot to kill Castro. Robert Kennedy did not want any investigation if it would lead to the plans made against Castro, to his own involvement and his brother's. The deep change in Robert's character seems to have come from a genuine recoil against such violence and scheming. From that point on, he would seek out those for whom Castro was a hero, not a villain. Such a change did not come from any gradual learning process. In fact, the harshness of this shock indicated Robert's *failure* to learn from the Bay of Pigs experience. That episode made him rely on counterinsurgency more fanatically, which opened the way to Vietnam. It made him ignore the lesson taught by the CIA's own Inspector General's report — that the overthrow of Castro should not have been undertaken in the first place — and seek that goal even more single-mindedly, forcing previously reluctant CIA officers into the effort. His response to failure at the Bay of Pigs was not detachment and a calm review of the CIA's murderous activities. The response was anger, and a call for greater efficiency in those activities.

But if the Kennedys learned nothing from their first crisis with Cuba, how did they respond so wisely in the second Cuban crisis, when Russian missiles had to be removed? The orthodoxy is that such wisdom could only have been derived from lessons of the earlier mistake. But the orthodoxy assumes that the missile crisis ended in a triumph for America, and that assumption needs some looking at.

21

"Triumph"

When a man concludes that any stick is good enough to beat his foe with — that is when he picks up a boomerang.

— GILBERT CHESTERTON

FOR ALL THE TALK of "learning" from the Bay of Pigs, and for all the earlier talk of seeking options, there is one option the Kennedys considered neither before *nor after* the failure of the Cuban invasion: leaving Castro alone. Some people — notably William Fulbright — tried to raise that option before the landing: Castro, said the Senator, is a thorn in America's side, not a dagger through the heart. After the landing, the CIA's own Inspector General had the same advice — which was not seriously considered. Perhaps the best lesson was presented gnomically by Clayton Fritchie, on Adlai Stevenson's staff at the UN. He told the President, "It could have been worse." Kennedy wondered how. "It might have succeeded."

Suppose the invaders had overthrown Castro's army, killed or imprisoned Castro himself, and ushered home the "government in exile." America would have produced José Miro Cardona, like a rabbit out of Uncle Sam's hat. Would he have commanded popular support in Cuba? He was opposed even by some of the exile invaders, even by some of the CIA organizers. No matter what his own qualifications, which were impressive, anyone would be tainted by the treatment he was given in America. The way he was shuttled from New York to Florida, after being kept ignorant of the invasion, would be an affront to Latin pride. That might not have been true before the revolution; but after it, his presence would have been a living sign of American imperialism. He would have been our puppet, and keeping him in power would have become a full-time American task — like propping up Thieu or Ky in Saigon. At a time when even the fading colonial regimes found it impossible to retain their former possessions, how could revolutionary Cuba submit to a new round of imperialism from America? Even if we succeeded in Cuba itself, the blatant effort involved would be feared and resented throughout Latin America and the Caribbean.

Robert Kennedy discovered that no serious estimate of the chances for a popular uprising had been asked for. Needless to say, the further chance of keeping an American surrogate in power could not have been considered, three or four steps further down the road from a hypothetical uprising. Hard as this is to credit, the Kennedys saw the elimination of Castro as a thing so obviously desirable in itself that no serious thinking went into the aftermath of that blessed event. The same thing continued true during the period when exotic poisons and sporadic sabotage and thousands of agents were used against Castro. For the New Frontier team, power meant doing what one wanted — and the team wanted to remove Castro.

The Kennedys thought power had only two components — ample resources, and the will to use them. In the Bay of Pigs affair, Kennedy was assured by Bissell that we had ample resources, so he concentrated on toughening his will. Then, when things began to go wrong, Robert Kennedy supplied the will and demanded that people in the control room come up with the mental and other resources: with all the famous talent around the table, *something* could be done. I once heard Eunice Kennedy say almost exactly the same thing at the head of her dining table. It is obviously a favorite line with the Kennedys. Nothing can withstand the direction of great talent by a will to win.

It is this attitude toward power that explains the frustrating, the almost literally maddening, impact of Castro on John and Robert Kennedy. Cuba obviously had fewer resources, of every sort, than America possessed. Yet Castro continued successfully to defy the giant — which meant that, being inferior in the one component of power, resources, Castro must have a compensatory superiority in the other component, force of will. The Kennedys were winners, yet *he* kept winning in his contest with them — proving that he was an even more determined winner. It was macho to macho, and he came off manlier, "ballsier," his charisma as intact as that beard the CIA scientists had tried to hex.

This Kennedy attitude was simply an exaggeration of a basically American attitude toward the postwar world. It would show up again during the Vietnam war — the fury that a "third-rate" nation could successfully defy us. Earlier, we had instituted a security program more stringent than the one imposed during the war itself, to retain our nuclear monopoly. Given that overwhelming resource, we could dispose of the world benignly, without resistance. As Philip Marlowe told the doctor, "When a man has a gun in his hand, you are supposed to do what he says." We had the nuclear gun in our hand — and, to our amazement, people still refused to do what we told them to. We had all the resources, so the failure must be in our will. McCarthyism was a great national search for the conspirators, the enemies within, who had sapped our will. That *had* to be the deficient component, since our resources were so great.

But the best students of power — Machiavelli and Hume, Clausewitz and Tolstoy — have always placed the source of power in the will of the commanded not of the commanding. Political power is the ability to get others to do your will. If they refuse, you may have the ability to destroy them; but that is not political power in any constructive sense. We can, at present, blow up the world with our nuclear weapons; but that does not mean we can rule the world. Conquest is not, automatically, control. Machiavelli is constantly teaching the difference between those two concepts: "Anyone comparing one of the countries with the other will recognize a great difficulty of conquering the Turks, but great ease in governing them once conquered. . . . But it is just the reverse with realms governed like that of France." The difference lies not in the resources of the conqueror, but in the disposition of the conquered. The docile Turks resist well, but easily conform; the French are easily divided by their conquerors, but rarely if at all united by their rulers. As Tolstoy wrote in *War and Peace:* "Power, from the standpoint of experience, is merely the relation that exists between the expression of someone's will and the execution of that will by others," and the second factor is more determinative than the first.

Because of the tremendous modern powers of destruction, those who look only to the resources and will of America's rulers are astonished at the impotence of power as they conceive it. The Russians, Cuba, any "third-rate nation" can refuse to obey us, even though we are able to obliterate them. Given the "realities" of the force-equation, we have tended to dismiss "world opinion" as something outside the calculus of coercion, though it is at the very center of power as a reality. People obey, said David Hume, *only* because of opinion — what he called opinion of right (one should obey) and opinion of interest (it will pay one to obey). Insofar as quantum-of-force theorists took opinion into account, they thought only of interest — obey us or we'll blow you up; obey us because we have economic advantages to bestow. Vaguer forces like anticolonialism were dismissed as mere sentiment. But Hume would have recognized in them the "opinion of right" that gives stability to political power (opinion of interest can shift as the "bribes" on either side are altered). So the project for getting rid of Castro was seen simply in terms of ability to kill him, disrupt his regime, remove his person. The will of the Cuban people was never taken seriously as a factor in the power situation. How they would be ruled after we had conquered their leader — whether power to influence was coordinate with, or at odds with, power to disrupt — never entered into the Kennedys' calculations.

From the time of *Why England Slept,* John Kennedy had not thought of power as the recruiting of people's opinion, but as the manipulation of their response by aristocrats who saw what the masses could not see. Relying on his own talent and will, the leader prods them, against their instincts, toward duty and empire. Thus, in the secret war on Castro, the American people were not informed of their government's activities — those "in the know" performed these services for people who could not understand the necessities of power. But this benevolent censorship left Americans unprepared to estimate the situation when Castro accepted Russian missiles onto his territory.

To the American public, this step looked unprovoked, mysteriously aggressive, threatening because it added resources to a side that clearly had a strong will already. There was no way for Americans to know — and, at that point, no way Kennedy could bring himself to inform them — that Cuban protestations of purely defensive purpose for the missiles were genuine. We did not know what Castro did — that thousands of agents were plotting his death, the destruction of his government's economy, the sabotaging of his mines and mills, the crippling of his sugar and copper industries. We had invaded Cuba once; officials high in Congress and the executive department thought we should have followed up with overwhelming support for that invasion; by our timetable of a year to bring Castro down, the pressure to supply that kind of support in a new "rebellion" was growing. All these realities were cloaked from the American people, though evident to the Russians and to the Cubans.

In this game of power used apart from popular support, the Kennedys looked like brave resisters of aggression, though they had actually been the causes of it. Herbert Dinerstein has established, from study of Russian materials, that the Soviet Union considered Latin America not ripe for large Communist influence until the Bay of Pigs failure. That gave them an opportunity, as continued American activity against Castro gave them an excuse, for large-scale intervention in this hemisphere.

The Russians were aiming at influence, by their support of the Cuban David against a Goliath too cowardly to strike in the daylight. Americans, unaware of all this, did not bother to ask themselves hard questions about the real intent of the missiles in Cuba. The President said the purpose of the missiles was "to provide a nuclear strike capability against the Western Hemisphere." But why would Castro launch missiles against even one of our cities, knowing that would be a suicidal act? Just one of our nuclear bombs on Havana would have destroyed his nation.

Well, then, if Castro did not have the missiles to conquer us (and how would he control us afterward, presuming that he could conquer us), was he making himself a willing hostage to Russia's designs? Would he launch his missiles in conjunction with a larger Russian attack — again, knowing that we could incinerate his island as a side-blow in our response to Russia? Even if Castro had wanted to immolate his nation that way, his missiles would not have helped the Russians — might, rather, have been a hindrance, because of the "ragged attack" problem. If missiles were launched simultaneously from Russia and Cuba, the Cuban ones, arriving first, would confirm the warnings of Russian attack. Or, if Cuba's missiles were to be launched later, radar warning of the Russian ones' firing would let us destroy the Cuban rockets in their silos.

Then why were the missiles there? For defensive purposes, just as the Cubans said. We refused to accept this explanation, because President Kennedy had arbitrarily defined ground-to-ground missiles as "offensive" after saying offensive weapons would not be tolerated. Yet we called our ground-to-ground missiles on the Soviets' Turkish border defensive. Deterrence — the threat of overwhelming response if attacked — is a category of defense when we apply it to our own weapons; but we denied the same definition to our opponents. Which meant that we blinded ourselves to the only reason Castro accepted (with some reluctance) the missiles over which Russians kept tight control. He wanted to force the Kennedys to stop plotting his overthrow, by threatening that, if worse came to worst and we were ready to crush him, he would take some of our cities down with him.

Americans watched this drama, as it were, through a glass pane, unable to hear the dialogue. Even after the crisis, we read Khrushchev's defense of his motives for placing the missiles, and considered it mere Communist propaganda:

> Cuba needed weapons as a means of containing the aggressors, and not as a means of attack. For Cuba was under a real threat of invasion. Piratical attacks were repeatedly made on her coasts, Havana was shelled, and airborne groups were dropped from planes to carry out sabotage. . . . Further events have shown that the failure of [the Bay of Pigs] invasion did not discourage the United States imperialists in their desire to strangle Cuba. (Speech of October 12, 1962)

Now we know that every factual statement in that list is true. But then we were unable to credit the rationale for Russia's advance to the defense of a Latin American country:

> What were our aims behind this decision? Naturally, neither we nor our Cuban friends had in mind that this small number of IRBMs, sent to Cuba, would be used for an attack on the United States or any other country. Our aim was only to defend Cuba.

It might be argued, now, that even if we knew about our own clandestine war against Castro, and admitted that the missiles were placed for deterrence, we could not tolerate their presence so near us. After all, accident or crazy leadership might launch them. The same thing is true of Russian missiles, of course. As Robert McNamara said at the time, a missile is a missile, whether fired at us from Russia or from Cuba. If mere proximity was the threat, we are in greater danger now than during the installation of those missiles, since Russian submarines cruise closer to our shores than the ninety-mile distance to Cuba. And the Kennedy administration knew that would soon be the situation.

In extraordinary interviews for *The New Yorker,* William Whitworth heard Eugene Rostow, part of Lyndon Johnson's war administration, defend the Vietnam commitment in terms of America's psychic needs, rather than outright military threat. Looking back to the Cuban decision his brother Walt took part in, Rostow admitted there was no direct danger from the missiles:

> "But during the Cuban missile crisis," I said, "were we more threatened from a technological standpoint than we had been before the missiles were installed?"
> "No, I think we were just touching a nerve of concern. . . . The missile crisis was a situation that I think is important for us to think about, because we were ready to go."

Rostow talks of America as feeling psychically crowded and on the edge of panic. To our citizens, uninformed of the American campaign on Castro, the Cuban provocation seemed unmotivated and therefore eerie. President Kennedy had to do something to reassure the frightened populace. His toughness calmed a people "ready to go."

That last phrase is a key one for Rostow in defending the Vietnam war. We could feel "crowded" even by forces halfway around the world. And when that happens, we become "ready to go" —leaving our rulers with only one pressing problem: how to channel our aggression into a limited expression. "The Cuban episode is worth studying because we were ready to go then. There was a rage in the

country and a sense of threat, and these were extremely dangerous."
In the same way, if the North Koreans had added one more insult to
the capture of the *Pueblo* in 1969, the American people would have
been unrestrainable: "There was a lot of rage in the country about
that. And my guess is that if the Koreans acted up the Americans
would hit very hard. Very hard. That would be natural, and human,
but it might be dangerous." In the same way, if South Vietnam fell
to the Communists, we would feel crowded. The problem, Rostow
admits, is not one of immediate military threat, but of a sense of in-
security:

> I think that if we faced that situation we would have to become a
> garrison state on a scale we can't even imagine now, and be con-
> cerned about threats from every quarter of the compass — be
> hemmed in. We couldn't be the kind of society we want to be.

> The trade that counts for the United States is with Canada, West-
> ern Europe and Japan. That's the bulk of it. And we could survive
> without most of that trade, I suppose. It isn't that. It's the sense of
> being hemmed in that becomes so dangerous.

By this reading, President Kennedy had two dangerous situations
to deal with simultaneously — the missile emplacements, and
American panic over those emplacements. Robert Kennedy implicitly agreed with Rostow when he told the President he had to remove the missiles or be impeached. In other words, the President
was a captive of his own people's panicky emotions. Options were
denied him by the American people — he could not even think of
leaving the missiles in place. That avenue was sealed from the outset.

Yet Kennedy had himself stirred up the feelings that limited his
freedom. He had called the missiles offensive and exaggerated their
range. It is understandable that he would not reveal all the American
provocation that explained the presence of the missiles. But why did
he have to *emphasize* the unprovoked character of their placement?
He told the nation that the Russians had lied to him in promising
not to send offensive weapons to Cuba. He said in his address on the
crisis: "The greatest danger of all would be to do nothing." If he was
chained to a necessity for acting, he forged the chains himself.

In this he was renewing a cycle that has bound all our postwar
Presidents. In order to have freedom of maneuver, a sense of crisis is

instilled; but once that sense is instilled, it commits the leader to actions he did not have in mind when he excited the fears. The most famous instance of this is Harry Truman's use of Senator Vandenberg's advice — if he wanted to rally support for anti-Communist aid to Greece and Turkey, he would have to "scare hell out of the country." But once Truman had raised the spectre of communism as an immediate threat to America, he had to calm the people by imposing a security program, establishing the Attorney General's List, setting up the machinery in 1947 that McCarthy would use in the 1950s.

Henry Kissinger assured his old academic friends, during the Vietnam war, that such a war must be prosecuted to the end, lest a new McCarthyism arise to ask "Who lost Vietnam?" as it had asked "Who lost China?" War became a homeopathic cure for American bellicosity — a little war taps the aggressiveness that, bottled up, might break out in a larger war. By a kind of devilish symmetry, the contemptuous manipulation of public opinion leads to a slavishness toward public opinion. Kennedy thought he could wage a war out of sight of the American people, for the people's good; but when the Cubans responded in open ways, he could not explain their effrontery, and had to ride the wave of public fear. All the talent and willpower of the best and brightest could not manipulate away the emotions they had aroused.

Kennedy thought of himself and Castro in charismatic terms — the two leaders using skill and will against each other, fencing over the heads of their respective peoples. But Castro was openly recruiting his people to a revolutionary cause while Kennedy was secretly scheming at assassination. The difference extends to more than tactics. The mere removal of Castro would not have dissipated the revolutionary élan. An "indispensable man" fallacy was at work in Kennedy's approach to Cuba. Meanwhile, by failing to recruit the will of the American people in an open way, Kennedy was put in the position of lying to his citizens at a time when Castro was telling the truth about American intentions and schemings. Having fooled the people in order to lead them, Kennedy was forced to serve the folly he had induced.

22

"Restraint"

IN DEALING WITH THE CUBAN MISSILES, John Kennedy displayed a restraint that has become legendary. It made Arthur Schlesinger rather weak in the knees:

> It was this combination of toughness and restraint, of will, nerve and wisdom, so brilliantly controlled, so matchlessly calibrated, that dazzled the world. Before the missile crisis people might have feared that we would use our power extravagantly or not use it at all. But the thirteen days gave the world — even the Soviet Union — a sense of American determination and responsibility in the use of power which, if sustained, might indeed become a turning point in the history of the relations between east and west.

Undoubtedly there was restraint exercised in the White House, most laudably when a U-2 plane was shot down during the tensest moments of the quarantine, before Russia had agreed to pull back. Although "ExCom," the ad hoc Executive Committee assembled to cope with the crisis, had earlier agreed to take out one of the surface-to-air (SAM) missile sites if this happened, the President wisely said he would wait for Khrushchev's response to the principal point of contention.

There was also restraint, of a sort, in the quick rejection of a plan for outright conquest of the island — though no one was very serious about proposing that. The option that did get serious consideration, and toward which the President at first inclined, was a preemptive air strike to destroy the missile launching pads. If the military had not suggested technical difficulties in this procedure, it would have been given even more serious attention — though Robert Kennedy's first reaction to the idea was to slip his brother a note saying, "I now know how Tojo felt when he was planning Pearl Harbor."

Though the air strike was rejected as a first step, it was prepared as the next step in case the blockade failed. Sorensen puts among the signs of Kennedy's restraint his use of the politer term quarantine instead of blockade — but this ranks rather with the counsels of prudence than of restraint. A blockade is, in international law, an act of war — the reason the administration had earlier given for not intercepting the shipments of SAMs to Castro. Kennedy was cautious in enforcing the blockade. But, with credit given for that, we have exhausted the evidences of Kennedy restraint. It is on the basis of these acts that he claimed, to his brother: "If anybody is around to write after this, they are going to understand that we made every effort to find peace and every effort to give our adversary room to move. I am not going to push the Russians an inch beyond what is necessary." That claim is demonstrably untrue, on at least five counts.

1. Kennedy could have explained to Americans that Castro was the object of secret warfare on the part of the CIA. This was something that would have been hard, and no doubt seemed impossible, to do. But the course was "unthinkable" only because Kennedy's search for "options" imprisoned him in the lies told to cover those options; and refusal to admit that his own acts caused the missile crisis in the first place makes it impossible to claim that *every* effort to make peace was explored and *every* possible chance for maneuver allowed to the other side.

2. Kennedy ruled out, instantly and without discussion, open diplomacy as a means of settling the crisis. When he learned of the

missiles' presence, he kept the knowledge secret — in the first place, to preserve the option of a sneak attack on the sites, what Robert Kennedy called "a Pearl Harbor." No attempt was made to negotiate with the Russians until an ultimatum had been secretly devised, then publicly delivered. This not only prevented prior diplomacy with the Russians, and forced them to capitulate; it excluded our allies from prior consultation, along with Congress and the UN. It is known that General de Gaulle's resentment of this act — the risking of nuclear war without consulting those endangered — confirmed him in the determination to carve out a separate nuclear role for France. Walter Lippmann quickly identified the weakness in Kennedy's approach. During the quarantine itself, he wrote:

> When the President saw Mr. Gromyko on Thursday [two days before the ultimatum], and had the evidence of the missile build-up in Cuba, he refrained from confronting Mr. Gromyko with this evidence. This was to suspend diplomacy. If it had not been suspended, the President would have shown Mr. Gromyko the pictures, and told him privately about the policy which in a few days he intended to announce publicly. This would have made it more likely that Moscow would order the ships not to push on to Cuba. But if such diplomatic action did not change the orders, if Mr. Khrushchev persisted in spite of it, the President's public speech would have been stronger. For it would not have been subject to the criticism that a great power had issued an ultimatum to another great power without first attempting to negotiate the issue. By confronting Mr. Gromyko privately, the President would have given Mr. Khrushchev what all wise statesmen give their adversaries — the chance to save face.

Later, of course, Kennedy would claim he *did* give Khrushchev every chance to save face. Lippmann, even before the crisis was over, proved that was not so. Later examples of preemptive strikes — Nixon's invasion of Cambodia, Israel's raids on an Iraqi power plant and Beirut — would invoke Kennedy's action in the Cuban crisis as a justification for neglecting diplomacy. In this respect, at least, the lesson conveyed by Kennedy's actions was not one of restraint but of unilateral boldness.

3. The decision-making body Kennedy set up was one that con-

duced toward boldness, not caution. When, in the spring of 1963, Theodore Sorensen gave a course of lectures at Columbia University celebrating the missile crisis as a model of decision-making, he praised the President for his lack of "preoccupation with form and structure" — proving he had learned nothing from the Bay of Pigs invasion. The "ExCom" was an informal body in more-or-less permanent session, without any order for screening and discussing advice. Its participants dropped in or out as they maintained prior commitments in order to keep the crisis secret. The President himself went off to Cleveland and Chicago while the ExCom debated life-and-death matters. Orderly inquest was at the mercy of separate schedules and improvised security. Roger Hilsman writes: "Everyone tried to keep up social engagements, although they sorely needed both the time and the rest that social engagements cost them. At one stage, nine members of the ExCom piled into a single limousine, sitting on each others' laps, to avoid attracting the attention that the whole fleet of long black cars would have done."

This hasty coming and going, in the back corridors, of men starved for sleep and rubbing against each other in different combinations, led to a blow-up when Adlai Stevenson joined them and suggested a diplomatic trade — removing the Marines from Guantanamo, or our missiles from Turkey, in exchange for Khrushchev's taking the missiles out. He was savagely denounced; even the President, according to Hilsman, showed his anger — and punished Stevenson through a friendly journalist, as he had done with Arthur Krock. Charles Bartlett was allowed to quote him as a "high official," in the *Saturday Evening Post,* saying, "Adlai wanted a Munich." The same pressures toward "macho" talk, the same inhibitions on any sign of weakness, were at work as in the Bay of Pigs sessions. Robert McNamara, after expressing his view that "a missile is a missile," was talked out of the recommendation to do nothing. For two days the President pushed for assurance that an air strike would work, and no one of sufficient weight was opposing him — no one but Robert. Though Sorensen later tried to credit the President's *procedures* with the happy outcome of the missile decision, that outcome — to the extent that it was happy — was the single accomplishment of Robert Kennedy.

What brought about this new restraint in the "bad Bobby" who was, even at the time of these sessions, urging Castro's overthrow? The explanation is almost surely the very fact that he *did* know how much the crisis owed to prior provocation on the CIA's part. The "mean altar boy" always had a lively moral strain in him — not enough to urge the admission (or even the suspension) of assaults on Castro, but enough to make him see that the Russians were not acting out of sheer malevolence, that they had some case, and were probably open to sensible bargaining. Mad as the President had been when Adlai Stevenson brought up the idea of trading Turkish missiles for the Cuban ones, Robert quietly assured Anatoly Dobrynin that America intended to remove the missiles from Turkey. Other ExCom people knew of the efforts being directed at Castro — Taylor and Helms and the President — but they do not seem to have felt this made it inappropriate to treat Russia as the aggressor. Only Robert Kennedy showed a dawning awareness that America might have been somewhat in the wrong. It would be a while before he began to sense the same thing about our course in Vietnam. But the "receiving equipment" for such moral signals was already in place; and that alone — plus Robert's influence with his brother — saved the ExCom from acting as recklessly as the Bay of Pigs advisers had. The veterans of the later sessions would make exaggerated claims for their own restraint — in part because they could easily have taken less prudent steps, but for one man. Against the background of other courses forcefully urged, the outcome did look so magnanimous as to seem self-denying.

4. Nonetheless, the course pursued was reckless. President Kennedy did not give the Russians the obvious opportunity to "save face." In the matter of the Turkish missiles, he humiliated them gratuitously, though the missiles had no military importance for us. Sorensen says the trade-off was one of the first things suggested as the ExCom began its considerations, but that "the President had rejected this course from the outset." His anger at Stevenson for proposing the trade seems to have come in part from the "nerve" he showed in raising again a possibility the President had ruled out. Some have said the President did not want to insult our allies by withdrawing the missiles without consulting them. But the secret sessions were an odd place for punctilious consultation of allies to become a great concern; and, even if this argument were made sin-

cerely, the hurt feelings of allies were little compared with the danger we put them in by serving an ultimatum rather than offering a deal. Besides, the argument is clearly not sincere. Kennedy had already ordered the Turkish missiles removed, and mere procedural delay had kept them in place to this point. Not only were they of no value; they were a source of possible trouble. Hilsman notes that they were "obsolete, unreliable, inaccurate, and very vulnerable — they could be knocked out by a sniper with a rifle and telescopic sights."

Though the Turkish missiles meant nothing to us, they were a symbolic grievance to the Soviet Union — in fact, exactly the kind of affront we were complaining of. We felt "crowded" by missiles ninety miles from our shore. The Russians had to live with the ignominy of hostile missiles right on their border. If Kennedy's first and only concern was the missiles' removal from Cuba — as he and his defenders proclaimed — then a trade was the safest, surest way to achieve that goal. But Kennedy clearly had other priorities in mind — he wanted to remove the missiles *provided* he did not appear forced to *bargain* with the Soviets to accomplish this. He must deliver the ultimatum, make demands that made Russia act submissively. He would not, as he put it, let Khrushchev rub his nose in the dirt. Which meant that he had to rub Khrushchev's nose in the dirt; and that Khrushchev had to put up with it. Kennedy would even risk nuclear war rather than admit that a trade of useless missiles near each other's countries was eminently fair. The restraint, then, was not shown by Kennedy, but by Khrushchev. He was the one who had to back down, admit his maneuver had failed, take the heat from internal critics for his policy.

It was not known at the time that Robert Kennedy informally told Dobrynin that the Turkish sites would be dismantled. Since that detail was published (after his death) in Kennedy's own account, it has been taken as a further sign of restraint on America's part. But the secrecy of the assurance is what mattered — along with its late informal relay to a secondary figure in the chess game. Removing the Turkish missiles had been part of the open trade proposed in the famous "second letter" of Khrushchev — the letter Robert Kennedy said should be ignored. When, one day before the President's deadline ran out, Robert Kennedy told Dobrynin that he thought the missiles would be removed, he expressly "said that there could be no quid pro quo or any arrangement made under this kind of threat or pressure." In short, the missiles would be removed so long as the Russians got no credit for their removal, could make no plausible claim that they were bargaining with an equal, not submitting to an ultimatum. It should be remembered that Robert Kennedy wrote his account of the missile crisis in the summer of 1967, five years after the event and when he was rethinking his own hawkish position on Vietnam. If all he could do to emphasize his own dovish behavior in the missile crisis was suggest this last-minute secret assurance to Dobrynin, there is no reason to think this represented a significant act of restraint on the part of the Kennedy administration itself. Kennedy still insisted on Russia's public humiliation over a symbol that had no real military importance for us — an insistence that faced us with a real military threat if the Russians did not accede to the harsh demand we made. Macho appearance, not true security, was the motive for Kennedy's act — surely the most reckless American act since the end of World War II.

5. To add injury to insult, Kennedy — with his insistence on crisis — sent his brother to Dobrynin to announce a twenty-four-hour deadline for Russia's response. This further "crowded" the Russians, made panicky response possible. It rubbed their noses a little deeper into the dirt. The justification for this hasty act was the possibility that some missiles might be armed and launchable within forty-eight hours. But what was the probability that Cuba would use a few short-range missiles, in a kamikaze attack, when America was in a state of alert, its SAC bombers in the air, its Polaris missiles prowling the waters around Cuba? It was surely less than the probability that Russia, backed into a corner and given a deadline, might make some hasty decision — perhaps to attack American troops in Germany — that could trigger World War III. Neither course of action made much sense. But the *less* probable was made the basis of our deadline, which threatened to trigger the *more* probable of two horrible possibilities. Kennedy, in other words, increased our danger by the deadline, on the chance that this would increase our victory, make it more total.

If the Russians had made even a *limited* attack in Europe or elsewhere, the Kennedy buildup of crisis rhetoric would have made it hard to refrain from nuclear response. After all, he felt unable to refrain from exaggerated response to the nonthreat in Cuba. He would have been *less* free to defy American "panic" if Khrushchev had imitated his bellicosity.

So the reaction to missiles in Cuba was not a model of restraint, of rational decision-making, of power used in peaceful ways. That it turned out "well" for us is a tribute to Khrushchev's restraint, not ours. And was the glorious victory so total after all? We have seen that it helped push de Gaulle farther down his independent path. Khrushchev's loss contributed, or appeared to contribute, to his own later downfall — depriving us of a leader who was easier to deal with than his successors. Besides, what was the lesson of the missile crisis for the Russians? That one should not back off in further confrontations over that island? When Jimmy Carter declared, in 1979, that the presence of Russian combat troops in Cuba was "intolerable," there was no sign of accommodation from Russian leaders. They have only two or three enthusiastic allies outside their own satellite system and Cuba is the most important one — one they cannot afford to fail again; one no Russian leader, with the example of Khrushchev before him, will abandon. We purchased submission at the price of later intransigence, which is often the case after gratuitous humiliation.

Praise of Kennedy for his conduct in the missile crisis often reaches the conclusion that he learned pacific ways in this "restrained" success. On the contrary, he must have learned that his own and his party's popularity soars when he can make an opponent visibly "eat crow," even if the only way to serve up that menu is to risk the national safety. But the argument for Kennedy can be put in a more persuasive way if we say that the totality of his victory gave him room to be more magnanimous in other areas, to make pacific overtures without looking dangerously weak or "dovish." The Kennedy literature makes his American University speech, in favor of negotiation and arms limitation, the fruit of the missile decision's outcome.

But if that is so, what lesson is taught? That one must never negotiate but in the wake of humiliating an enemy? Surely that is the lesson applied year after year in Vietnam. We must never negotiate from weakness, went the slogan; so, after sedating the war during elections, there was a heavy bombing schedule every November and December of the even-numbered years, culminating in the "Christmas bombing" of 1972. Negotiation, which should mean the achievement of mutual benefit by diplomatic means, has become for Americans the negotiation of the other side's surrender after a defeat. We could never go to the negotiating table as equals — that would look like trading missile for missile as equals in 1962.

Some critics, notably Ronald Steel, have accused Kennedy of pushing for a knockout blow late in October of 1962 in order to affect the congressional elections. Put so crudely, the charge is unfair. Rather, an eye on domestic response locked Kennedy into the cycle which makes it impossible for American leaders to make peaceful moves except in the aftermath of bellicose ones successfully carried out. Steel notes that even Sorensen quoted a Republican ExCom member (probably Douglas Dillon) during the crisis:

> Ted, have you considered the very real possibility that if we allow Cuba to complete installation and operational readiness of missile bases, the next House of Representatives is likely to have a Republican majority? This would completely paralyze our ability to react sensibly and coherently to further Soviet advances.

Roger Hilsman, too, admits that domestic pressures affected Kennedy's judgment during the crisis. To some extent, he was still the prisoner of his rhetoric, making an apparently "soft" attitude toward Cuba impossible:

> The fact of the matter was that President Kennedy and his administration were peculiarly vulnerable on Cuba. He had used it in his own campaign against Nixon to great effect, asking over and over why a Communist regime had been permitted to come to power just ninety miles off our coast.

Furthermore, in order to restrain the calls for interdiction of SAMs to Cuba, Kennedy had exaggerated the danger of ground-to-ground missiles (thinking they would not be installed):

Thus in trying to meet the opposition's charges and to reassure the public without actually saying why it was so confident, the administration fell into the semantic trap of trying to distinguish between "offensive" and "defensive" weapons.

Kennedy was soon stuck with his own claim that ground-to-ground missiles were offensive: "If the missiles were not important enough strategically to justify a confrontation with the Soviet Union, as McNamara initially thought, yet were 'offensive,' then the United States might not be in mortal danger but the administration most certainly was." When Ronald Steel quoted that sentence to show that Kennedy was affected by electoral pressures, Hilsman replied with the claim that he had larger issues of political support in mind: "I meant that the administration would be faced with a revolt from the military, from the hardliners in the other departments, both State and CIA, from not only Republicans on Capitol Hill but some Democrats too." Kennedy, who boasted that McNamara had brought the military people under control, had to please them, or they would "revolt."

Over and over in our recent history Presidents have claimed they had to act tough in order to *disarm* those demanding that they act tough. The only way to become a peacemaker is first to disarm the warmakers by making a little successful war. And if the little war becomes a big one, it must be pursued energetically or the "hawks" will capitalize on the failure. War wins, either way. If you are for it, you wage it. And if you are against it, you wage it. So Kennedy is given credit for making overtures to lessen the threat of nuclear weapons only after he risked nuclear war to get the "capacity" to make a mild disarmament proposal. That was the obvious lesson of the missile crisis. Even Sorensen had to admit it was the moral many people derived: "Ever since the successful resolution of that crisis, I have noted among many political and military figures a Cuban-missile-crisis syndrome, which calls for a repetition in some other conflict of 'Jack Kennedy's tough stand of October 1962 when he told the Russians with their missiles either to pull out or look out!' Some observers even attributed Lyndon Johnson's decision to escalate in Vietnam to a conviction that America's military superiority could bring him a 'victory' comparable to JFK's." Sorensen thinks that was not the lesson that *should* have been learned. But it is the lesson that *was* learned. Assertions of power rarely teach what the powerful intended.

23
Charismatic Nation

His success was the immediate cause of his destruction.

— GIBBON, of the Emperor Maximus

THE KENNEDYS RIGHTLY DAZZLED America. We thought it was our own light being reflected back on us. The charismatic claims looked natural to a charismatic country. America, we like to think, has been specially "graced." Set apart. The first child of the Enlightenment, it was "declared" to others as the harbinger of a new order. Yet this rationally founded nation was also deeply devotional, a redeemer nation. Reason and religion, which should have contended near our cradle, conspired instead. If we kept ourself isolated from others, it was to avoid contamination. If we engaged others, we did so from above, to bring light into their darkness. To deal with others as equals would betray our mission.

So, in the missile crisis, some asked why we should resent missiles near our shores more than Russians were allowed to resent missiles on their border. But to most Americans the answer was obvious. We are not like other nations. We can be trusted to use our power virtuously. Our missiles were not offensive because they were *ours*. As Hanson Baldwin wrote, after the crisis, in the New York *Times:* "The real measure of the overseas base therefore is its purpose. The United States contention, shared by its allies, has always been that its overseas bases were established solely in answer to Communist aggressive expansionism and at the request of the countries concerned." The distinction between missiles depended less on their structure and range than on the character of the country producing them. And who could doubt our good character?

If we refuse to "negotiate from weakness" (i.e., from parity with the negotiating partner), that is because we are not simply one more member of the community of nations scrambling for narrow advantage. It is our task to think for all those involved, to keep scavengers away from the world's developing nations, to uphold freedom around the globe. Charisma exempts from normal process. The sense of a "graced" country lay behind our dispatching of Peace Corps youths to dazzle the world with our virtue. The implicit message, underneath the laudable desire to serve, was anti-Communist even when crude propagandizing was excluded. The message was: Be like us.

The sign of grace is luck, and who could be luckier than Americans? Given a vast continent to explore and exploit in comparative isolation from the rest of the world, we entered the game of the great powers only when we were ready to — on our own schedule, for our own purposes. Our first major intervention in this century was for the rescue of democracy; but the old system of power relations thwarted us at Versailles. A whole generation of rising leaders vowed that would not happen next time, and the "lesson of Versailles" made us conduct our very own war to a conclusion that left us masters of the world. In 1945, America — which had entered the war still reeling from the Depression — stood at the pinnacle of power, with resources no other nation ever possessed. Our enemies had been defeated by a policy of total war carried through to unconditional surrender. Our allies had been invaded and weakened. Our military apparatus was the greatest ever assembled; and nuclear weaponry was added to it in the climactic last act of our Pacific campaign.

Total war was waged to insure the totality of our control afterward. Those defending the unconditional surrender policy, against military and intelligence people who said it would prolong the war, maintained that only this would give America a "clean slate" for building a world order of peace. The fascist philosophy had to be destroyed, erased, removed from the world like a cancer. This was not simply a war for trade rights, or ports, or access to material resources. The American *vision* had to prevail.

Our power had created expectations which alone can explain the panic of America in 1947. We were still the economic and military master of the world. No one could threaten our shores. We had a nuclear monopoly. Our prosperity continued. No other country could impose its will on us. Yet in an extraordinary series of moves, President Truman followed Senator Vandenberg's advice and scared the hell out of the country. Solidifying new prerogatives from this sense of crisis, he instituted the security system, established the CIA (which began building resistance centers for World War III), and opened a campaign to avoid "losing" Turkey and Greece as we were losing China.

Why this panic in the very heart of power? We were hostages to our own broad claims. By attempting total control, we felt imperiled *anywhere* when *anything* went against our will. We were illustrating a truth that Gibbon taught in various ways. The expansion of one's rim of power diffuses internal resources, stretches the thin periphery ever farther out, so that a small concentration of hostile force can burst the bubble of empire. Since "the increasing circle must be involved in a larger sphere of hostility," the entirety is risked at each isolable point along the rim.

The Eisenhower years represented a tacit acceptance of limits, at odds with this aspiration toward universal control. That is what Senator Kennedy complained of when he said the country must get moving again (Walt Rostow's phrase). A new generation must take up again the torch that had guttered out. Massive retaliation had become an excuse for inaction. Little challenges around our periphery of influence were being neglected, cumulative losses not redressed. Maxwell Taylor complained of the cuts in defense spending. Space did not command any enthusiasm on Eisenhower's part, even after Russia's Sputnik "victory."

We now know that Eisenhower let Allen Dulles initiate secret coups or coup attempts in Iran and Guatemala, Indonesia and the Congo. But, despicable as these were, they were kept secret precisely because there was no public policy of engagement everywhere, no mystique of countering any guerrillas who might pop up. The Dulles operations were small enough, and tailored to the individual situation, for "success" (as in Iran) to cause no widespread outcry against the United States and failure (as in Indonesia) to let us cut our losses with no great public humiliation. Eisenhower's attitude toward intervention in a colonial war was made clear when he over-ruled all the advisers asking him to rescue the French at Dien Bien Phu.

Eisenhower admitted there is a "tyranny of the weak," an ability of massed little forces to trouble the thin-drawn periphery of American concerns, for which there is no properly "calibrated" response. The gnats could be smashed, but only in ways that made the giant look worse than its challengers. Short of obliteration, no intimidation was credible for most of these enclaves of defiance. Recruiting their will was either impossible or would be made impossible by military threat. There was nothing to do but ignore what could not be controlled in any useful way. That was the advice of a man who understood power, its meaning and limits.

But John Kennedy had different teachers on the nature of power. They thought any recognition of limits signaled a failure of nerve. For them the question was not *can* you do everything, but *will* you do everything? The American resources were limitless — brains, science, talent, tricks, technology, money, virtuosity. The only thing to decide was whether one had the *courage* to use all that might — and John Kennedy, in his inaugural address, assured us that he had. In his first major speech on defense, he said: "Any potential aggressor contemplating an attack on any part of the free world with any kind of weapons, conventional or nuclear, must know that our response will be suitable, selective, swift, and effective." Anywhere along the outmost sweep of our vast reach, we would strike if provoked.

It might not have been possible for the Romans to protect an expanding perimeter of power, one thinned by its extension to enclose the known world. But America could protect the whole world, because we had things the Romans lacked — jet planes, helicopters, napalm, defoliants, one-man water-walking rockets, computers, and theoreticians of the strategic hamlet. We could do everything, it was believed, so long as we never did, in any one spot, more than was absolutely necessary. That is where Robert McNamara's computers came into play — for dispatching the exactly right-sized teams to troubled spots. Admittedly the computers could not measure things like the strength of anticolonial feeling. But that was considered an advantage by Kennedy's "pragmatic" nonideologists. For them, the hard facts of cash and firepower spoke louder than sentiment.

The Americans would come with "clean hands," as Pyle says in the Greene novel — not apostles of capitalism, like Eisenhower's big businessmen; not preachers of world ideals, like Wilson. We were just technicians of development in the age of Rostow; producers of what mankind wants, said McNamara of Detroit. This was the policy Arthur Schlesinger had proclaimed, as part of the "end of ideology," in his book *The Vital Center:* World War II veterans who had "learned the facts of life through the exercise of power" realized that life "is sometimes more complicated than one would gather from the liberal weeklies."

For men holding such views, Vietnam was an ideal place to try out new tools of power — a place to prove that development could be encouraged without colonial exploitation; a place where mobility and concentration of firepower could do more than massive armies and huge weapons; a place where infiltrating North Vietnamese could be interdicted. Jungle and swamp would train our new guerrillas to all kinds of conditions. Despite later talk of a "quagmire" that sucked us in, Americans actually charged into Vietnam — thinking, as we did of Cuba, that a few men brilliantly directed could wrap the whole thing swiftly up. Officers were cycled through to observe the process because the opportunity would not last forever.

A speech written for Kennedy's delivery on the day he died boasted that he had "increased our special counterinsurgency forces which are now engaged in South Vietnam by 600 percent." The administration was still presenting Vietnam as a symbol of Kennedy's success in the books written just after his death. Hugh Sidey, for instance, puts this in his list of breakthrough achievements:

> A deep pride in the state of our armed forces really was the biggest factor in the underlying serenity. Our superiority in missiles, our improved conventional fighting capability and the new emphasis on guerrilla warfare, all carefully tailored by Robert McNamara, reestablished confidence in our strength. In Southeast Asia the enemy had been engaged on his own terms, and though there still was no victory in Vietnam or Laos, we were no longer losing.

William Kaufmann, celebrating the success of *The McNamara Strategy,* wrote in 1964:

In fact, the war in South Vietnam, if it has done nothing else, illustrates how the Military Assistance Program and an American military advisory group can produce an indigenous combat force of significant power with a relatively small commitment of American manpower. But the real test of South Vietnam is less of the Military Assistance Program than it is of the ability of the United States to deal effectively with all the related aspects of subversion and guerrilla warfare.

The unhappy later progress of the Vietnam war made Kennedy's defenders claim he would have withdrawn from the contest after committing 16,500 troops to it. The only positive evidence that is offered for this view is Kennedy's assurance to Senator Mansfield that he would have to get out of Vietnam sometime after the 1964 election. But the year intervening between his death and that election would have involved further commitments of the sort that President Johnson (despite his initial distaste for the idea of a larger war) made, on the advice of Kennedy's most trusted counselors. And Kennedy's "commitment" would have been even more binding. Not only was he the initiator of the process Lyndon Johnson took over; it was an initiative formulated in the terms of the "flexible response" by which Kennedy hoped to justify his whole military program and foreign policy. Was he going to let Green Berets, too, learn "that Superman is a fairy"? Any withdrawal would have been a confession that his overarching strategy — with Rostow's rationale, and Taylor's strategy, and McNamara's reorganization — was feckless: it could not deal with precisely the kind of problem it was framed for.

Not only Kennedy's advisers, but the Kennedy brothers, supported the Vietnam war for years after John Kennedy's death. As late as 1966, Robert was still applying the wrong "lesson of the missile crisis" to Vietnam: "As a far larger and more powerful nation learned in October of 1962, surrender of a vital interest of the United States is an objective which cannot be achieved." This was said to assure people that his proposal for negotiating with the Communists did not mean a surrender — though that proposal was itself no guarantee of a quick solution, as Richard Nixon and Henry Kissinger would find to their sorrow. If it took so long for Robert

Kennedy to disengage, even under President Johnson, whose skill at conducting his brother's policy could be blamed for its mishaps, it would have been impossible to disengage with his brother still in charge and hoping to "win."

John Kenneth Galbraith has suggested that Kennedy was about to change his policies because he had expressed a desire to get rid of Dean Rusk after the 1964 election. But that desire signals the opposite of any withdrawal from Vietnam. The man he wanted in Rusk's place was McNamara, than whom there was no more "hawkish" adviser in 1964. Rusk, despite his hawkish line under President Johnson, was unacceptable to the Kennedys because he seemed too *timid* and irresolute.

That Kennedy would have started disengaging from Vietnam, at the very time when he had hope of building a new administration there in the wake of Diem's overthrow, is unlikely. Though America did not engineer Diem's assassination, we allowed it, hoping for better things. As Roger Hilsman wrote in 1964: "The downfall of the Diem regime gave Vietnam and the United States a second chance to carry out an effective program to defeat the Communist guerrillas and win the people. Ambassador Lodge and whomever Kennedy might have chosen to replace General Harkins, whose tour of duty was coming to an end, might well have done the trick — if Kennedy had lived." It should be remembered that Hilsman was considered a "dove." There was no dove position in Kennedy's administration that stood for withdrawal. The doves were for winning the war by gentler methods. If Kennedy had wanted to make withdrawal possible, he would have had to invent a new position out of thin air — against all the forces unleashed by his own rhetoric and planning, conveyed through his network of advisers.

The principal division between Kennedy's advisers just before his death pitted the "political solution" people against the "military solution" people. But the political solution was for further intervention, more central American command, and increased activity. Hilsman, for instance, thought that more men rather than more bombs were needed:

Our proposal was to put a division of American ground forces into Thailand as a warning and couple it with communications to

North Vietnamese representatives in the various Communist and neutral capitals. If the warning was not heeded, that division could be moved right up to the Laos border, and a second division could be introduced into Thailand. If that set of warnings was also ignored, a division could be introduced into Vietnam, and so on — not to fight the Viet Cong, which should remain the task of the South Vietnamese, but to deter the north from escalating.

Meanwhile, our "advisers" would direct an illegal "Bay of Pigs" operation into Laos, keeping our involvement clandestine:

> To help protect the more northern portions of South Vietnam, it might be necessary to do the ambushing in Laos. But there was a world of international political difference between a black-clad company of South Vietnamese rangers ambushing a black-clad unit of Viet Cong infiltrators on a jungle trail in Laos and American jets dropping bombs in Laos.

The "political" solution promised more for less, but involved an even more complete control of the situation. We needed better puppets in Saigon, to be treated as José Miro Cardona had been in New York. Hilsman's own hope was for the strategic hamlet approach ("clear and hold" rather than "search and destroy"), which had only failed because of a lack of the central discipline Americans must supply: "The major weakness of the program under the previous [Diem] regime, [R. K. G.] Thompson reported, had been the lack of overall strategic direction and Nhu's policy of creating hamlets haphazardly all over the country."

This "lesser" option actually involved greater interference in the entire life of the country — we would build it up from scratch in hamlets we sited and ruled — and a great arrogance about America's ability to dispose of all things sweetly with minimal violence. The "doves" had decided that the Ngo family could not shed the taint of collaboration with the French colonizers (something America was not guilty of), so they had to go. But Arthur Schlesinger, in his life of Robert Kennedy, points out that the Ngos were showing a willingness to negotiate with the North, rather than allow America to take away the rule of their country, just at the time America helped topple the Ngos. Bad as their family's record had been, in the eyes of their countrymen, they were at least Vietnamese, and did not want to accept de facto dictatorship by American proconsuls:

> The Ngo brothers were, in their anachronistic fashion, authentic Vietnamese nationalists. They were reluctant about American troops and resistant to American interference. "Those who knew Diem best," Robert Shaplen of the *New Yorker* wrote after twenty years in Vietnam, "felt that neither he nor Nhu would ever have invited or allowed 550,000 American soldiers to fight in their country and to permit the devastation caused by air attacks." Diem may also have felt, as Bui Kien Thanh has suggested, that massive American intervention would provoke massive Chinese intervention and deliver Vietnam to its historic enemy. In May 1963 Nhu proposed publicly that the United States start withdrawing its troops. In the summer he told [Michael] Forrestal in his "hooded" way that the United States did not understand Vietnam; "sooner or later we Vietnamese will settle our differences between us." "Even during the most ferocious battle," Nhu said to Mieczyslaw Maneli, the Polish member of the International Control Commission established in 1954 to supervise the Geneva agreement, "the Vietnamese never forget who is a Vietnamese and who is a foreigner."

Maneli was a go-between in the diplomatic feelers the Ngos had put out to Ho Chi Minh just before Diem was killed. It was to prevent more negotiating of that sort that General Khanh engineered an anti-Minh coup after the anti-Diem coup had succeeded.

The self-styled doves were drawing us deeper in while they thought they were getting us out. This corresponds to the general pattern of Kennedy's administration. It was not the military that caused most trouble, but the civilians; not the bureaucrats but the "best and brightest" who thought they were beating the bureaucracy; not the Joint Chiefs of Staff but their "tamer," Robert McNamara; not Curtis LeMay, whose thirst to bomb was self-defeating because self-caricaturing, but Rostow and Taylor, who promised that we could get into Vietnam and never feel the urge to bomb. The advocates of "lesser" action envisioned the possibility of greater control — which always (just) slipped their grasp. Attempts at total control always do.

We have seen that Hilsman wanted to introduce one, or two, or three divisions as a buffer, so his pacification program would have a chance to be tried. The real story of Vietnam is not that of counterinsurgency yielding to regular troops. From the outset, the counterinsurgents needed regular troops to scale the fighting down to a point where the counterinsurgents could be effective. Guerrillas need water to swim in, or an umbrella for their actions. Regular troops were, from the outset, that umbrella. Schlesinger says:

> As for counterinsurgency, it was never really tried in Vietnam. Taylor and Rostow, for all their counterinsurgency enthusiasm in Washington, roared home from Saigon [in 1961] dreaming of big battalions. . . . The Special Forces were sent to remote regions to help peripheral groups like the Montagnards. At the end of 1963 there were only one hundred Green Berets left in South Vietnam.

The other "advisers" sent in were regular troops; partly because the Special Forces training program was still in its infancy, but mainly because the circumstances for using the Special Forces had to be *created* — Diem had to be "controlled," we had to give him reinforcements for his army, stiffen his morale, while trying to refashion his regime.

So much for the lesson of the Bay of Pigs. We were still trying to find a situation that would not call for heavy military commitment, and using heavy military commitment in order to create that situation. The whole mystique of flexible response was that it would fit each contingency with the appropriate force. But rather than adapt to reality, we ended up trying to make reality adapt to our preconceptions.

At home, the Kennedy people thought they could apply "surgical" control to problems while ignoring the bureaucracy. Problems were isolable, to be removed from prior context and given a neat technical solution. That was a questionable approach even in our own country. "Break the Rules Committee" and you have not solved the problem of congressional recalcitrance — you have only embittered congressmen, who will resist more stubbornly. To think we could go into an alien culture and manipulate the "hearts and minds" of its inhabitants by technical skill — remove a Castro here, put up a strategic hamlet there — was always a delusion. Once again, confidence in our resources and will had made the complex interplay of millions of other wills seem irrelevant. Even the guerrilla experts who talked of winning the hearts of other people thought this could be done by image-manipulation on a level with American campaign tricks. General Lansdale, the most respected of the "hearts and minds" school, ran Operation Mongoose on the assumption that he could woo the people of Cuba from Castro by a religious indoctrination program that presented him as the Antichrist. Other Green Berets naturally reverted to the saying, "If you have them by the balls, their minds and hearts will follow." The Kennedy pursuit of power never got far away from balls.

There is no way of knowing what President Kennedy might have done had he lived. Could he have withdrawn from Vietnam without losing face? He thought he could not trade Turkish missiles for Cuban without being impeached, so necessary was it to keep America's hawks happy with his toughness. Would he have disowned his own policies and advisers in Vietnam, and done it in time to leave him any choice in the matter? Perhaps; there is no knowing. But he did not live — and the lessons of power, the men of power, the examples of power he left behind him gave us the war in Vietnam. Even when a Republican President, after four years of negotiation and bombing, disengaged from Vietnam, some of his critics blamed America for the bloody turmoil in Vietnam and Kampuchea. We never consider that other countries, freed from a colonial framework, must work out their own tribal and historical grievances without regard for us. If anything happens in the world, America must get the credit or the blame — we did not act, or we did not take the right actions. It never occurs to us that we are not all-important in the long-range tides of particular peoples' histories. Kennedy, though he might eventually have freed himself from these illusions of total American control, helped to strengthen them in other Americans. His real legacy was to teach the wrong lesson, over and over. The attempt at total control does not merely corrupt, as Acton said; it debilitates. It undoes itself.

24

The Prisoner of Power

Those whom the splendour of their rank, or the extent of their capacity, have placed upon the summit of human life have not often given any just occasion to envy in those who look up to them from a lower station.

— SAMUEL JOHNSON, "Life of Richard Savage"

HARRY TRUMAN ESTABLISHED for ex-Presidents the embarrassing custom of building libraries to themselves (Truman used to act as guide through his own shrine, signing things in the imitated Oval Office, or playing the piano). President Kennedy did not live to preside over his library's construction or arrangement; but one hopes he would have eliminated the more grandiose touches. The worst aspect of the exhibits is an illuminated dateline that runs over all the cases of memorabilia. Below a dividing line are important family dates (from the landing of the first Kennedy on America's shore), correlated, above the line, with events in world history. So, for 1917, we read "John F. Kennedy born in Brookline," conjoined with "Russian Revolution," as if Clio viewed history stereoscopically with a Kennedy always in one slide.

The pairings suggest, in places, more than coincidence — as when, late in 1963, we read below the line "President and Mrs. Kennedy arrive in Texas for political tour" just after reading, above the line, "Diem government in South Vietnam is overthrown."

The events in Edward Kennedy's life march side by side with history's major happenings. The Kennedy family's importance is asserted through this equal billing with World History. But it is hard to shine when one is sharing the stage, always, with Historical Events. Edward Kennedy enters the world, in 1932, partnered with "The New Deal comes to Washington." Some think he is fading from our politics in the same company. And, even aside from such particular chimings, it must be unsettling for one's life to be measured out on such a macroscopic scale — to have wars for playmates, manifestos shuffled with the dance cards, weddings woven into the rise and fall of nations. No man's life should be drawn across the rack of Everything Important supplied by this schedule.

Even if the exhibit were not there, I suppose, people would construct something like it in their minds. Edward Kennedy lives with two great growth charts traced behind him in the air. In every situation, whomever he is meeting, the implicit question hangs there: How does he measure up? Has he got the stuff to be another John F. Kennedy? Somehow Edward acquired, through his late twenties and early thirties, the reputation of being "the family's best politician"; but the 1980 race seems to have destroyed that claim. He lacks the John Kennedy flair, the knowing suggestion of familiarity with ideas, the witty aside that reinforced his poised air of dignity. When Edward poses as an intellectual, he looks uncomfortable. He is not dumb, by any means; but his political feel is for people — preferably other politicians — not for books. His "deep" speeches tend to be delivered woodenly. My wife and I saw that at a 1978 meeting in Philadelphia, where Kennedy addressed a group launching "Project '87" to prepare for the bicentennial of the Constitution's drafting. The audience was made up of fat cats and scholars. For the scholars he met (James MacGregor Burns pointing them out to him), he ran a tape recorder in his head, the importance of the Constitution today, a perfunctory recital for which he had been programmed.

That night's speech was well researched and well written — a timely argument against calling a new constitutional convention. But the audience was cool, made up of conservative Philadelphia money types (some at our table spoke well of the town's pistol-packing mayor, Frank Rizzo). Those who knew Edward Kennedy only from political rallies full of his supporters were dumbfounded when he spoke so poorly in the 1980 campaign. I was partly prepared for that by his failure to reach out to a skeptical audience in Philadelphia, even with good material prepared for him.

The demands to live up to the President's memory make Edward alternate exaggerated efforts at seriousness with collapses into rowdy relaxation; one minute Peck's Bad Boy, the next an Elder Statesman. When, for instance, he went to a reunion of his Virginia Law School classmates, the same year as that Philadelphia speech, his fellow alumni came to rib him about his school days and his presidential chances. The university president, Dr. Hereford, introduced him by remembering how, as a young faculty member, he rented his home during a sabbatical year to Kennedy and John Tunney. Hereford had some misgivings about turning his house over to students, but these were mollified when he heard that the Kennedy son was bringing a family maid to care for the place. The misgivings revived when he came back to town and heard, from the cabbie who picked him up at the airport, that his address was famous now for the parties thrown, the bands hired, the jolly crowds. As jocular reminiscences were exchanged, Kennedy rose and gave a stiff recital on the privilege of legal training. Just as he is invisibly manacled in the public company of women, so reports of his Charlottesville speeding tickets made him almost a caricature of sober responsibility when he went back to that scene. His name and his past imprison him. It is hard to cross every stage escorting History on your arm.

If Edward is not another poised John Kennedy, he is even less a rumpled and plunging Robert. Robert was a prematurely serious child and he aged into even more childlike earnestness. His haste to be with Cesar Chavez breaking a fast seemed to reflect a desire to make up for lost time, for the vigils in southern churches that Robert had not shared with Dr. King. In the Senate, Robert, the elder, was defiant of custom and lacking in respect for ancient colleagues. Edward, the younger brother, went around picking up Robert's broken crockery. Edward is temperamentally a joiner — Robert was a resigner. I remember speaking just after Edward Kennedy, in 1972, at an antiwar protest held in the Senate caucus room. Kennedy was one of only two Senators who showed up, and he spoke earnestly against the war. But the group, which was petitioning for redress of the constitutional grievance of undeclared war, got no encouragement from him in its determination to commit civil disobedience. That is not Edward's way. If Robert had been there, he would have made it clear he shared the group's gut feelings, even if he did not agree with their tactics. Edward Kennedy is a dutiful liberal, not a natural radical. He will be courageous in his choice of goals, but conventional in his pursuit of them. He stands true to old positions — not breaking into new territory, like Robert. His health plan, for instance, is an old measure adopted in most industrial democracies, and he has maneuvered for it in the accepted Senate ways. But in a period of economic retrenchment and noisy "antigovernment" rhetoric, this essentially centrist politician is thought of as the leftwardmost major figure in our politics, the principal target of right-wing political action committees. With a compromise abortion stand close to the majority position, he is considered a villain by antiabortion groups, in part because of his religion. The gun lovers love to haunt his campaigns. He *is* the Left to much of the Right, and his downfall would signal the permanent fall of the Left. It is interesting to see how, as his own position has been eroded, the stature of people scheming against him has diminished. At first it was Lyndon Johnson, who tried to oust the Kennedys and establish his own legitimacy. Then it was Richard Nixon, a President hiring gumshoes to pad around Chappaquiddick. Then Jimmy Carter devoted disproportionate time and effort to the project of "whipping his ass." Now it is John Dolan of the National Conservative Political Action Committee who thinks he holds Kennedy's fate in his hands. Just by bearing his name, Kennedy has come to resemble the aging gunfighter of western movies, the one every young punk wants to beat as a way of making his reputation.

I asked him, in his Virginia home, if he ever thought of his family legacy as a burden, something that hampers him, by now, more than it helps. "I can't think of my brothers that way. I'm just grateful for all the things they taught me, all the experiences we shared. For the rest, you just have to take that." It was mid-February of 1981, and defenders of the new Reagan administration had claimed *they* were heirs to whatever was good in the Kennedy presidency — leaving the actual Kennedy to take blame for all that was bad. Arthur Laffer, the prophet of Reagan's "supply side" economics, continually invoked the 1963 tax cut as the cause of America's last spurt of prosperity. Kennedy laughed at that: "It is one thing to have a tax cut while maintaining inflation at less than 3.6 percent for three years. It is another matter to impose one with double-digit inflation."

Columnist George Will, who threw a party for the incoming Reagan administration, said that the Republicans now uphold President Kennedy's tough stance against the Russians, the determination to close a defense gap. Edward Kennedy tries to recapture his own name, but is resigned about the prospects of success: "President Kennedy believed the nation must be strong; but he was willing to take imaginative steps like the nuclear test ban." When I press him on the differences between John Kennedy in 1960 and Robert Kennedy in 1968, he says that naturally both men changed with the experience of new things. But Robert underwent especially deep changes in his last years? "He certainly did." One is to presume that John Kennedy would have taken the same course — though it is hard to imagine him at a Cesar Chavez rally.

Edward Kennedy has to keep living three lives at once — or keep giving an account of the lives the other men lived for him. Walking through his empty house, crammed with pictures of the family, one realizes how much of his life has already been lived for him, off in directions he can neither take, anymore, nor renounce. At one time, the same-and-different Kennedy smile coming from so many faces clustered on mantel or shelf must have intensified his presence, replicating every aspect of family influence he could bring to bear. Now they seem to drain him — he seeps off into their fading images.

His divorce proceedings have been announced. Only one son is living with him at the moment, and he is at school. Today the Senator's press secretary, Robert Shrum, has come out for lunch with us. Otherwise Kennedy lives here alone. But his family is never far from his conversation. He has just come back from a visit with his mother in Florida, where the February rain and cold kept most people from swimming — but not the ninety-year-old Rose. "When she took me to church, there was no one at the altar with the priest, so she said, 'Teddy?' You would have been proud of me, Bob, serving mass." I said I would not know how to serve Mass in the new liturgy, not since Latin went out. *"Ad Deum qui laetificat juventutem meam,"* Kennedy rattles off, in schoolboy tones. Shrum takes up the next response, and I the third. We all agree the *"Suscipiat"* was the toughest response, and prove our point by variously misremembering it.

It was an unnaturally warm day in February: I had seen three chairs lined up before the front door when I parked my car — like deck chairs on a liner, each with its own giant blanket. I went in through the open door and found Shrum, who said, "The Senator likes to be outdoors every minute he can." We sat down like a silly version of the three leaders lined up at Yalta, to talk about nuclear disarmament. Kennedy favors a comprehensive test ban (CTB): "President Kennedy took the initiative which led to the first test ban. We need to have some of that imagination."

Is CTB feasible? "In 1974, I explained my proposal to Brezhnev in Moscow, and he said, 'If you had that in your pocket, I could sign it right now' — which surprised me. When I went back in 1978, I asked him why the Russians were opposing our CTB proposal. He said, 'You have changed the terms, from five years to three years. You have added to the number of on-site inspections' — the agreement to have any on-site inspections was a breakthrough that we wasted. 'You have changed from no explosions allowed to none above three kilotons.' "

Why did Kennedy think these changes had been made? "Brzezinski told me we had to get SALT II first, and go for CTB later." In fact the Carter administration, like the Nixon administration before it, resented Kennedy's dealings with Russian leaders as an infringement on their own power to make foreign policy. Kennedy is one of the few men who can be welcomed by foreign leaders as a kind of surrogate President — which infuriates real Presidents. He can hurt his own proposals simply by advancing them in his own name. He continues to live inside the pressures that made Robert fear the cause of peace would be hurt with President Johnson if a Kennedy carried its banner. When Edward Kennedy took up the cause of wage and price controls in the 1980 election, he guaranteed that President Carter would never consider that course. Such power to initiate is easily translated into a powerlessness to conclude.

I asked Kennedy if his belief that wage and price controls were needed had been dispelled by the election. "No." Will you continue to call for them while President Reagan actually takes off controls? "I believe in deregulation. We deregulated the airlines and that was even more successful than it appears — part of the savings were eaten up by the increase in fuel costs. But there are forty or so more areas where we can deregulate." Why beat one's head against a wall? If the mood is for deregulation, then deregulate — something, at least, gets done.

Did Kennedy feel the liberal cause was badly damaged by Reagan's triumph, by the loss of so many of Kennedy's liberal colleagues in the Senate? He denies that any overwhelming mandate was won. After all, who can expect an incumbent to win with thirteen percent inflation? "Twelve Democratic Senators lost by less than four percent." A few votes here or there and the Senate would still be Democratic. Yet Kennedy is a centrist politician. He says President Reagan should be given a chance to show whether he has a cure for the nation's economic troubles. "I hope he does. We are looking for grounds of agreement. Maybe President Reagan can bring about voluntary price restraint." He does not sound very hopeful. "Well, I guess it can be done; but that would take a tremendous investment of the government's time and energy. I asked Helmut Schmidt how he controls prices in Germany. He said it takes two hundred hours of his personal time during the working year, to keep after labor and business — I wonder how he keeps track of the exact hours?"

Attempts at accommodation with the Reagan people are part of Edward Kennedy's temperament. But a man who could not elicit cooperation from the preceding Democratic administration is unlikely to get much from a White House stocked with right-wing types who think of him as the personification of the Left, or as the heir to certain historical stands — the defense-gap shrillness, the tax cut — they want to *detach* from him and claim as their own. Besides, any chumminess with them would offend his own constituency, labor and blacks and the tattered remains of the New Deal generation. Kennedy shows no desire or design for forging an entirely new coalition. In fact, Gary Hart — one of the few liberal Senators to survive the 1980 election — expressly excludes Kennedy as "old fashioned" when he talks of forming a new Democratic program in the Senate. He thinks Kennedy's appeal is based on nostalgia, something that does not stir young politicians trying to build new careers.

If the Right transfers irrational grudges against this or that Kennedy to Edward, the Left nurses an intermittently hopeful disappointment at his failure to live up to its dreams for him. A few liberals are continually running him for President, and he must encourage them (mildly) to protect his eroding position in the Senate. His problem, for a long time, was how to keep running for President without actually having to *run*. In 1980, that difficult juggling act became an impossible one. President Carter gave him no "out" of loyalty or partnership with the Democratic incumbent. And Carter's disastrous personal polls left him no excuse to be drawn from party discipline. All those who had waited for years to see Kennedy run told him, in effect, that it was time to put up or shut up. I saw how these converging pressures worked during the summer of 1979 (that period of "malaise" when President Carter retreated to his mountaintop and consulted every important person in his party except Kennedy). In May, I rode from Washington to Baltimore with Douglas Fraser of the United Auto Workers, Kennedy's principal noncongressional ally in the campaign for governmental health insurance. Kennedy was announcing his health plan, to put it in competition with the President's — and he expected Fraser to be with him in the Senate caucus room when he answered press questions. But Fraser said he could not come unless Kennedy was a declared candidate for President. "If you are not going to take on Carter, I may have to live with him for another four years." Carter was cultivating Fraser with phone calls and White House meetings, which gave labor access and leverage. Fraser would sacrifice that to stand with a *campaigning* Kennedy, but not to help a mere Senator promote this bill with a slim chance of passage. At some point, even to advance his Senate projects, Kennedy had to say yes to all those begging him to run.

Fraser was dutiful, rather than begging; he still doubted Kennedy could live down Chappaquiddick. But he joined with Kennedy when he announced. Others were less calm in their advocacy. Multiply the kind of pressure Fraser was exerting a thousandfold, and one sees that Kennedy really had no choice to make in 1980 — he had to run for President. He was not free *not* to. His own lack of enthusiasm for the task showed in the poor preparation he had made. He was only running because everyone assumed Carter had to lose; why prepare for a rough race? Kennedy wants the presidency, if it comes to him by the pressure of events; but he does not have the fire in his belly to rule, like John Kennedy, or the determination of an underdog, like Robert in 1968. Edward rented a private "Air Force One," early in the fall of 1980, and campaigned as an incumbent. The same forces that left him no real choice about running debilitated him when he began the campaign. He was trapped in a race he could not win because he would only undertake a race he thought he could not lose.

It is hard for some to realize that Edward Kennedy is hobbled by his own apparent power. They saw him deliver a stunning speech to the 1980 Democratic convention, and watched the crowd on the floor go crazy with affection for the man and his heritage. Many of those who merely accepted Jimmy Carter as a candidate almost fanatically desired Edward Kennedy. He speaks to them with a voice no one else can equal. That was apparent not only at the party convention of 1980, but at the midterm meeting of Democrats in Memphis two years earlier. Kennedy stole that show with a single speech, in some ways a more powerful one than the televised 1980 address.

President Carter, fearing a mini-convention revolt in 1978, dispatched his entire White House operation to Memphis; then came himself, to sit meekly in two "workshops" while people criticized his record ("Can you imagine Lyndon Johnson sitting there letting others attack his performance?"); and gave a speech too fervent in its rhetoric and too tepid in its delivery. Jerry Rafshoon produced a presidential movie to awe the crowds. Eleven White House aides were given the job of countering Kennedy's single appearance at a health-care discussion. To an overflow audience in the largest hall off the convention floor itself, the moderator admitted the reality behind the discussion of various health programs: Governor-Elect Bill Clinton of Arkansas said there had been a change in the program, that they were really going to discuss "the relative merits of Georgia peanuts and Massachusetts cranberries."

Joseph Califano led off for the White House, arguing that the economy would not allow any more in health care than the administration was proposing. Kennedy, following, thundered against that timid position. His prepared text, distributed to the press, distilled all his long advocacy on the subject. Charts showed his plan's feasibility. And then, his voice rising, face reddening, Kennedy abandoned his text, stepped forward of the lectern, his voice booming out unaided to the back rows, shouting that every family has disabling illnesses, the Kennedys had, but Kennedys can pay, and Senators have illnesses, but Senators have ample health insurance, but what of people without these advantages, isn't what's good enough for Congress good enough for *any American citizen?* The audience was up with him, shouting too, euphoric, happily angry. All the exaggerated talk of Kennedy style seemed vindicated. All the memories of his family's suffering, and its sense of caring, all the happier times of social concern at the heart of Democratic politics, made Democrats feel good again — all but dour White House aide Stuart Eisenstadt, who glowered at this demonstration against his boss.

And then the convention went off to vote with Carter on the key measure before it. There had been a moment of rapturous nostalgia, outside the everyday world of political bargaining. They were happy to forget the price tag while Kennedy orated — and were careful to remember it when the vote came. Kennedy was gone from Memphis by the time the real action took place. He had done his job. He had kept alive some memories. The deals were cut without him.

A pattern is emerging. Kennedy is at his best when he is not in the running. That is true not only in Memphis, or at the New York convention; the reporters following him in 1980 noticed a sense of freedom growing on him as his chances faded. He performed best when he was showing his mettle as a survivor, not bidding to take over. Forced by fame, by his name, toward power, he tightens up. Allowed to back off, he relaxes. This is not surrender. He still takes a role, subordinate, one where he can maneuver against the pressures that would *make* him succeed. He seems to be acquiring a sense of power's last paradox — that it is most a prison when one thinks of it as a *passepartout.* When one thinks of it as a prison, one is already partway free.

Epilogue

Brotherhood

There are secret aspects, beyond divining, in all we do — in the makeup of humans above all; aspects mute and invisible, unknown to their own possessors, brought forth only under the incitements of circumstance.

— MONTAIGNE

THERE IS SOMETHING TWISTABLE in the hand about power — something tricky and unpredictable, "amphisbaenic," backward-striking. And that is as it should be. Remember, after all, what power is — getting others to do one's will. There is something obviously unhealthy in the concept of a whole world ready to do one nation's will. Yet America has yearned toward that unnatural condition, trying to force on others the relation of children to a parent. The American mission preached by recent Presidents — most fetchingly by John F. Kennedy — would benignly coerce others "for their own good," freezing the exercise of their wills in a state of incomplete development.

Power, if it is just the mobilization of resources by one's own will, has no internal check at all. Economy dictates the best use of resources, and to have any identity at all is to will one's own good. Such power must push out endlessly — which means it is not free. It must spread ever wider its periphery of influence — which means it will be dispersed. But power as the interaction with other wills is fundamentally suasive, which means it must surrender in order to rule. This formulation sounds paradoxical, yet we all have intimate experience of its truth.

A parent can have every resource of coercion, along with the will to coerce, in dealing with a child; he or she can "ground" the child, spank, take away toys, allowance, privileges. But this combination of resources with will does not equal power, in the sense of getting another to do one's will, if the child keeps saying *no*. One can kill the beast in a frenzy of impotence brought on by the attempt to use power at its utmost reach of determination. But real power depends on the checking of such unilateral ferocity of purpose, such indiscriminate use of available physical resource.

The parent who exerts his or her power over children most drastically loses all power over them, except the power to twist and hurt and destroy. This power to destroy — to wound, to sever bridges, to end lives — is easily wielded; and we tend to call this real power since it has such an instant, spectacular effect, dependent only on our will. We can all smash a TV set, a computer, a friendship, a marriage. Few of us can build a workable computer or rewarding marriage. Any idiot can wreck what only a genius can make.

In the case of political order, obedience comes to a leader only if he shows the respect for his followers that encourages opinions of right and interest in them — i.e., the belief that they ought to follow him, and that it will help them to do so. Thus Machiavelli, celebrating the ruthless prince, said that his highest skill was in gaining a reputation based on the solid opinion of his subjects. Even when the prince inspires fear, it must be a respectful fear without hatred. Helots and mercenaries, like compelled allies or satellites, weaken the state they seem to aggrandize. "Therefore the best fortress there can be is not to be hated by the people; for if you have fortresses, but the people hate you, the forts cannot save you." American politicians, including the Kennedys, tend to remember these truths when recruiting domestic support. But the ideal of foreign power has been to approximate our assertiveness to our powers of destruction, to equate ability to destroy with right to control. There, *our* will is being tested, not *other* wills recruited.

If sheer assertion of power results in its abdication, the reverse of that is also true: real power is gained by yielding one's own will in the persuasion of others. As Tolstoy said, "The strongest, most indissoluble, most burdensome and constant bond with other men is what is called power over them, which in its real meaning is only the greatest dependence on them" ("Words About *War and Peace*"). The best witness to this truth is the real source of American power in the Kennedy era. The 1960s was a period obsessed with power — the power of the American system, or power to be sought by working outside it; the power of insurgency, or of counterinsurgency; the power of rhetoric and "image" and charisma and technology. The attempt to fashion power solely out of resource and will led to the celebration of power as destruction — as assassination of leaders, the sabotage of rival economies, the poising of opponent missiles.

The equation of real power with power to destroy reached its unheard refutation in the death of our charismatic leader. As children can wreck TV sets, so Oswalds can shoot Kennedys. The need to believe in some conspiracy behind the assassination is understandable in an age of charismatic pretensions. The "graced" man validates his power by success, by luck. Oswald, by canceling the luck, struck at the very principle of government, and it was hard to admit that he was not asserting (or being used by) some *alternative* principle of rule. Oswald was a brutal restatement of the idea of power as the combination of resource with will. Put at its simplest, this became the combination of a Mannlicher-Carcano with one man's mad assertiveness. Power as the power to *conquer* was totally separated, at last, from ability to control.

Robert Kennedy's assassination gave lesser scope to conspiracy theorists — no one knew, beforehand, his route through the kitchen. With him, the effect of sheer chaos was easier to acknowledge (though some still do not acknowledge it — they think purposive will rules everything). What was lost with Robert Kennedy was not so much a legacy of power asserted as the glimpse of a deeper understanding, the beginnings of a belief in power as surrender of the will. He died, after all, opposing the caricatures of power enacted in our wars and official violence.

But another man was killed in the 1960s who did not offer mere *promise* of performance. He was even younger than the Kennedys — thirty-nine when he was shot, in the year of Robert's death at forty-three. There were many links between the Kennedys and Martin Luther King — links admirably traced in Harris Wofford's book on the three men. Together, they summed up much of the nobler purpose in American life during the 1960s. Yet there was opposition, too — Dr. King, more radical in his push for racial justice, was far more peaceful in his methods. Robert Kennedy, however reluctantly, used the police powers of John F. Kennedy's state to spy on Dr. King, to put in official hands the instruments of slander. King was a critic of the space program and war expenditures. King, though more revolutionary in some people's eyes, was not "charismatic" in the sense of replacing traditional and legal power with his personal will. He relied on the deep traditions of his church, on the preaching power of a Baptist minister; and he appealed to the rational order of the liberal state for peaceful adjustment of claims advanced by the wronged. His death, as tragic as Kennedy's, did not leave so large an absence. His work has outlasted him; more than any single person he changed the way Americans lived with each other in the sixties. His power was real, because it was not mere assertion — it was a persuasive *yielding* of private will through nonviolent advocacy.

Since he relied less on power as mere assertiveness of will, mere assertiveness of will could not entirely erase what he accomplished. He had already surrendered his life to bring about large social changes, constructive, not destructive. He forged ties of friendship and social affection. He did not want to force change by violence or stealth, by manipulation or technological tricks. His power was the power to suffer, and his killer only increased that power.

The speeches of John F. Kennedy are studied, now, by people who trace their unintended effects in Vietnam and elsewhere. The speeches of Martin Luther King are memorized at schools as living documents — my son could recite them in high school. "Flexible response" and "counterinsurgency" are tragicomic episodes of our history. But the Gandhian nonviolence preached by Dr. King is a doctrine that still inspires Americans. My children cannot believe that I grew up in a society where blacks could not drink at public water fountains, eat in "white" restaurants, get their hair cut in white barber shops, sit in white theaters, play on white football teams. The changes King wrought are so large as to be almost invisible.

He was helped, of course — he was not a single mover of the charismatic sort. And he was helped not so much by talented aides as by his fellow martyrs, by all those who died or risked dying for their children or their fellow citizens. While Washington's "best and brightest" worked us into Vietnam, an obscure army of virtue arose in the South and took the longer spiritual trip inside a public bathroom or toward the front of a bus. King rallied the strength of broken men, transmuting an imposed squalor into the beauty of chosen suffering. No one did it for his followers. They did it for themselves. Yet, in helping them, he exercised real power, achieved changes that dwarf the moon shot as an American achievement. The "Kennedy era" was really the age of Dr. King.

The famous antitheses and alliterations of John Kennedy's rhetoric sound tinny now. But King's eloquence endures, drawn as it was from ancient sources — the Bible, the spirituals, the hymns and folk songs. He was young at his death, younger than either Kennedy; but he had traveled farther. He did fewer things; but those things last. A mule team drew his coffin in a rough cart; not the sleek military horses and the artillery caisson. He has no eternal flame — and no wonder. He is not dead.

We see in Bolingbroke's case that a life of brilliant licence is really compatible with a life of brilliant statesmanship; that licence itself may even be thought to quicken the imagination for oratorical efforts; that an intellect similarly aroused may, at exciting conjunctures, perceive possibilities which are hidden from duller men; that the favourite of society will be able to use his companionship with men and his power over women so as much to aid his strokes of policy, but, on the other hand, that these secondary aids and occasional advantages are purchased by the total sacrifice of a primary necessity; that a life of great excitement is incompatible with the calm circumspection and sound estimate of probability essential to great affairs; that though the excited hero may perceive distant things which others overlook, he will overlook near things that others see; that though he may be stimulated to great speeches which others could not make, he will also be irritated to petty speeches which others would not; that he will attract enmities, but not confidence; that he will not observe how few and plain are the alternatives to common business, and how little even genius can enlarge them; that his prosperity will be a wild dream of unattainable possibilities, and his adversity a long regret that those possibilities are departed.

— WALTER BAGEHOT, on Bolingbroke

Acknowledgments

The author is grateful to the following for permission to quote: *The Search for JFK* by Joan and Clay Blair, Jr., Berkley Publishing Corp., 1976. Reprinted by permission of Berkley, the authors, and Scott Meredith Literary Agency, Inc.

"For John F. Kennedy His Inauguration," from *The Poetry of Robert Frost* edited by Edward Connery Lathem. Copyright © 1961, 1962 by Robert Frost. Copyright © 1969 by Holt, Rinehart and Winston. Reprinted by permission of Holt, Rinehart and Winston, Publishers.

To Move a Nation by Roger Hilsman. Copyright © 1964, 1967 by Roger Hilsman. Reprinted by permission of Doubleday & Company, Inc. and The Lantz Office Incorporated.

Why England Slept by John F. Kennedy (Funk & Wagnalls). Copyright © 1961 by Harper & Row, Publishers, Inc. Reprinted by permission of Harper & Row, Publishers, Inc.

Presidential Power by Richard Neustadt. Reprinted by permission, from *Presidential Power* by Richard Neustadt. Copyright © 1960, 1976, 1980 by John Wiley & Sons, Inc.

Robert Kennedy and His Times by Arthur M. Schlesinger, Jr. Copyright © 1978 by Arthur M. Schlesinger, Jr. Reprinted by permission of Houghton Mifflin Company.

A Thousand Days by Arthur M. Schlesinger, Jr. Copyright © 1965 by Arthur M. Schlesinger, Jr. Reprinted by permission of Houghton Mifflin Company.

Kennedy by Theodore C. Sorensen. Copyright © 1965 by Theodore C. Sorensen. Reprinted by permission of Harper & Row, Publishers, Inc.

Index